Psychoanalysis:
Critical Explorations in Contemporary Theory and Practice

Edited by

Alan M. Jacobson, M.D.

and

Dean X. Parmelee, M.D.

BRUNNER/MAZEL, *Publishers* • New York

Library of Congress Cataloging in Publication Data

Main entry under title:

Psychoanalysis, critical explorations in
    contemporary theory and practice.

    Includes bibliographical references and
index.
    1. Psychoanalysis—Addresses, essays,
lectures. I. Jacobson, Alan M.
II. Parmelee, Dean X., 1947 -   [DNLM:
1. Psychoanalysis.   WM 460 E96]
RC509.P83   616.89'17   81-17991
ISBN 0-87630-269-X   AACR2

Copyright © 1982 by Alan M. Jacobson and Dean X. Parmelee

Published by
BRUNNER/MAZEL, INC.
19 Union Square
New York, New York 10003

MANUFACTURED IN THE UNITED STATES OF AMERICA

Contents

Preface

The psychiatric clinician practices in a field beset by conflict. Competing theories and techniques from the biological and social sciences have primed this conflict. It is an inordinate task for the conscientious clinician to sort through the explosion of information to determine what is applicable to one's work, while keeping an open mind about the ideas of tomorrow.

For the clinician whose interest and mode of practice is in the psychoanalytic sphere, conflict is particularly acute. During the past two decades the entire theoretical construct of psychoanalysis and the efficacy of psychoanalytically-based treatments have been challenged. In addition, the principles of psychoanalytic technique have undergone modification and adaptation to fit a more varied group of persons seeking psychiatric help.

It is our hope that this volume on psychoanalysis will provide psychiatric clinicians of varied theoretical orientation with a review of the status of basic psychoanalytic theory and a perspective on its range and depth for clinical application. The chapters presented here are drawn from a Psychiatry Department Grand Rounds Series at the Massachusetts General Hospital. It was our goal for the Series and for this collection to have each contributor address contemporary psychoanalytic concepts and practices in a useful and meaningful way. Topics of identified importance for the mental health professional were chosen.

In Chapter 1, William W. Meissner examines, with a historical perspective, changing models in psychoanalysis with special reference to the relationship of these changes and conceptualizations to treatment. He begins with a review of Freud's early work on hysteria, traces the building of concepts of the unconscious, id, superego and ego, and concludes with an examination of modern concepts of object relations. This chapter, therefore, provides an introduction to this volume by presenting the broad scope of the development of psychoanalytic ideas.

Malkah T. Notman, in Chapter 2, focuses on a particular segment of psychoanalytic ideas—the psychology of women. She investigates the special issues involving the development of the psychology of women from the early psychoanalytic literature to the present. Including some of the current data from the social and biological sciences, she considers the implications of these changing views for the psychotherapy of women today.

Gerald L. Klerman examines the problems of psychoanalytic propositions in Chapter 3. Are they testable hypotheses? If testable, what are the implications for the field? He uses the psychoanalytic theory of depression as the focus for his discussion. We have included this chapter because books on psychoanalytic theory and clinical material often leave aside issues of the very nature of the scientific bases of psychoanalysis.

In Chapter 4, Steven B. Bernstein provides an in-depth look at the psychoanalytic understanding and treatment of primitive personalities. He focuses his discussion on Kohut and Kernberg, reviewing and explaining the essential principles of their works. In addition, he compares and contrasts their views on borderline and narcissistic character disorders. Bernstein presents a clear and readable review of their major concepts, which are often complex and difficult to comprehend. Bernstein's work is at the cutting-edge of psychoanalytic theory development and, as such, is an important addition to any volume exploring new directions in psychoanalysis.

Chapter 5 is a personalized examination of the origin and course of psychoanalytic child psychotherapy by Eveoleen Rexford. She opens with a review of the case history of Hans, Freud's first attempt to use his speculations about adult neurosis derived from adults in understanding children. She demonstrates the necessary ingredients for child psychotherapy and follows this with a review of child psychiatry, including its current directions and its relationship to psychoanalysis.

Readers will find Max Day's Chapter 6 a rewarding exploration of his application of psychoanalysis to groups. Day demonstrates the salient features and dynamics of psychoanalytic group psychotherapy, using his rich clinical experience. This presents the reader with an application of psychoanalytic principles to a different model of practice.

In Chapter 7 Lee Birk shares his ideas and expertise on the blending of psychoanalytic theory and technique with a behavior therapy approach in groups or family treatment. This represents an interesting and unusual approach to clinical practice. Without diminishing the importance of psychoanalytic methods and concepts, Birk discusses the value of behavioral techniques in helping patients in psychoanalytically-oriented treatment. Such thoughtful blending of divergent treatment methods provides an exciting model for consideration by mental health clinicians.

In Chapter 8, Christopher Gordon and Edward Messner present a model and method for psychotherapy supervision based on their concept of the "therapeutic contract." With so many divergent approaches to therapy being taught and used today, their contribution is useful for students and teachers of a variety of psychotherapies. This chapter extends modern psychoanalytic concepts to the important area of supervision.

The editors conclude this volume of essays with an examination of the nature of psychoanalysis and possible future influences on the social sciences. They discuss, in particular, the value of developmental psychology and techniques for observing family and dyadic discussions for refining psychoanalytic models and techniques of therapy. This chapter also pursues issues raised by Klerman in Chapter 3 regarding the scientific evaluation of psychoanalytic principles. They conclude with some remarks about the future impact of psychoanalysis on clinical psychiatry.

ACKNOWLEDGMENTS

We wish to record our deep appreciation to the nine contributors to this book. Throughout the many revisions of the manuscript, they have been patient and always put forth their best.

Dr. Thomas P. Hackett, Chief of Psychiatry at Massachusetts General Hospital, enthusiastically supported our starting this project, and the Charles River Hospital and the Joslin Diabetes Center provided us administrative support to complete it. Dr. Jacobson's time was supported in part by Diabetes Research and Training Grant No. AM 20530 from NIAMDD.

We wish to thank Drs. Stuart Hauser and Gil Noam, who exposed us to structural theories of ego and moral development which we examined in Chapter 9.

Finally, we thank our wives who helped us in many ways throughout.

A.M.J.
D.X.P.

Contributors

STEPHEN B. BERNSTEIN, M.D.
*Faculty, Boston
Psychoanalytic Society
and Institute;
Associate Clinical Professor of
Psychiatry,
Tufts University School of Medicine*

LEE BIRK, M.D.
*Associate Clinical Professor of
Psychiatry,
Harvard Medical School*

MAX DAY, M.D.
*Assistant Clinical Professor of
Psychiatry,
Harvard Medical School;
Associate Psychiatrist,
Massachusetts General Hospital;
Member of Faculty,
Boston Psychoanalytic Institute*

CHRISTOPHER GORDON, M.D.
*Clinical Instructor of Psychiatry,
Harvard Medical School;
Clinical Associate,
Massachusetts General Hospital*

ALAN M. JACOBSON, M.D.
*Consulting and Research Psychiatrist,
Joslin Diabetes Center, Boston;
Assistant Professor of Psychiatry,
Harvard Medical School*

GERALD L. KLERMAN, M.D.
*Director of Research,
Stanley Cobb Psychiatric
Research Laboratories,
Massachusetts General Hospital;
Professor of Psychiatry,
Harvard Medical School*

WILLIAM W. MEISSNER, S.J., M.D.
*Associate Clinical Professor of
Psychiatry,
Harvard Medical School;
Member of Faculty,
Boston Psychoanalytic Institute*

EDWARD MESSNER, M.D.
*Assistant Clinical Professor of
Psychiatry,
Harvard Medical School;
Associate Psychiatrist,
Massachusetts General Hospital*

MALKAH T. NOTMAN, M.D.
Clinical Professor of Psychiatry,
Tufts University Medical School;
Training and Supervising Analyst,
Boston Psychoanalytic Institute

DEAN X. PARMELEE, M.D.
Director of Child and Adolescent
Inpatient Services,
Charles River Hospital;
Clinical Instructor of Child Psychiatry,
Boston University School of Medicine

EVEOLEEN N. REXFORD, M.D.
Professor Emerita of Psychiatry and
Child Psychiatry,
Boston University School of Medicine

Psychoanalysis:

*Critical Explorations
in Contemporary
Theory and Practice*

Chapter 1

The History of the
Psychoanalytic Movement

William W. Meissner S.J., M.D.

INTRODUCTION

Psychoanalysis is a field of changing concepts and perspectives. Contemporary aspects of psychoanalysis cannot be understood without reference to its history. History, however, in terms of names and dates is well documented in other places and confines the subject to being a type of psychiatric antiquity. Beyond historical description lies the lively development of psychoanalytic ideas.

It is a history of these ideas that I wish to present in this chapter. Moreover, I propose to adopt a very specific perspective having to do with the interaction between psychoanalytic theory and psychoanalytic therapy. If there is any point that I would like to convey to you in presenting this material, it is that psychoanalysis is fundamentally and at root a clinical theory. When psychoanalysis withdraws from the hard-rock clinical data it deals with, it begins to become wan and pale. When it can put its taproot into that rich clinical material of the immediate interaction between analyst and patient, then it flourishes. As Goethe observed long ago, all theory is gray—reality is green. In psychoanalysis, as in all science, this is an anomaly. It is a constant problem in the methodology of psychoanalysis. It creates special difficulties in trying to assess what psychoanalysis is and what it does, because there is also a mandate that says that I cannot simply test out hypotheses in one isolated context, particularly just the context from which those hypotheses are derived.

Consequently, psychoanalytic theory has to become a general theory, rather than a specific theory of how analysis works in the analytic situation. Further, it has to be tested and validated as a general theory. It is in that transition, in that interface between the concrete reality of clinical data and immediate clinical experience, on one level, and the formulations of the general theory, on another level, that many of the problems in trying to understand and validate psychoanalysis arise. So if you think about analysis as authentically a clinical theory and think about the problems of methodology that are involved in translating it into other kinds of testing situations, other kinds of validating situations, experimental contexts where it becomes necessary to define, delineate, specify, and clarify variables and their functional interrelationships, the enterprise becomes very difficult indeed.

In sum, I would like to emphasize in this discussion that psychoanalytic theory does not arise in a vacuum; it arises out of the clinical context. The interaction between theory and practice, between the theory and the therapy, is extremely complex and has to involve very difficult reciprocal patterns of interaction between what is going on in the analyst's mind and what is going on in the interaction with his patient—and these may be quite different. It is that interesting interface and the difficulties and differences involved in it that provide a continual stimulus to analytic thinking. This has been true historically as well as in the conduct of specific analyses.

ORIGINS IN HYPNOSIS: THE CATHARTIC MODEL

Freud was first trained as a neurologist and was interested in trying to understand the functioning of the human brain and its role in various forms of human behavior. His substantial work on aphasia (1) for example, was an important and ground-breaking contribution to the understanding of the role of cortical functions in the use of speech and language.

After he had finished his training, Freud had the opportunity to study with the French neurologist Charcot. Charcot is noteworthy in the history of neurology for one very important contribution among many others—he re-established hysteria as a legitimate medical diagnosis. There was a tendency in medical circles of the time to regard hysteria as a form of malingering without much intrinsic medical interest. Charcot's realization that many of his patients in his neurological clinic at the Salpêtrière (most of whom were female) manifested hysterical symptoms led him to study these patients more carefully. His dramatic case presentations, in which he showed that even the most striking hysterical manifestations could be reproduced by hypnosis, added a new dimension to the study of hysteria.

Charcot was most interested in defining the parameters and mechanisms of hysteria. In French neurological circles of the time, the interest in hypnosis was very much at large. Charcot established that hysteria had something to do with the patient's individual psychology, that it was not simply due to some kind of neurological lesion or a form of malingering, but that it was, at least in part, a psychological phenomenon. He also pointed the study of hysteria in a new direction; it was Charcot who observed that hysteria was "une chose génitale," a genital or sexual matter. Thus, he identified the role of sexuality in hysterical symptomatology. Freud studied with Charcot at the Salpêtrière. He listened to the lectures, examined the patients, and became very interested in the problem of hysteria and its relation to hypnosis. When he returned to Vienna, Freud met Josef Breuer, who also had been interested in this phenomenon for some years. Together they elaborated a theory of hysteria that was essentially psychological—even though they cloaked their descriptions in neurological language. The modality of therapeutic intervention they used was hypnosis based on Breuer's notion of catharsis.

The issue was a basic question of how the mind operates. Breuer's theory reflects the predominant trend of theorizing among late nineteenth century physiologists, dominated by the thinking of the physicist Helmholtz. Helmholtzian principles demanded that all formulations be translated or translatable into terms of neural energies and processes. No other basis of explanation or understanding was acceptable. Breuer's translation of emotions and psychic states into the language of neural excitations, distribution of neural energies and neural processes has logical difficulties and it would presumably have faded into history were it not for the fact that Breuer's colleague in this effort was Sigmund Freud.

Because of its influence on Freud's thinking, Breuer's theory has become an interesting historical footnote. In fact, it is an interesting intellectual exercise to read Breuer's theoretical chapter in the *Studies on*

Hysteria (2). His explanation of why hysteria occurs, the language he uses, and the conceptualization that he presents are almost identical to the theory that Freud formulated about the same time in writing his Project for a Scientific Psychology (3). There is some question as to who was influencing whom at the time, since both men shared the Helmholtzian convictions. The earlier cathartic theory seems to have been Breuer's—at least he was the one to formulate it. As we shall see, Freud found it necessary to abandon this hypothesis; in fact, the indications of Freud's dissatisfaction with it can be found quite clearly in the *Studies on Hysteria* (2).

The model of hysteria Breuer proposed was based on the model of hypnosis—an essentially repressive model. In this model, hysterical symptoms arose not only when a traumatic experience occurred, but more specifically when the experience occurred in a prepared state of mind. The experience had to be a form of severe emotional disturbance, had to be a traumatic event, and had to occur in the context of what Breuer called a "hypnoid state." The very term "hypnoid" evokes associations of hypnosis. In fact, Breuer was appealing to a hypnosis-like state of mind to explain hysteria. He felt that hypnosis produced a state of dissociation in the mind in which part of the mind was split off from normal integration with consciousness and cut off from normal voluntary control. The idea of the hypnoid state was similar. This was a state of weakness or dissociation in the mental apparatus which meant that, when the traumatic event occurred, it somehow impinged on the dissociated area of the mind, so that the normal processes by which the mind was able to encompass and work through a traumatic experience were cut off and the traumatic experience then became embedded in this area of mental functioning without being worked through and integrated.

Consequently, in this segregated area of the mind, there was something occurring that was outside of the normal functioning of the rest of the mind and was expressing itself of the realm of normal consciousness and voluntary execution. This was his explanation of how a hysterical symptom occurred. For example, paralysis of the hand would suggest that the hand was under control of the dissociated area of the mind which cut off the normal motor impulses, and that it was unavailable to motor impulses from the rest of the mind. His notion was that if one could identify the traumatic memory, undo this hypnoid dissociation, and allow the bound-up energy, the bound-up affects which were so cut off from the rest of the mental apparatus, a channel of release so that they could come forth, they would be expressed and become conscious. This was termed an abreaction. The recovery of the traumatic memory and its re-experiencing, together with the painful affects connected with it, made it possible to adequately discharge these strangulated affects, thus offering the possibility of more effective processing and integration of these pathogenic residues. The symptoms would then disappear; insofar as the connections were re-established, and the dissociation was overcome, the affective material tied up in this state was now available to be worked on and ready to become integrated with the rest of the individual's ongoing experience.

Although Freud had difficulty accepting the concept of hypnoid states, he used it because it did offer a partial explanation of sorts, and because the theory of catharsis and abreaction seemed to be supported by clinical experience. His acquiescence was grudging at best. It is very clear that even in the "Preliminary Communication," which was the first discussion that Breuer and Freud published about their study of this phenomenon, Freud had reservations about Breuer's formulation[2]. The parts of it that we can attribute to Freud make it clear that Freud did not quite agree. He felt that the so-called "hypnoid states" were simply a given, that there was no explanation for them, that consequently the hypnoid state was simply a postulate. Freud found the explanations, which Breuer accepted, to be incomplete. These explanations presumed ill-defined genetic and hereditary dispositions, a "dégénerance mentale" that represented a built-in hereditarily determined weakness in the nervous system of hysterical patients. This was simply a postulate; you believed it or you didn't. Freud could not remain satisfied with such an unsupported postulate; he felt there had to be some explanations for this phenomenon.

THE REPRESSIVE MODEL

The next step in the process of discovery was important and of the utmost signifance in the development of psychoanalytic thinking. Recall that it was in the context of work with patients that Freud ultimately moved from this hypnoid model to a model of defense, in which repression was no longer a passive occurrence that was simply the result of hypnoid dissociation, a given dissociation, but became an active, defensively motivated process. It was the essential notion of defense that he offered to explain why it was that this phenomenon of dissociation occurred.

A question at this point is what brought about this transition in Freud's thinking. There are many factors which contributed to this change. I will mention two. First, use of hypnosis was not altogether successful; it didn't work for all patients. Some patients simply could not be hypnotized or could not be put into a deep enough trance to recover the traumatic memories. Second, some patients for whom the symptomatology would disappear as a result of catharsis and abreaction of the strangulated affect would have a return of symptoms, often in full force. This left Freud wondering: What's wrong with the theory? You do everything you are supposed to do and the effects aren't always satisfactory; the theory doesn't always work. When it does seem to work, in many cases the symptoms come back again. If the theory were correct, there should be no reason for the symptoms to return. Something was wrong with the model.

As a result, Freud retreated from the use of hypnosis. The process of change went on for a decade or more and reflected Freud's continued attempts to work through this problem. As he retreated from his reliance on hypnosis, he began to experiment with various modifications of his technique. One of the modifications included having the patient lie down, with him sitting behind and out of the patient's line of vision. At times, when the patient had nothing further to say or was blocked so that access to the crucial memories seemed cut off, or when Freud felt that the patient was getting close to some important material but some resistance was preventing further progress, he resorted to a form of suggestion. He would press firmly on the patient's forehead and insist that as a result of this pressure some relevant thought would come into the patient's mind (2). Of course, the patient would compliantly oblige with the required production. Freud was not satisfied with this because the approach was not scientific, but rather magical. We can add that, from our more contemporary perspective, we might have even harsher criticism to make of Freud's attempts, which seem so manipulative, controlling, authoritarian.

The second, more relevant influence on Freud's developing views was his radical experience of struggling with the patient's often powerful resistance to his efforts to uncover the repressed traumatic memories. Freud began to think that there were forces of resistance in the patient that not only accounted for the resistance to remembering, but also may have contributed to the original repression and the production of symptoms. Something was going on in the patient that not only allowed for the traumatic memories to be cut off, but also actively cut them off and kept them cut off.

The major point of difference between the cathartic model and Freud's repressive model was that in the cathartic model the vulnerability to dissociative splitting was postulated, but in the repressive model it was the result of active defensive forces which also became resistance to the therapeutic process. By way of analogy, in Breuer's model it was as though someone closed a door in the mansion of the mind and closed off that room in the mind from the rest of the mind. All you had to do was open the door and everything would be fine, contact with the rest of the house would be re-established. In contrast, in Freud's model, not only did somebody close the door, but somebody was still holding it shut. To open the door you had to overcome the patient's resistance.

As Freud retreated from the use of hypnosis and began searching for other ways of dealing with this phenomenon, he began to realize that there were other inner resistances to his efforts to uncover the critical pathogenic memories. The primary source of resistance was repression, which Freud saw as an active defense. Freud tried to find ways to get at this resistance, to overcome it and thus gain access to the pathogenic material. It was in the course of these attempts that his technique gradually evolved from hypnosis to free association. He slowly came to realize that his attempts to struggle with the patient's resistances were not altogether successful and, in addition, were introducing extraneous influences that contaminated the therapeutic situation. He began taking a different tack. He would say to his patients, "Now look, all I want you to do is lie here and relax and tell me anything that comes into your mind." "Anything?" "Yes, anything—as if you were sitting on a train watching the countryside go by and giving a description of what you saw as the train went along." The emphasis shifted to putting the patient in a position of relaxed passivity, a set of mind in which collaboration with the analyst was encouraged by an atmosphere of complete openness and permissiveness, such that the patient could say whatever came into his or her mind without exception, and without qualification, shame, or embarrassment.

So Freud became interested not in the fact that there was something repressed, but in the fact that there was some repressing force or agency. His attention shifted from what was unconscious, that is, from the content of what was repressed and its meaning in the patient's past experience, to what it was that was creating this split in the mind and keeping that material repressed. To Freud's way of thinking, it must be the same forces of repression which produced and maintained the split that he found offering resistance to his efforts to get at the unconscious material.

THE SEDUCTION THEORY: RESISTANCE AS DEFENSE

An important related change that emerged in this context was the rejection of the so-called seduction hypothesis. Freud partly based his thinking in this period on the idea that, in order for this defensive apparatus to be thrown into operation in a way that could bring about such a pathological dissociation, the original trauma that was postulated in this context had to be something overwhelming to the patient's defenses. It had to take place at a point of the patient's experience where the defensive organization was vulnerable, and it had to be such as to arouse a high degree of anxiety. It had to be of such a nature as to be very threatening to the patient. What he heard from many of his patients in searching out this kind of traumatic phenomenon was a tale of seduction. In the life histories of these individuals, he would recover apparent memories of how they had been seduced one way or another by adults who were in charge of them as children—parental seductions, seductions by nursemaids, aunts, uncles, etc. A whole range of early traumatic sexual experiences came into view which seemed to provide the traumatic stimulus for which Freud was looking. He became convinced that this early sexual trauma was the root of a neurotic reaction, and it was the defense against the excessive stimulation created in the situation of traumatic seduction that resulted in the hysterical disposition. In patient after patient, using his pressure technique and other more subtle forms of suggestion, Freud was able to recover such seductive accounts and he became solidly convinced that he had found the key to the neuroses. Note also that he became interested in dreams as important products of this unconscious realm of mental activity. He began to analyze himself and to analyze his own dreams. We know that almost all of the content of the *Interpretation of Dreams* (4) was based on Freud's own dreaming experience. This provided him with a unique source of material which shed considerable fresh light on mental processes and advanced Freud's understanding of how these things worked.

The analysis of his own dreams and mental content led Freud to an important discovery. He found these same resistances in himself. He found different kinds of content which seemed to parallel the sorts of infantile material he had been hearing from his patients. He was able to recover early sexual wishes and memories in his own life experience. One of the interesting things that was involved in this was that he recognized evidence of hysterical symptoms in his own family—clearly there was no evidence of seduction there. He began to wonder: Was it really possible that infantile sexual seduction could be so widespread? He began to ask himself: What are we really talking about here? Can it be that all these upstanding, respectable, moral people are going around committing perverted acts and even incest?

The idea occurred to him that his patients were not telling him historical recountings of real events, that is, real sexual seductions, but rather that the infantile material was the product of infantile sexual wishes and was caught up in a fantasy of seduction rather than actual seductions. This was a momentous realization, because it meant that the basis for his theory of repression—the mind's reaction to his real trauma in early childhood—had to be altered. Instead, the focus of his work had to be the nature of the organization of the child's mind such that it would create such sexualized fantasies. It was a decisive shift in emphasis, and one that was of major significance for psychoanalysis. Freud broke the news of this stunning abandonment of his seduction hypthesis in a now famous letter to his confidant, Wilhelm Fliess. He wrote:

> Let me tell you straight away the great secret which has been slowly dawning on me in recent months. I no longer believe in my *neurotica*. This is hardly intelligible without an explanation; you yourself found what I told you credible. So I shall start at the beginning and tell you the whole story of how the reasons for rejecting it arose. The first group of factors were the continual disappointment of my attempts to bring my analyses to a real conclusion, the running away of people who for a time had seemed my most favorably inclined patients, the lack of the complete success on which I had counted, and the possibility of explaining my partial success in other, familiar ways. Then there was the astonishing thing that in every case . . . blame was laid on perverse acts by the father, and realization of the unexpected frequency of hysteria, in every case of which the same thing applied, though it was hardly credible that perverted acts against children were so general . . . . Thirdly, there was the definite realization that there is no "indication of reality" in the unconscious, so that it is impossible to distinguish between truth and emotionally-charged fiction. (This leaves open the possible explanation that sexual phantasy regularly makes use of the theme of the parents.) Fourthly, there was the consideration that even in the most deep-reaching psychoses the unconscious memory does not break through, so that the secret of infantile experiences is not revealed even in the most confused states of delirium. When one thus sees that the unconscious never overcomes the resistance of the conscious, one must abandon the expectation that in treatment the reverse process will take place to the extent that the conscious will fully dominate the unconscious (5).

This shift in orientation meant that a fresh emphasis had to be drawn toward an understanding of the repressing mechanisms of the mind rather than of the repressed content. Now, in terms of what we understand today, that involves a shift from looking at the repressed and unconscious memories, along with a therapeutic emphasis on the recovery of such memories and the abreactive discharge of the associated affects, to an attempt to discover *the mechanisms and motives of the repression itself*. This was a much more difficult undertaking. It also involved a *definite shift* in the way he went about conducting an analysis.

An important point about this is that when you are dealing with the recovery of unconscious material and are concerned only with the relief of symptoms, the task is theoretically easy. All you have to do is get to those memories and allow adequate discharge, and you have a patient who is improved. Analysis could be short and quick, and in those days analyses were relatively short and quick. But as soon as you shift to a concern with the forces and mechanisms of repression and resistance, the task becomes more difficult because then you have to work through those resistances and motivations of the mind in order to get a therapeutic effect. So that the shift is not just theoretical, but more importantly involves practical therapeutic questions concerning the motives and processes of the original repression and the motives and processes of the patient's present and continuing resistance and repression. The shift brought into focus basic questions as to how a patient's mind functions and how it got to be that way. This involved a shift from a symptomatic emphasis to an emphasis on organizational and structural aspects of the psychic apparatus. The implications of this change only became apparent for Freud gradually and are oversimplified here for reasons of clarity and emphasis.

One of the resistances that proved to be very important was the resistance that arose only when Freud began to change his methodology and his approach to patients and to allow them to free associate. What he found was that patients became attached to the analyst, that, in fact, they developed a loving relationship with the analyst. Remember, most of these patients were female and most of them young.

Freud found that their sexual impulses were readily mobilized in relation to the therapist, and they developed intense, loving and often idealized attachments to the therapist. In retrospect, the observation was not new. Years before, Breuer had treated an hysterical young woman, who has become known as Anna O. Over the months of her treatment, she had become increasingly attached to Breuer and finally began to express her loving feelings. He was a very distinguished and respected man in the Viennese medical community, and suddenly he found himself with this young girl making a play for him. As the relationship became increasingly erotic, he became upset—it was affecting his relationship to his wife, it was getting him into all kinds of trouble, and when she professed her love for him and wanted him to marry her, that was it! He couldn't take it anymore. He stopped the therapy and went off on a vacation with his wife (2).

This is one of those interesting points where the interaction of aspects of human personality and the process of scientific discovery plays a significant role. Both Freud and Breuer experienced the same erotic attachment from their patients. Breuer was forced to discontinue his pioneering investigations of hysteria. But Freud did not lose his balance and perspective as a scientific investigator and observer. He realized that he was experiencing an important psychological phenomenon, which required further exploration and understanding rather than fright and flight. Freud realized that very intense emotional responses were being generated and that they were offering a very powerful resistance to the course of the therapy. What evolved was a situation in which the patient didn't care about what the analyst thought or said and didn't care about the symptoms; all she was interested in was her relationship with the therapist and making it a personal, living, intimate relationship. Now, obviously, that would destroy any kind of therapeutic situation and create a major resistance to any effective therapeutic work.

INFANTILE SEXUALITY

Freud was able to connect the development of these transference feelings to his other important realizations regarding the role of infantile sexual impulses. His basic insight was that the transference was equivalently a transferring of sexual, erotic impulses originally directed toward a parental object to the relationship with the analyst. This resulted in a more or less conscious wish for loving, sexualized or intimate relationship with the analyst. In other words, the emergence of the transference reproduced the emotional configuration from earlier emotional and sexually based attachments to significant objects of dependency in the patient's childhood experience.

Freud believed that the forces generating the phenomenon of transference were the very same forces that generate the fantasies of seduction. The common element behind both these phenomena was an infantile sexualized wish. From my own experience, Freud's theory about actual infantile seduction is a very attractive hypothesis. A young woman, whom I later analyzed, came to me as an outpatient. She presented a very disturbing, upsetting memory of having been penetrated by her father as a young child. This traumatic memory revived in the context of her engagement to a young man and stimulated an intense libidinal fantasy of early seduction and incestuous experience. During her therapy we found that she and her father would take showers together when she was three or four years old, and he would wash her. In washing her he would presumably touch her genital area and the excitement, the fascination with his penis, and the sexual wishes that were stimulated in this context laid the groundwork for the generation of this fantasy. This infantile fantasy emerged later on, stimulated by more intimate involvement, under the guise of an apparent memory.

If we put ourselves back into Freud's pioneering shoes, cases of this sort might easily seduce one into thinking of early infantile seduction as an important determinant of pathological symptoms. Although Freud was wrong about the role of seduction and had to revise his approach, the seduction hypothesis still has its derivatives in more contemporary perspectives. We think of seduction today in more nuanced terms. We don't think about actual parent-child intercourse so much, but we do think about seduction. Incestuous relations do occur, of course, but they are relatively rare exceptions to the rule, and certainly could not be appealed to as a determining cause for neurotic symptoms that are so pervasive in our society. Nonetheless, the seduction of children by parents is a very important issue in almost all the patients we see. The seductions take many forms that are often subtle and implicitly interwoven with the fabric of dependency which is characteristic of the more or less normal relations between parents and children.

For example, not infrequently we find, in an adolescent, unwillingness to give up his dependency on libidinal ties to his parents and establish himself as a separate, individuated adult. Difficulties in establishing a loving relationship to another non-incestuous libidinal object occur concomitantly in this situation. These problems relate back to what has gone on between parent and child during the earlier course of childhood development that has reinforced libidinal attachments and patterns of dependency. Often this is very subtle, mixing with other kinds of developmental issues. Still, there is a kind of parental seduction that may encourage or reinforce more infantile forms of involvement and attachment and may resist the young person's attempts to become more independent and autonomous. So it wasn't that Freud was off base, but that he didn't have our more modern perspective on this. He couldn't fit it into any larger perspective and at the same time deal with the phenomenon that he was facing. However, we must admire Freud's remarkable capacity to remain open to the continuing input of evidence derived from his experience with patients, as well as his ability and willingness to abandon even long-cherished convictions when the theory did not fit the facts.

THE STRUCTUAL MODEL

That same remarkable capacity led to even further changes in Freud's thinking as the years went on. For most of these early years, Freud's notion of how the mind was put together was organized in terms of unconscious, conscious, and preconscious levels of mental operation. This topographic model, which served as the organizing principle of Freud's thinking for a quarter of a century, organized the mind in terms of consciousness. The model was essentially an elaboration of the basic distinction between the repressed and the repressing aspects of the psyche. The unconscious level was the level of repressed content and its associated instincts. The preconscious and conscious levels contained the mechanisms and processes by which the unconscious was regulated and controlled, as well as integrated with the demands of reality.

In looking at the distinction between what is repressed and what is repressing, the model required that he postulate some basic differences between them. If he were to put them altogether in the unconscious, then he would have difficulty conceptualizing how they might be in conflict with each other. Freud's theory was essentially a theory of conflict—in its earliest and most basic form, as exemplified in his early theory of hysteria, the conflict was envisioned as arising between instinctual impulses seeking immediate discharge under the pleasure principle and the controlling regulation of more conscious mechanisms of the mind operating in terms of the reality principle. As long as these sides of the conflict could be segregated into separate areas of functioning, so that unconscious impulses were kept separate from and opposed to conscious mechanisms, the theory seemed adequate.

A problem arose, however, as Freud's experience with forms of resistance expanded. He came to realize that frequently enough the resistances of his patients were also unconscious, and often remained so even in the face of conscious efforts to overcome them. Moreover, these unconscious resistances often resulted from guilt feelings. This discovery of unconscious guilt opened new areas of complexity in the understanding of neurosis and neurotic conflict. There was no longer simply conflict between pleasure and reality. Moreover, it demonstrated that conflict could persist entirely in the unconscious. When he found both the repressed and the repressing elements ending up in the unconscious, he began to reconsider his model of how the mind was structured. The topographic model of unconscious, preconscious and conscious no longer seemed adequate. Since the repressing mechanisms were also to some degree unconscious, a more adequate model was called for which would account for the operation of such mechanisms in both conscious and unconscious terms. So Freud had to offer a new model which accounted for this complexity. The new model was the very familiar one that still dominates most of our thinking about mental functioning: the structural theory which organizes mental functions in terms of separate agencies, the id, ego, and superego.

This creation of the tripartite structural model was a definite step forward, because it meant that Freud was more explicitly and specifically concerned with matters pertaining to the organization and integration of mental functions and structures and with an attempt to understand how they came to be. In other words, the shift in theoretical emphasis carried with it a shift from concern with the development of neurotic conflicts to a concern with the development of mental structures and operations themselves. No longer was it simply a matter of instinctual forces impinging on the mind; it wasn't just a matter of counterforces pushing this other force out of the way, keeping those instinctually derived ideas repressed into the unconscious; it wasn't just the dynamic configuration of conflict between these forces—he was now talking about how the mind is organized, how it comes to function as it does, how such organization and patterns of functioning come about, how it is actually put together.

This marked a milestone because it entailed a marked shift in therapeutic orientation. The earlier theory had directed efforts to the recovery and discharge of unconscious content. In parallel with the theoretical shifts—or, more correctly, a step or two ahead of the changes in theoretical orientation—Freud realized that the overcoming of the patient's resistance was an important step in this process. As he continued to meet with new kinds and complexities of defense, the focus of analytic work shifted to these defenses. This shift was prompted in part by the problem of unconscious guilt, which brought into focus the whole question of superego. Because Freud had to deal with the phenomenon of unconscious guilt and the effects it had in the therapeutic process, his understanding of depression, masochism, and the negative therapeutic reaction all seemed to gain new clarity in relation to unconscious guilt. We know now that these phenomena are considerably more complex, but for Freud this insight opened new vistas of understanding and called for important therapeutic modifications.

NEGATIVE THERAPEUTIC REACTION: THE ROLE OF GUILT

Let us consider for a moment the negative therapeutic reaction. By this term Freud meant to describe a situation in which all the indices for a good therapeutic response are present—the resistances apparently worked through, correct interpretations made and seemingly good insight achieved—but the patient not only does not get better but may even get worse. These patients ought to respond positively to the therapist, but they don't. Freud found this phenomenon puzzling. Why don't they respond? Something must have been going on in their minds that stood in the way of responding positively to the therapist's interventions.

These observations and questions forced Freud to go back and rethink his understanding of how the therapeutic process worked. His original idea, following Breuer's notion of catharsis, was that the therapeutic effect was achieved by the retrieval and abreactive discharge of traumatic memories and the related dammed-up affects. As he shifted away from a model of retrieval and discharge, he became increasingly aware of the role of resistance, and particularly unconscious resistances. Once he shifted this level of looking at resistances, he had to deal with them and achieve some understanding of them in analytic terms. What are the resistances? How are they operating and affecting the work of analysis? How can we get through them so that the repressed material can become available and be adequately discharged? In other words, analysis became equivalent to analysis of the resistances. According to the model, once the resistances were removed, the repressed material would be remembered, and all you had to do then was interpret this material and the patient would gain the necessary insight.

Well, among the resistances was the factor of unconscious guilt, and along with it other unconscious aspects became much more apparent. Freud began to see that there was an additional source of these resistances that had not been accounted for in his previous theory. This source was particularly involved in unconscious opposition to the ego and was specifically the source of unconscious guilt. Furthermore, as a source of resistance it was clearly different in character and, in fact, opposed to the instincts and their imperative need for discharge and immediate gratification as expressions of the pleasure principle. Thus, the stage was set for an additional, separate psychic agency, the superego, to account for these observations. The therapeutic focus now shifted to the effort to take the superego apart, to work on it, and then through that approach to allow the resistances to diminish.

It was out of this welter of observations that Freud finally formulated his structural hypothesis. The emphasis on defense had turned his attention to the ego and how it works, so that he began to think in terms of different aspects of ego functioning as they played a role in the organization and maintenance of defenses and resistances. He gradually realized that there were qualitatively different kinds of resistance which could not be simply attributed to the functions of the ego, but seemed more appropriately delegated to some part of the ego that not only played a different role in the process of defense and repression, but also occupied a position of conflict over against both the instincts and the ego. This theoretical distinction between so-called ego and superego resistances entailed another major shift in orientation to a strong emphasis on the analysis of the superego in both its resistances within the analysis and its general functioning. In fact, many clinicians, following Freud's lead in this matter, began to see the analytic work as focusing primarily, if not exclusively, on the working through and resolution of superego conflicts.

MODEL OF AUTONOMOUS EGO FUNCTIONING

The refocusing provided by the shift to a structural hypothesis opened up new areas of consideration and of awareness in the analytic work itself. The clarification of the ego as structurally independent opened the way for an increasing awareness of the more autonomous areas of ego functioning, over and above its traditionally recognized defensive functions. It became possible to think about areas of autonomous functioning in the individual personality that might play a role in the therapeutic process. The ego was not a unitary structure with a single or unitary function, but rather it was a complex entity with many functions that could operate in different ways in different situations, and these functions could carry out their activity with varying degrees of autonomy and independence either from drive influences or from the governance of superego.

Consequently, the matter of therapeutic change was no longer simply a question of the resolution of conflicts that might arise between unconscious repressed content and more or less conscious or even preconscious repressing mechanisms; it was also a question of how the various parts of the ego related to each other and worked in terms of each other. Thus, the analyst not only had to become much more sensitive to the indications of conflicts between each of the three systems (as, for example, between superego and id—e.g., in the case of superego functioning leading to a feeling of guilt for an instinctual impulse—this we would call an intersystemic conflict), but he also had to be aware of conflicts that arose between the various functioning parts of the ego itself (intrasystemic conflicts).

It immediately becomes apparent that the therapeutic enterprise in this frame of reference is considerably more complex and difficult than that predicated by Freud's earlier model. The earlier model had predicated the simple recovery of traumatic memories and their adequate abreactive discharge as the central modality of therapeutic change. The new model, however, suggested that the therapeutic effort was caught up in the complex interaction of various parts of the patient's functioning psyche so that if one were able to achieve some degree of release or resolution in one area of psychic function, that modification would have important reverberations and set up significant reactions in other areas of the patient's psychic functioning. Consequently, if one were to try to interpret or clarify one aspect of the patient's conflict, one had to take into account at the same time the multiple ramifications of that input for all the various levels and areas of functioning that were also going on in the patient's mind at the same time—both consciously and unconsciously.

There emerged from this the important analytic principle, enunciated so clearly by Anna Freud (6), of equidistance; that is, if one were to think of the psychic agencies as arranged somehow in a mental space, the analyst figuratively tries to keep himself equidistant from all of these areas of functioning without allowing himself to become excessively involved in or attentive to any one of them, thus allowing all of them to have their proper play and interaction within the analytic process. If, for example, the analyst were to ally himself too closely with the patient's ego, the potential for expression of both instinctually derived material and superego inputs would be correspondingly diminished. Similarly, if the analyst were to ally himself excessively with a superego position, repressive forces would be introduced into the analysis that would have important consequences for the analytic process. Even if the analyst were to excessively ally himself with a given ego position, this might serve only to short-circuit or undermine other operating ego positions and thus allow potential areas of intrasystemic conflict to go unattended. So the analytic principle of equidistance maximizes not only the availability of inputs from various areas of psychic functioning, but also the potential for therapeutic change in all significant areas of psychic functioning.

TRANSFERENCE AND THE THERAPEUTIC ALLIANCE

Transference is central to the analytic process and in the overall understanding of the shifts in the analytic model from the cathartic to the most recent ego psychology model. When Freud began to make the distinction between areas of unconscious functioning related to instinctual drives and other areas of the psychic apparatus like ego and superego, he laid the foundation for an extremely important therapeutic distinction, namely the distinction between the transference neurosis and the therapeutic alliance. In the ego psychology approach, this distinction looms large. The infantile, more regressive aspects of the patient's functioning that are related to early ontogenetic levels and derived from instinctual sources become channeled over time into the transference neurosis, so that there is recreated in relationship to the analyst a kind of unique relationship that is not simply based on the here-and-now exchange between two personalities, but also involves derivatives from the infantile level of experience.

This conception of transference is similar to that formulated by Freud in the understanding of the genesis of neurosis: The affective involvement with and attachment to the original infantile object are cut off, repressed, and then re-expressed in a repetition of the qualities of that original relation within the current relationship to the analyst. This model of transference is relatively limited, as we understand it today, and suffers from many of the basic inadequacies of that earlier Freudian model. The earlier model is based on a fundamentally economic notion of repetition. That is, it postulates that the earlier infantile impulses are regenerated and reactivated in the analytic situation and are subsequently funneled into a new relationship with the analyst—as though the affective experience of and attachment to the analyst were simply a repetition of the patient's infantile experience.

This was accounted for on simply economic bases—by economic here I mean that the early theory focused simply on the mechanics, if you will, of repression and discharge, the well-known "return of the repressed." However, the new relationship to the analyst is not simply a repetition, but is, in fact, a new relationship that has its own unique set of motivations, its own inherent implications, its own complications and elaborations. In other words, it is a new interpersonal experience in which something new is created between patient and analyst that did not exist before in any previous relationship. This implies a considerable shift in theoretical orientation, specifically from an economic theory of repression and discharge to a much more genetically-based theory in which the residues of earlier infantile genetic experience are seen as now re-elaborated and reformed in a new developmental context.

But the fact remains that the transference neurosis is a privileged area of dynamic significance insofar as the unconsciously transferred elements are determined very largely and predominantly by infantile residues. This provides the analyst with the opportunity, when the transference neurosis finally emerges and becomes defined and clarified, to be able to explore the forces in the mind that underlie this phenomenon. There is a common misunderstanding, even among analysts, that an adequate transference interpretation need only concern itself with the element of repetition in the transference neurosis. So an analyst might observe that some part of the patient's response to the analyst is similar to certain aspects of the patient's interaction with a parental figure. But such an interpretation remains fragmentary and partial, simply because the transference manifestation has its own inherent motivations in the present which call into play a whole different set of variables than those involved in the earlier developmental object relationship.

Let me try to be clear about the point I am making here. In looking at transference from the repressed side, we are talking about an early emotional attachment that is somehow cut off, repressed, and resurfaces in the current relationship to the analyst. Between that point of view and the point of view that would look at the phenomenon in terms of an understanding of the processes and mechanisms of the mind, particularly the ways in which the mind deals with and integrates levels and aspects of its experience in the current context of a newly experienced relationship, we can see that the new relationship which is emerging may have many similar characteristics to a previous one, but that it has its own peculiar characteristics that cannot simply be reduced to that other previous relationship. Furthermore, as soon as you decide that the model of the mind that you are providing for yourself has autonomous areas of conflict-free functioning (something that can be found in almost all patients), you have the basis for understanding formation of such new relationships unrelated to the previous considerations of repetition and infantile determinants. That area of therapeutic interaction which is not reducible to the terms of transference and which calls into play other areas of relatively autonomous functioning within the patient in the relationship with the analyst is called the *therapeutic alliance.*

Without the theory of independent structure in the ego, and perhaps to some extent in the superego, one would have to maintain the position that it would be impossible for any patient to become involved with and relate to the analyst in any terms that would not be subject to the determinants and vicissitudes of transference. This is very much the position that is maintained currently by Kleinian theorists. The strong emphasis on unconscious fantasy in all aspects of mental functioning—a core supposition of the Kleinian approach—means that in their therapeutic approach the Kleinians, for all practical purposes, ignore any aspects of autonomous function that we might describe as related to the therapeutic alliance and focus their attention almost exclusively on transference phenomena. Indeed, such clinicians interpret these in terms of the most primitive instinctual determinants. But if one acknowledges theoretically the autonomous existence of ego structure as an operative part of the mental apparatus which plays a determining role in the shaping of the therapeutic relationship, then one opens up a whole different area of understanding of the complexities of the therapeutic relationship, as well as a quite different understanding of what therapy is about, how it works, and how change is brought about within the patient.

In his still marvelous paper on transference love, Freud (7) pointed out that the transference was not only the most powerful motivating force in the analysis, but also the source of the most powerful resistance to therapeutic progress. What he referred to as "positive transference" makes it possible for the analysis to occur at all, and provides the basic motivation for the patient's continuing involvement in the analytic process. Without this positive transferential attachment to the analyst, the resistances that are stirred up by the analytic process would simply be too strong and the patient would not be able to tolerate it.

Remember that Freud was operating with a relatively simple model of the mind that did not leave room for any kind of positive involvement with the analyst other than the unconsciously derived and instinctually-based positive transference. If, however, you are working with a more differentiated model that allows for areas of autonomous ego function in addition to instinctual attachments, the way is open to a more complex understanding of the patient's relationship to the therapist and particularly of the patient's positive involvement. In other words, the patient's positive involvement in the analytic process may not simply be a reflection of positive transference, but may also involve other elements and other aspects of the patient's functioning which allow him to engage in the analytic process as a positive collaboration with the analyst so that they can settle down and accomplish the analytic work together. The shift to a structural hypothesis and particularly the development of a functional concept of the ego led in the direction of this more differentiated understanding of the analytic process, and thus evolved the concept of the therapeutic alliance.

Once these two different aspects of positive involvement in the analytic process have been established, they must be identified and differentiated further. Because the concept of transference neurosis was formulated very early in Freud's own experience and has been utilized as a central principle of clinical work since then, its varieties and vicissitudes are quite familiar and well understood. The notion of the therapeutic alliance has been available for a lesser time and its use does not have such an extensive history as the use of transference neurosis. Indeed, there has been a tendency to take the therapeutic alliance for granted. There is general agreement that the areas of ego functioning that I have discussed to this point do have a role in the analytic process and for a good treatment there must be a reasonably solid alliance; however, in a relatively healthy and well functioning neurotic patient, there is generally a fairly solid alliance formed without too much difficulty and relatively automatically, so that there is not the concern about whether the alliance is going to be formed or maintained. Attention then is much more explicitly focused on the complexities and vicissitudes of the transference.

It is evident, however, that many patients do not have this automatic ability to develop and maintain a therapeutic alliance. Rather, they may have a variety of characterologic dysfunctions representing more complex psychopathology. These patients tend to have considerably greater difficulties with the therapeutic alliance. In working with these patients, the concern has shifted to an understanding of those factors which contribute to the therapeutic alliance, how the therapeutic alliance can be established and maintained, and also how the variety of therapeutic misalliances which arise so easily and frequently in the treatment of these patients can be addressed, resolved, and worked through. It remains a solidly established analytic principle that a reasonably firm and constant therapeutic alliance is required for the work of the analysis. But what happens when the patient's pathology is such that the therapeutic alliance itself is tenuous, unable to be maintained, inconsistent, fluctuating and easily subject to regression?

This is a shift away from a model which emphasizes intrapsychic conflicts exclusively. Freud's early model for explaining hysteria is based on the conflict between instinct and defense, and even later in the structural theory the element of conflict remains central, particularly in the intersystemic conflicts between the respective psychic agencies, as, for example, between ego and superego. This sort of conflict model operates best when you have more or less articulated and structuralized agencies which are brought into interaction and opposition in such a way that functioning in one area of psychic activity runs into conflict with psychic functioning in some other area. Moreover, these conflicts are essentially intrapsychic.

We have come to recognize this structure of psychic agencies with its emphasis on intrapsychic conflict as characteristic of neurotic personalities. Thus, the structural and conflict-based models operate optimally when we are dealing with such reasonably well-developed neurotic personalities. In fact, these models were developed in an effort to understand precisely these personalities. But in other areas of psychopathology, which are recognized more commonly now, the problem involves not so much intrapsychic conflict, but, rather, the difficulties that are inherent in establishing and maintaining relationships with other significant human beings.

It is this area of the patient's pathology that seems to bring into focus most acutely problems related to the therapeutic alliance. Consequently, the issues in such patients are no longer primarily those of impulse and defense, but relate to difficulties that cut below the level of such conflicts. It is not that such patients do not have issues of conflict—these are often extremely important at some point in the patient's therapeutic work; however, the more pressing and more important difficulties have to do with the inability of the patient to relate in a meaningful, consistent and cooperative manner with the therapist.

The problems and challenges presented by the therapeutic alliance form a major focus of psychoanalytic research in the contemporary scene. Obviously, with the patients we have been discussing, the problems related to development and maintaining of a therapeutic alliance take precedence over more specifically conflict-related issues impinging on the transference neurosis. Unless the alliance is established and maintained effectively, no useful therapeutic work can be accomplished and there is little chance that issues that may relate to problems in dealing with the transference will be explored or resolved. The levels of pathological defect that underlie these difficulties with the alliance appear to stem from extremely early strata of the patient's developmental experience.

One of the major problems in such patients, for example, is their difficulty in generating any sense of enduring trust in the therapist. Such a deficit of basic trust stems, to the best of our knowledge, from very early interchanges between the needy infant and the mothering figure.

The classical transference distortions that derive from oedipal fixations were difficult enough in terms of the task of gaining some understanding of them through analytic work and later from study of children's oedipal development. But the defects that impinge upon the therapeutic alliance are considerably more primitive and involve much earlier developmental levels that are certainly pregenital and, by and large, preverbal. Not only are such levels considerably more difficult to work with in the analytic situation, but attempts to gain some understanding or some toehold in this difficult area from the observation of children or from other forms of developmental research have been extremely limited in effectiveness.

OBJECT RELATIONS THEORY

In the current context, analytic thinking is astir with a vigorous re-casting and rethinking of traditional notions in an attempt to gain some better understanding of these more primitive areas of psychic functioning and their genesis. Discussions about the role of narcissism and of early object-related experience dominate much of the current analytic ferment. The structural theory articulated in terms of the classic tripartite agencies, the id, ego and superego, have had to give way in only the last few years to a consideration and reformulation of intrapsychic activity that is recast more in terms of the organization and functioning of the self. The psychology of the self, related in complex and still not thoroughly formulated ways to the development of narcissism, has become an exciting new area for the generation of analytic insights. The further integration of insights developed out of a self-versus-object frame of theoretical consideration with the more established and traditional body of classical ego psychology, still firmly rooted in the structural and tripartite theory, remains a critical theoretical problem. (See Chapter 4.)

The emergence of the structural theory prepared the way for a more specific emphasis on the role of internalized objects and an increasing awareness, particularly in the wake of Freud's The Ego and the Id (8), of the significance in the transference of early object relations in the development of both ego and superego. The analyst not only is an object for the displacement of infantile attitudes and wishes, but also substitutes by projection for the idealized or prohibiting parental objects. Loewald (9) has pointed out that the transference is really a new object relationship which facilitates the regressive crisis of the transference neurosis with its accompanying infantile anxieties. In some respects, then, the analytic situation can be viewed as a form of repetition of certain aspects of the mother-child relationship. With this consideration, emphasis in the understanding of therapeutic effectiveness shifted from matters of simple interpretation to include concepts related to the introjection of the analyst with the resulting alteration of superego severity.

Thus, the effect of interpretations in analysis could be seen as serving to facilitate this analytic internalization and the subsequent structural modification (10). Within the framework of object relations, interpretation has the function of facilitating understanding and working-through of the transference neurosis. The transference is effectively a form of resistance which must be analyzed. However, a higher priority is placed on forming and maintaining a stable working relationship between the analyst and patient. Thus, early work in the analytic process is concerned with analysis of defense and with building and reinforcing an effective therapeutic alliance rather than with interpretation of unconscious fantasy material. In dealing with patients whose object relations conflicts and self-integration are on a more primitive level, the emphasis in the therapeutic effort shifts even more to the creation of a "holding" environment within which the patient can be unthreatened and secure and which provides a matrix within which some attempt can be made to undo and rework the early trauma in the mother-child relationship.

The greatest resistance in this context is shown in the patient's attempt to maintain his internal world of internalized and split objects. This forms a closed system which isolates the patient from difficult interactions with his environment, and provides a locus within which the closed system dynamics of Freud can have their play. The therapeutic aim is to create a breach in this internal world, this closed system, and to make it accessible to the influence of reality. The reality principle, in opposition to the pleasure principle, operates more in an open system fashion in which inner and outer realities can be brought into meaningful relationship and approximation. The transference neurosis tends to flourish within the closed system context, so that the relationship with the external object is available more in terms of transference distortions than reality. Interpretation in this context is inadequate for promoting therapeutic change. Rather, the patient's relationship to the analyst must develop in such a way that the transference can be gradually worked through and replaced by a real relationship. This can only be accomplished by disruption of the patient's artificially closed system and replacement of it with a more open system of relationship and engagement in meaningful and adaptive ways with external objects.

Thus, it can be seen readily enough that the growth of analytic experience—particularly the growth in experience with the more difficult forms of character pathology, in which the issues of developmental

deficits, conflicts in object relationships, and impairments in the organization and functioning of the self-system play a predominant role—has
led analysts to formulate a quite different and broader-reaching theoretical perspective to give support to their continuing therapeutic efforts.
It is important to note in all of this that very little of the analytic acquisition is left behind in this process. Rather, the previous forms and levels
of understanding have to be reintegrated as parts of a more extensive,
more far-reaching explanatory framework, which enjoys increasingly
greater power both in theoretical understanding and therapeutic effectiveness.

This chapter emphasizes the evolution of analytic ideas and the development of more differentiated and more sophisticated models of how
the mental apparatus functions. This evolution has developed from a
process of continual interaction with clinical experience. Not only has
the deepening and broadening of clinical experience led to a gradual
and continual modification of the theory, but the emergence of certain
kinds of theoretical formulations has laid the ground for new appreciation of certain clinical observations and has at frequent junctures in the
history of psychoanalysis resulted in significant shifts in therapeutic
orientation.

This has been true from the very beginning of psychoanalysis, and
I would like to think that that spirit of open inquiry which constantly
seeks to learn more and more about how the human mind functions,
both in illness and in health, has not faded from the psychoanalytic
scene. I can tell you from my own personal experience that work in
psychoanalysis has been challenging and exciting from the first day I
came into contact with it over a score of years ago, and it remains today
no less challenging, no less stimulating, no less provocative, and no less
engrossing. No one who has any familiarity with the contemporary
psychoanalytic literature could even begin to think of it as static or
unproblematic. The challenge to learn and to constantly gain new understanding and perspective and the continual opportunity to deepen,
enrich, probe and question our current understanding of the human
psyche are presented with every patient and arise almost daily in the
experience of every thinking analyst. It is this unique openness, closeness and intimate interworking with clinical data and clinical experience
that give psychoanalysis its unique stamp. It is in that close contact with
the clinical world that psychoanalysis lives. The further scientific question is whether it can continue to live and breathe in other less clinical
contexts.

REFERENCES

1. Freud, S.: *On Aphasia*, New York: International Universities Press, 1953.
2. Breuer, J. and Freud, S.: Studies on hysteria, *Standard Edition*, 2. London: Hogarth, 1955.
3. Freud, S.: Project for a scientific psychology, *Standard Edition*, 1: 281-397, London: Hogarth, 1966.
4. Freud, S.: The interpretation of dreams, *Standard Edition*, 4 and 5, London: Hogarth, 1953.
5. Freud, S.: *The Origins of Psychoanalysis* M. Bonaparte et al. (Eds.) Garden City: Doubleday, Letter 69.
6. Freud, A.: *The Ego and the Mechanisms of Defense*. New York: International Universities Press, 1966.
7. Freud, S.: Papers on technique. Observations on transference-love, Standard Edition, 12: 157-171. London: Hogarth, 1958.
8. Freud, S.: The ego and the id, *Standard Edition*, 19, London: Hogarth, 1961.
9. Loewald, H.: On the therapeutic action of psychoanalysis. *Int. J. Psychoanalysis*, 41: 16-33, 1960.
10. Strachey, J.: The nature of the therapeutic action of psychoanalysis. *Int. J. Psychoanalysis*, 50: 275-291, 1969.

Chapter 2

The Psychology of Women:
A Contemporary Appraisal

Malkah T. Notman, M.D.

INTRODUCTION

Psychoanalysis has been a constantly changing discipline. Since its inception with the original discoveries of Freud, modifications have been continual. This has been true in all areas of psychoanalysis—theory, therapy and research. Psychoanalytic theory about women also has undergone many changes, during Freud's time and afterward. In fact, Freud himself noted that he did not feel he understood women's psychology well. Recently, responding in part to the impact of the women's movement, psychoanalytic views about women have received particular attention. Since many of the original ideas were developed in the culture of Freud's time, they reflected the phallocentric aspects of that culture. With the exceptions of criticism and modifications from Karen Horney (1), Ernest Jones (2), and a few others later, such as Clara Thompson (3) and Gregory Zilboorg (4), the ideas were rarely questioned from positions outside that culture until recently.

It is interesting to note the extent to which the male's development and psychic structure were placed centrally in theoretical formulations, and how little this was recognized or then thought inappropriate, even though the majority of patients were women. That is, the ideas of how a human being developed were conceptualized as if this person were male. The female version was then presented as a "variant" of the male. Freud did state explicitly that he thought he did not understand women well and that he felt little was known about women; he stressed the need for knowledge about women's biology and psychology (5). He presented some excellent clinical descriptions, based on his and others' observations, which are still valid today; however, he drew a particular set of conclusions from those observations and presented them as if they were universally valid. It is possible to draw alternative conclusions from these same observations, conclusions which are not as influenced by the same cultural stereotypes, which take into account the impact of so-cialization on what were thought to be innate processes, and which also include more contemporary sophistication about biology and develop-ment.

Psychoanalysis is still identified by some as a field which depreciates women. However, there have been a number of recent contributions which have re-examined old ideas and made major revisions. The early formulations were frequently based on reconstructions of child devel-opment from clinical experience with adults. In recent years, careful infant observations have contributed to major revisions about devel-opment and psychoanalytic theory. The disciplines of biology, anthro-pology and sociology, which were not as well developed in the period of Freud's first writing, have contributed further new data. Modern technical advances have made more sophisticated tools available for observation and experimentation in the biological sciences and related fields.

In this chapter, I shall address several major concepts and indicate the changes which have occurred in contemporary psychoanalysis. To do so, I will present a discussion of "femininity" to guide our thinking, review what Freud and other classical analysts thought about the con-cepts of passivity, masochism, narcissism, penis envy, and bisexuality, which have become such pivotal terms in current discussions, relate recent evidence to this material, and conclude with some contemporary ideas about feminine development and what are, in turn, special issues for the psychotherapy/psychoanalysis of contemporary women.

DEFINITION OF FEMININITY

Femininity is a very difficult subject to define because the word is

used in a number of ways. It is used descriptively, normatively, diagnostically, clinically and colloquially. The confusion of descriptive and
normative has long been a problem (6). When one attempts to focus on
"essential" descriptive components, a new complexity emerges, that of
drawing boundaries between the effects of socialization and inherent
biological determinants. For example, it is clear from many studies of
very early, postnatal interaction of caretakers and infants that expectations exist in parents which are related to the gender of the infant and
which affect the behavior of the caretakers (7). Infant development is
now understood to be a reciprocal process in which the infant also
stimulates responses in the caretaker, who further engages the infant
and thus contributes to his/her development.

It may be more appropriate to consider femininity as a fluctuating
concept involving reciprocally interrelated processes, with mutually interacting influences of determinants from genetic, anatomical and instinctual sources, with interpersonal and social forces. Being born as a
girl, then, means being an individual with a specific genetic composition
and anatomical structures, with the potential for their further development in a recognized feminine direction under the influence of specific
hormones, which are present prenatally and postnatally. At the same
time, being born as a girl activates particular expectations in parents and
others, stimulating responses which are different in many ways from
those that are aroused towards a boy baby (5, 9). These are culturally
determined as well, having origins in each individual's personal and
family history, and they, in turn, affect the development of the individual
into someone appearing and behaving as a "feminine" person.

In an attempt to describe "feminine" behavior, one still resorts to
stereotypes which may, indeed, remain clinically valid, although one is
really describing a behavioral and responsive continuum. The descriptive norms of femininity are often difficult to separate from the pros-
criptive ones. For instance, many women are indeed more passive and
less manifestly aggressive than most men. This is clinically true; at the
same time it probably also represents an expression of lifelong restric-
tions against expressing aggression and activity directly, and also against
being self-assertive where this behavior would be judged appropriate
for males.

FREUD'S AND OTHER EARLY CONCEPTS OF FEMININITY

Freud's original description of femininity involved a triad of characteristics: passivity, masochism and narcissism (10, 11). His original for-

mulation also characterized femininity as giving preference to "passive aims," which he distinguished from passivity itself, saying that to achieve a passive aim may demand a great deal of activity and acknowledging the activity involved in maternal behavior. Although he warned against equating masculinity with activity and femininity with passivity, he himself did not heed the warning and often used "passive" for "feminine" and "active" for "masculine."

Passivity

In understanding the differences between men and women, Freud turned to their early development. He believed that girls and boys develop similarly for the first three years, until they become fully aware of anatomical differences. He thought that children assumed that everyone started life with the same form of genital, a penis, and that the discovery of the female body with the missing genital constituted a "castration shock" for both boys and girls. The girl thought she had a penis originally and lost it, for which she blamed her mother and felt angry, envious and defective. This Freud saw as a turning point in the little girl's growth. He viewed her early development as essentially "masculine," with her pleasurable sexual sensations deriving from her clitoris as parallel to the boy's phallic experiences. Masturbation initially was also viewed as "masculine" because it was primarily clitoral. Her early relationship with her mother was profoundly affected by this discovery of her "inferiority."

Freud believed that the feelings of inferiority led to a renunciation of sexuality for the little girl. It is important to remember that Freud was the first to recognize the importance of infantile sexuality and of masturbation as part of the development of normal sexual feelings and expression. He discussed masturbation and its significance in three phases—an infantile phase, a childhood phase and then a new phase in adolescence. He believed that early masturbation for girls was clitoral and not vaginal. This also entered into the body image of the girl, that is, how the girl viewed herself and her body, particularly her genitals. Since he thought of the clitoris as an inferior, small penis, he assumed that the little girl experienced this in the same way and inevitably felt disappointed. As a consequence of this disappointment, she renounced some of her sexuality, and at least some of her masturbation as well (5, 10, 11).

Another important consequence of this experience was the little girl's turning away from her mother, whom she also devalued, as she realized her mother did not have a penis either, and she turned towards her father, beginning her oedipus complex (or electra complex as others have referred to this in women). In the process, her earlier activity was given up and "passivity" gained the "upper hand," leading her eventually to give up the wish for a penis and substitute the wish for a baby in the course of her development towards femininity.

These ideas were shared by other analysts, although they were challenged to some extent by Karen Horney and Ernest Jones. Jones, Kleeman (12) and some others stressed the relationship with the mother, which they believed played a preponderant role in the child's life in the first year; they also felt that the little girl was from birth more feminine than masculine.

Freud (10) and other early analysts believed that the little girl was not really aware of her inner sexual organs or of her vagina and did not integrate these in her self-image, which could therefore not involve a positive feeling about her anatomy. As it was observed, female masturbation was clitoral and thus fitted these ideas about "early masculinity." In the shift which was to occur later, from the clitoris to the vagina, Freud saw a renunciation of what he called the "early masculine phase" of femininity, or "childish masculinity," and this shift from clitoris to vagina was related to true feminine development. Little girls were therefore thought of as if they were "castrated" boys. Femininity came after disappointment with oneself and conflict. The wish for a baby, an important component of feminine identity, was thought to be a replacement for what the girl did not have. The development necessary for successful parenthood and its positive experience was not considered at this point.

So, in girls, the castration complex and penis envy led to turning away from the mother and towards the father and thus initiated the Oedipus complex. In boys, the oedipal development was different. The growing sexualized attachment to the mother and consequent rivalry with the father intensified the little boy's anxiety and fear of punishment. He developed castration anxiety as a result of learning about sex differences and interpreting the girl's lack of a penis as a castration, which he then feared for himself. Castration anxiety constituted a powerful motivation for renouncing his oedipal wishes for his mother—thus encouraging his movement out of the oedipal phase.

In attempting to understand femininity and the role of reproduction and the genitals, divergent psychoanalytic theories about feminine development centered for a time around the questions of whether early vaginal sensations existed and whether the little girl was aware of the vagina and uterus as organs which could contain a baby (13). Those who believed that she *did* have this awareness assumed an early development of what was considered femininity. Freud's view was that the vagina was discovered only at puberty and "true" femininity accepted only then. There was some disagreement about this. However, pregnancy and mothering, the awareness of the vagina and the expectation of future babies were seen as central to feminine identity.

Others, such as Benedek (14) and Bonaparte (15) sought some explanation for women's drive organization and maternal behavior in biological and instinctual determinants. Benedek thought that the major basis for the biological roots of the feelings associated with pregnancy and motherhood was to be found in the fluctuation of the female endocrine cycle. She studied this cycle and concluded that the "deep-rooted passivity" and "tendency toward introversion," described by Helene Deutsch (16) as characteristic of the female psyche, appeared mostly in connection with the post-ovulative phase of the menstrual cycle. Benedek also looked for some connections between feminine characteristics and cyclical changes and studied hormonal variations and psychological material, attempting to establish relationships, using relatively crude hormonal assays of the 1940s. She thought she did find connections between cyclic variations in psychic states and she concluded that "the emotional manifestations of the 'specific receptive tendency' and the 'self-centered retentive tendency' are the psychodynamic correlates of a biologic need for motherhood," and that therefore motherhood is not secondary or a substitute for the missing penis, but it is the manifestation of an "instinct for survival in the child that is the primary organizer of the women's sexual drive and her personality" (17). In this, she anticipated current writers who stress the non-substitutive nature of the wish for a child and who describe the reciprocal nature of the development of motherly feelings as a response to the infant's needs (18, 19, 20). Although developmental identification with one's mother was seen by her and others as an important determinant of a woman's emotional attitude toward motherhood and of her mothering behavior, the central role of the pre-oedipal identification with the mother was not emphasized as much by earlier writers as was the biological, if not instinctual, origins of mothering behavior and of the female drive organization. Adult women's psychological attitudes were thought to be dependent on a hormonal or some other biological basis. Another view of the source of the wish for a child was that the baby was a replacement for the organ the girl did not have. This was prevalent in the literature.

Masochism

A second component of Freud's and Deutsch's "feminine triad" was masochism. Freud regarded masochism as due to "the suppression of women's aggressiveness which is prescribed for them constitutionally and imposed on them socially which favors the development of powerful masochistic impulses" (5, p. 116). He went on to say that masochism was "truly feminine" (5).

There was, also, in the early literature some discussion as to whether masochism was at all biologically determined and whether feminine masochism represented an adaptation to the inevitable pain of child-bearing or other feminine experiences. Helene Deutsch (16) considered "feminine masochism" as parallel to "activity directed inward"; that is, a woman's masochism is parallel to the man's intensified aggression which accompanies his activity directed outward at the end of adolescence. Thus she distinguished feminine masochism from the neurotic masochism which manifested itself in perversions and neurotic suffering and pain. She spoke instead of a passive-masochistic character type characterizing the feminine physiological structure.

Narcissism

The third element in Freud's and Deutsch's feminine triad was narcissism. The concept of narcissism has acquired different contemporary meanings, relating to descriptions of personality types and diagnoses; these will not be discussed here. In describing feminine narcissism, Freud said that one attributes a larger amount of narcissism to femininity, which also affects women's choice of object, so that to be loved is a stronger need for women than to love (5, 16). "The effect of penis envy has a share in the physical vanity of women, since they are bound to value their charms more highly as a late compensation for their original sexual inferiority" (3). He was both describing clinical phenomena and ascribing dynamic reasons for them in these statements. It is a narcissistic disappointment which, according to Freud, leads the little girl to withdraw from her mother and to turn to her father when she discovers her lack of penis.

There is a strong association in this thinking between the sexual anatomical situation in which a woman receives the male sperm in the sexual act and the personality attributes thought to characterize femininity. Freud really saw feminine love as passive and narcissistic where the woman lets herself be loved (7).

As is clear from what has been said, although Freud respected individual women, valued them as colleagues and was one of the first physicians to take many baffling problems of women seriously, he really did
feel that many "feminine" characteristics were due to an actual genital
inferiority, which women also believed, and the consequences of this
inferiority led to the need to overcome or hide these facts. He thought
women were fully satisfied only when they had a son, compensating
for penis envy and feelings of inferiority. The greater cultural value and
status of a male child over a female child did not seem to enter his
arguments.

CURRENT PSYCHOANALYTIC THINKING

There have been successive changes in many areas of thinking in
regard to women (21). Questions and modifications came from within
psychoanalytic movements, expressed in its early days by Jones, Horney, Thompson and others, from data from other fields, and from an
evolution of thinking as social changes had an impact on sex roles, family
patterns, and other societal realities.

Recent writers have presented evidence to clarify feminine development and challenge some of the early analytic views. The image of
women as anatomically defective because of the absence of the penis
and the substitutive nature of childbearing, for example, have been
questioned extensively (21, 22, 23). Chasseget-Smirgel (24) says: "Images
of women as deficient or castrated are a denial for both sexes of the
images of the primitive mother, the good omnipotent mother, symbol-
ized by the generous breast, fruitful womb, wholeness, abundance."

Many recent authors have addressed themselves to the question of
feminine identity, its sources and childhood manifestations, and have
attempted to create a concept of femininity and an understanding of
feminine development based on knowledge of the female rather than
on the model of the male. However, the components of femininity are
not uniformly agreed upon. Even the role of reproduction, in which
women have a unique function, has not occupied an undisputed place.

In attempting to arrive at a contemporary definition of femininity, one
must include a number of components. One group consists of those
behaviors, attitudes and styles presented as feminine in a given culture.
Those are, in turn, related to physical functions which are exclusively
female, such as reproduction, and any others dynamically related to
these reproductive roles. Is it necessary to have a dichotomy between
masculine and feminine? Although many distinctions between mascu-

line and feminine are blurring and there may be fewer inherent differences between the capacities of men and women, there do appear to be some differences. Certainly, many differences have in the past been used to justify inequities. However, some tendency to polarize may be universal, although this is more limited than in the past. This tendency may derive from the male-female differences in relation to childbearing, intimacy with the very young child, and some blurring of the distinctions between oneself and others in pregnancy. The early differences between boys' and girls' relationships to male and female parents may have also been an important basis for developmentally different outcomes. For example, in separating himself from an early attachment and early identification with a female parent, the little boy must differentiate himself from the feminine personality (21).

It is difficult to describe femininity without including some reference to the reproductive functions of the woman and the identification with and anticipation of these by the little girl. It is also difficult to discuss femininity apart from masculinity, which has also been a changing concept in recent years. One might question whether a woman's self-esteem must be as closely bound up as it has been with her attractiveness and relationships to men, or whether having children will actually be achieved by all women in this period of a declining birth rate. Recent concepts seek to define femininity in terms which do not use as a basis a substitution of reproduction, or the baby, for a defect the girl feels she has, or the missing penis; that is, these theorists attempt to describe and understand a separate line of feminine development (22, 25, 26). However, reproductive capacity and choice do seem to be important components of femininity in a developing girl, whether or not that choice is actually exercised by an adult women. At least at present, there is considerable evidence that women do make choices about themselves in relation to others which are different from the choices made by men (25, 27) and which can be said to be important components of femininity.

Data from the Biological Sciences

It is obvious that men and women are anatomically and biologically different. The extent to which the behavioral and personality differences which accompany sex roles are biologically determined is far from resolved. The role of hormones and the developmental consequences of anatomical differences need to be studied further. Many manifest sex differences are the result of interaction between the biological determinants and the social factors.

However, there are clear maturational and neurological differences from birth, with girls born neurologically more mature. Left brain hemisphere maturation is also reported to be earlier in girls, with consequent behavioral and skill differences, which in turn elicit different responses from their caretakers (28). The implications of these differences for later development are not entirely possible to determine at this time.

Freud believed that bisexuality was a constitutional biological potential upon which later psychological development rests, and that it was characteristic of all individuals to have both "masculine" and "feminine" traits, although these were not clearly defined (29). Data from studies of embryological development have seemed to confirm this idea, since the reproductive organs of each sex develop from undifferentiated precursors, which, in the presence of appropriate hormones, can appear to develop into either male or female organs. Actually, it is the genetic composition which determines the sex—with two X chromosomes constituting females and XY chromosomes constituting males. However, the potential exists for modifying the cells, tissues and organs of each sex in the direction of the opposite sex by introducing appropriate hormones (26).

The mechanisms of the differentiation into male and female are interesting. The genetic composition of XX or XY determines the initial differentiation of ovaries or testes from the primitive undifferentiated tissue. The circulating hormones produced by these organs in the fetus then determine further differentiation into recognizable sex organs. If the embryo is to be male, the testes differentiate earlier than the ovaries and secrete both androgen and a hormone which produces regression of the Mullerian duct system. In the absence of androgens, the individual appears female. Rather than considering this to be bisexuality, more recent investigators have labeled this "sexual bipotentiality" (29). Furthermore, the resting or primary state androgens must be present at a particular time in fetal development. It is thus possible to have an individual who is genetically male but appears female, in that external genitalia are undeveloped and the penis looks like a clitoris (29, 30).

The implications of these data for psychological development are not immediately apparent. However, this approach does represent a contrast to the point of view in which normal female development is seen as a variant of the male. Continuing research in this area is resulting in many new findings. There appear to be some central nervous system effects of these fetal hormones as well, such as those changes which are precursors of cycling in the female, leading in later life to menstrual cycles under the subsequent influence of the hypothalamic-pituitary-ovarian interrelationships.

Gender Identity

The establishment of gender identity has been clarified and distinguished from femininity or masculinity. This concept involves the cognitive awareness of the sex one is. In rare instances this varies from one's "true" sex, as the phenotype may be different from the genotype because an endocrine or anatomical problem distorts the genitals as seen at birth, but the sex the infant is decided to be (called the "sex assignment"), which is the sex in which a child is reared, exerts a predominant influence on the individual's self-concept. Gender identity development is accompanied by awareness of sex roles, that is, the behaviors, attitudes, expectations, appearance which accompany each sex. It is firmly established by about 18 months (30).

Stoller regards this development as untraumatic and unconflicted. He speaks of "primary femininity" as representing the first stage in female development. It consists of the establishment of a sense of being rightfully a female, based on the combination of biological factors, sex assignment at birth, parental attitudes, early postnatal effects and developing bodily sensations, especially from the genitals. However, he believes the second stage of feminine development is the result of conflicts, particularly oedipal conflict, and the resolution of these conflicts produces a more complicated and richer femininity. This idea of a "primary femininity" has gained considerable acceptance (26).

Significance of Early Relationships

The importance of the early pre-oedipal attachment to the mother has received increased recognition, supporting some of the early ideas of Jones and Klein, but with some different emphasis. There is also acknowledgment of the degree and significance of the little girl's early attachment to her father. Abelin (31) states that the little girl develops a differentiated relationship to the father before her first birthday. Little girls tend to be generally more discriminating than little boys with regard to unfamiliar persons. Observations of children in the 10- to 18-month period indicate that the mother is perceived as the expressive affectional parent and the father as the instrumental parent (32). This confirms the establishment of the awareness of sex-role differences early and clearly is in the context of sex-role stereotyping of the predominant styles of women and men.

The importance of infant development is better understood in current theory and the contribution of pre-oedipal experience is, in general, acknowledged more fully than in early psychoanalytic theory. The importance of these pre-oedipal relationships before the conflicts of the phallic phase have been recently reviewed by Galenson (33). The girl's identification with her mother forms an important early component of her feminine identity and her sense of gender identity is partly based on this identification. The impact of external reality and relationships with others has been increasingly recognized.

There is abundant evidence that pre-oedipal, as well as oedipal, experience and interactions differ for boys and girls. Their relationship to the mother is necessarily different. The mother's own relationship with her mother is recreated by having a daughter. This also enables her to identify with her own child and re-experience the past, as well as to restitute it, perhaps, by becoming a better mother and daughter (34, 35). There is likely to be a different, and perhaps more intense, tie between a mother and a daughter (35) than between a mother and a son. This had been less emphasized in the past than the importance of the son in supplying the "missing penis." This process of close identification with the daughter may result, however, in increased difficulty for the mother in permitting and supporting differentiation and separation-individuation in her daughter, with the resultant persistence of strong pre-oedipal attachments to the mother. This phenomenon has been described by many psychoanalytic writers (2, 5, 16, 36).

Chodorow (37) points to aspects of the difference in male and female development which may partly account for the affective and relational identifications between women and their mothers, as opposed to the "positional" identifications boys have with their fathers (i.e., relating to their status and role). She feels that the close tie which has been established and the availability of the mother are important factors. The father, less available in traditionally organized families, is defined more by fantasy, as well as via values and behavior. Because of this difference and the potential regressive appeal of the mother, the need to reject the feminine may be more pronounced in boys than the need to reject the masculine in girls. In this way, boys preserve their masculine identification. The identification with father is made in negative rather than positive terms, i.e., by avoidance of the feminine, in this view. Women, by contrast, may have more problems with their separation and individuation.

Body Image

An additional set of important developmental influences derives from the experience of having a female body, with a vaginal opening, rather than the protruding genitals (26). The relationship of this to the learned expectations of one's inner potential—that is, that one has the potential to bear children—and also to body changes which are expected later, including the growth of a new structure, breasts, also forms part of feminine self-concept. In turn, there are certain sex-related personality traits measured by psychological tests, such as the tendency to make less sharp differentiations of figure-ground perceptions, greater dependence on and investment in relationships, and greater affiliativeness, as well as other female-male differences which may also be influenced by these anatomical differences and their consequent subtle effects on one's perception of life. That is, if one's body presents some hidden organs and potential, possibly this has an effect on certain perceptual tendencies. This is not to minimize the powerful socializing factors which are in effect, including the different ways boys and girls are treated from their earliest days (38).

An important area of recent research is the documentation of sex differences in the rearing of children, not only as toddlers or school children but from birth on. Parental expectations are different for boys and girls even prenatally. Although Freud was obviously aware that parents treat little boys and girls differently, it has only been in the past 15-20 years that a considerable literature has developed which indicates the extent, depth, subtlety and significance of these differences. For example, Moss (39) observed infants and mothers over the first three months of life and found profound differences in maternal behavior toward male and female babies, as well as pronounced shifts from the way the infants were treated at three weeks to the way they were treated at three months. He felt that initially conditions are set by the infant, with its state, such as fussing, sleeping, waking, acting as an important variable. He found that mothers initially responded more to male infants, who were generally more irritable. By three months the mothers were responding less to them, and more "contingently" to females, resulting in conditions which he thought would make females "more amenable to the effects of social reinforcement and manifest a higher degree of attachment behavior" (39, p. 28). In another study (40), a six-month-old infant was dressed in girls' clothes and handed to a group of mothers, none of whom was the mother of this infant. This same infant was then dressed in boys' clothes and handed to the same group of mothers. The mothers responded differently to the boy than to the girl and described "him" as "different" from "her."

Other experiments indicate that adults who do not know the sex of an infant have difficulty relating to that infant at all because their responses are so heavily influenced by sex-role expectations.

Studies of older children confirm the differences in rearing and indicate that many more subtle socialization pressures are operating. For example, girls are clearly taught at an early age to deal with aggression indirectly. There is at present no clear evidence that there are sex differences in the innate potential for aggression, although some authors feel there might be, but there is strong evidence that males behave more aggressively than females (30). It is apparent that behavior of parents and other important people in a child's life has enormous impact, and that studies to assess sex differences are reaching older children and adults who have already lived through years of differentiated experiences. This knowledge contributes to the greater emphasis in recent theory on the importance of object relations and real experience, in contrast to the earlier focus on the development of the drives.

The importance of early learning, based on the maturation of cognitive capacities, has been recently stressed (33, 41). It was not really taken into account by early theorists. This includes the importance of language development with the concomitant categorizations which have become possible.

We have mentioned that the body image representation divides girls and boys early and that observations support the view that young children have differentiated relationships with each parent, male and female. From their studies of preschool children, Galenson and Roiphe (42) observe what they consider castration anxieties by the second half of the second year. They become apparent at the time the child develops anxiety about fears of losing the people who are important to him/her and are perceived as dangers to the self because of the child's still unstable sense of differentiation of self and others. Castration fears are strongly influenced by the child's life experience, such as the nature of his/her relationships, their constancy and the amount of stability or real loss which has occurred in that child's life.

In contrast to the early speculations about masturbation in little girls, data from clinical and research observations support the early awareness of the vagina in girls and confirm that girls' masturbation sometimes involves vaginal fantasies and play, so that the vagina does form part of the self-image (23, 38). The confusion many girls feel about their genitals is partly based on their hidden location and the taboos about examining them. The little girl cannot actually see the organ she is told about (43). This confusion is added to by parental mislabeling, using the term vagina to refer to the female genitals as a whole, without differentiating labia, vulva, vagina, uterus, etc.

Penis Envy

The central position given to conflicts of the oedipal stage and to penis envy as a stimulus to feminine development has shifted. Penis envy is no longer seen by most analysts as occupying as pivotal a position in women's psychological organization. It certainly exists as a concern for many women consciously or unconsciously; however, if it is a major problem in an adult woman, it is generally in connection with other conflicts in which early deprivation, intense envy, and separation problems are important components. For some women, it is an issue which may be present to various degrees but is not the critical determinant of feminine development. Identity and self-esteem are not thought to be necessarily related to a sense of defectiveness because of anatomical inferiority. In fact, the degree of penis envy Freud considered normal and necessary for the girl to achieve femininity is considered depressive by Clower (23), and to be an indication of pathological envy or the incomplete resolution of separation-individuation. That is to say, the woman does not feel "whole" on her own.

Passivity

Passivity as a description of the central aspect of adult femininity is incomplete, since it does not include the normal, active maternal behavior with which the young child identifies, which is part of even the early psychoanalytic views. It also does not address autonomous, assertive individuated development in women. It is perhaps less valid as a description of most women than it once was. Yet, many women do feel conflicted about aggression and do not easily use what abilities and talents they have to change social patterns regarding acceptable sex-role behavior. Conflicts around passivity persist clinically, although many women now perceive them and wish to change (8).

Self-Esteem

Recent psychoanalytic development has given considerable attention to "self psychology," in Kohut's (44) terms, and to the "awareness of self" and self-esteem. Self-esteem is difficult to define precisely, but for our purposes it can be defined as an ego state, involving an assessment of how one measures up to one's ego ideal or to the internalized values, goals, standards of parents and others. It is also an indication of how one wants to be.

Self-esteem is defined by Jacobson (45) as the ideational, especially the emotional, expression of self-evaluation. Self-esteem fluctuates within certain limits, depending on responses of others and one's own feelings of accomplishment, mastery, and value in a variety of ways.

Gender identity is inseparable from issues of self-esteem. An individual can feel good about herself if she feels adequate "as a woman"—whatever the definition of that may be. "Unfeminine" is usually a term of criticism. Physical and sexual experiences, bodily gratifications, acceptance of one's body and all its functions were stressed by Thompson as basic to the establishment of self-respect and self-esteem (3). Women have found it difficult to acquire ease and pleasure from their bodies and satisfaction with their body image or to experience gratification and pleasure from the sensations emanating from their bodies (3, 22). They have often felt self-critical and depreciated and this does not contribute to feeling good about oneself. A self-image as a "castrated" individual certainly lowers self-esteem. It implies that one is not whole or perfect or even as one "should be."

Kohut (44) believes that self-esteem derives from a stable system of firmly idealized values. Under favorable circumstances, such as appropriate selective parental responses to the child's demands and to the manifestations of the child's grandiose fantasies, the child learns to accept his/her realistic limitations and recognize his/her grandiose fantasies. Then the crude, immature, exhibitionistic demands are given up and replaced by ego-syntonic goals and purposes, by pleasure in his/her functions and activities and by realistic self-esteem.

Therefore, major influences in the development of self-esteem are attitudes of parents and identifications with them, as well as "original narcissism," used here in a positive sense. George Mead in 1934 stated a similar view, namely that the child "has achieved something of a self concept through reacting to and internalizing the attitudes of family members to him" (46). He feels that self-esteem is gradually modified by experiences with peers and others but that the basic link to parents is critical. Bibring (47) speaks of the achievement of mastery which also leads to self-esteem by diminishing helplessness. Jacobson (45) considers self-esteem to be modulated by the superego and modified in response to actual experience. It is more fluctuating when unconscious conflicts exist. She believes that, during the process described by Mahler (20) as separation-individuation, the child gradually moves from the wish to be symbiotically tied to the parent toward acquiring the attributes of the parent and selectively identifying with that parent.

Since the child needs and depends on parental love, help and approval, and desires to live up to gradually internalized parental expectations and standards, the state of parental self-esteem and self-image is extremely important. For a woman whose mother had a self-concept as someone who was devalued, which is true for many women, the struggle for positive self-esteem may mean a psychic separation from and even a rejection of the mother. Generally this is not a conscious process, but an unconscious one manifested in a sense of distance or hostility. During adolescence, the individual separates and individuates and at the same time identifies. If a parent is devalued, the child's self-image, or that fraction of it derived from identification with the parent, is affected.

Another possibility for a woman whose mother is depressed for a significant part of her childhood is to move closer to the father and identify primarily with him. The inherent difficulties in this situation emerge in the resolution of the oedipus complex. For example, identification with the father may lead to conflicts about "femininity" and difficulties with men.

Depression is a widespread problem for women. Weissman describes the implications of maternal depression for children (48). The woman who has had a depressed or devalued mother will have problems with her own self-esteem unless other identification models are available. Then she must also have the capacity to integrate these new relationships and experiences. Since the mother is the object of identification and a source of ego growth and support, many women in this situation do not develop the resources necessary for the development of ego autonomy and may have difficulty working through self-esteem problems.

A discussion of self-esteem also involves some consideration of aggression. As indicated earlier, women have not been permitted the direct expression of aggression in the same way as men. Women who do express aggression directly often feel guilty or unfeminine (49). Kaplan (50) speaks of the inhibition of aggressive impulses in latency girls. She describes these impulses as either self-directed or followed by guilt if they are directed against others. Aggression in this context means not only hostility, competitiveness and destructive impulses and acts, but also the assertiveness and free expression sometimes labeled self-actualization. To the extent that mastery, competence, the pursuit of personal goals and competitive activity require the recognition and expression of aggression or its derivatives, this awareness of being aggressive is likely to diminish self-esteem and the woman will feel a sense of worthlessness or wrongdoing. This can lead to conflicts between the assertiveness required in work or other situations and internalized prohibitions.

In contemporary views of women there is a trend toward acknowledgment of the importance of self-actualization and greater acceptance
of aggression and its expression as appropriate. This has taken the form
of increased tolerance of or even support for competitiveness in sports,
professional or business pursuits and other areas. However, women's
anger is still feared, and the openly aggressive woman will have difficulties. This can create inhibitions in her work and other functioning.
Horner (51) has described the "fear of success" in a population of bright,
achieving girls who were inhibited and blocked in their achievements,
particularly when working with male students, because they perceived
success would cost them the relationship with males and the esteem of
people around them. They were concerned that they would be seen as
unfeminine. In fact, they may have been correct, since many of the male
students at that time were uncomfortable with women they saw as
competitive.

In the development of women, dependency has been supported and
reinforced. The concept of "learned helplessness" is one way of describing this process (52). Little girls are also kept closer to their mothers
than are little boys; they are encouraged to seek support and express
dependency needs (53). They have, in the past, grown up expecting
they will be cared for by men, although in other ways they are the
providers of nurturance. Functioning more autonomously and independently can threaten the individual woman's sense of "femininity."
In classical theory, the penis was valued for a variety of reasons: because
it gave the little boy a special advantage in urination and showing off;
because of its "fanciness"; because of its greater availability as a source
of sexual pleasure and masturbation; and because it was a symbol of
masculine status and power. The girl's lack of a penis was considered
a realistic and self-evident reason for her sense of powerlessness. Current theory takes into account the effects of socialization to a greater
degree. One might, therefore, take a somewhat different position, focusing on the girl's concern with her weakness and devalued state, in
which she sees herself as in need of some source of strength and specialness outside herself. Without this she sees herself as defective or
vulnerable. One can broaden this concept to pay attention to the
woman's central concern with her weakness and devalued status rather
than her literal envy of someone who has a penis.

Masochism, viewed in this context, is considered differently from in
the past. A truly masochistic individual, whether male or female, is
considered pathological. Blum states that "masochism is a residue of
unresolved invantile conflict and is neither essentially feminine nor a

valuable component of mature female function and character. Though the female might be more predisposed to masochism, there is no evidence of particular female pleasure in pain" (21, p. 188). It is important to distinguish between masochistic suffering as a goal in itself and tolerance for a discomfort or deprivation in the service of the ego or ego ideal. Frequently, an experience which may be termed heroic suffering if it is some effort a man makes, for instance in an athletic pursuit, might be termed "masochistic suffering" in another context, such as a woman's tolerating the pain of childbearing.

Women do characteristically find more fulfillment in doing for others than in acting for themselves. They support their husbands, live through their children and enter service-oriented work. In doing so they may give up what might be fulfillment of their own needs for the sake of the relationships which are central to their lives (25). Insofar as relationships and concern for the needs of others are central, it might be argued that women fulfill important humanistic values. This surrendering one's own goals must be distinguished from masochism in its classical sense.

Erikson addressed himself to female personality development, although most of his work, as is true of that of most theorists, has been concerned with men (54). His theories integrated the individual's development with social practices, customs and beliefs; he saw an individual as adapting throughout to a particular societal context. He stressed the sex differences in childrearing in several cultures and connected these with the kind of men and women who developed in each culture. Data from studies of play in 12- and 13-year-old American children led him to focus on differences in spatial tendencies which he saw as analogous to anatomical differences. He spoke of the "inner space" of the woman, reflected in the emphasis on enclosure, protection, and receptivity in the constructions of girls, in contrast to the protrusion, activity and projection in the productions of boys. The emptiness which remained a potential for women led to a potential for depression and despair. He commented on the greater skills of women in those areas which enhanced their ability to respond to the needs of others. Although he was clearly aware of socialization in the development of these traits, he did not acknowledge this in his formulation. There was an anatomical basis to his theory and, although it was presented in positive terms, with stress on the capacity for nurturance and the value of intimacy and cooperation, it provoked attack from feminists who objected to the biological determinism which had been used in the past to support inequality rather than to emphasize positive differences.

Erikson formulated eight stages in normal development, with a focus on ego qualities which emerge from each (55): 1) Basic Trust, 2) Autonomy, 3) Initiative, 4) Industry, 5) Identity, 6) Intimacy, 7) Generativity, and 8) Ego Integrity. These eight stages have been criticized as applying more accurately to the development of males where, for instance, the stage of identity precedes the stage of intimacy. Women's identity has been related to the achievement of intimacy with another (55). Because of the importance of relationships in feminine development, Gilligan has proposed that intimacy and identity are "fused" and develop together (56). Erikson has also been criticized for his persistent identification of "woman" with "mother" and his emphasis on the achievement of identity primarily through motherhood.

The Significance of Reproduction

The importance of childbearing in feminine identity has always been assumed. A woman's expectation of being able to bear children has been considered critical in the development of gender identity, femininity and self-esteem. Nevertheless, in spite of their importance for human survival and the fact that fertility has been worshipped and considered sacred throughout history, childbearing and caretaking functions have generally occupied a lower place in the scale of status and prestige in most societies. Recent social changes that have diminished emphasis on reproduction and have resulted in the emergence of other alternatives for women have provoked questions about life choices which were previously felt to be automatic and about the concepts of femininity and feminine identity that were formerly accepted as fundamental (57).

Psychoanalytic theory has contributed to our understanding of the significance of childbearing for individual development. However, this has not been a central area of exploration and most early writers have seen motivations for motherhood as derivative of other developmental experiences. Although female sexuality was a critical area of investigation for Freud, Kestenberg points to the relative scarcity of references to maternal needs and motherhood (13).

Contemporary psychoanalytic thinking has also addressed the role of childbearing and childrearing in feminine identity. There have been some major changes in family patterns and fertility, with a dramatic decline in the birth rate. Many children do not have the opportunity to observe pregnant women at close range—not even their own mothers pregnant with younger siblings. Many young adult women are in conflict about a decision which used to be assumed, namely, that they would marry and have children. For them, femininity and fulfillment as a woman seem to require some revisions of self-image. It seems likely that the capacity to bear children is significant, whether or not this is realized as an adult choice. It is important to know that one's body can work right. Margaret Mead said, in criticism of Freud's views, that the vagina was seen by him as merely a displacement from the clitoris rather than a passage into the womb (58). Mead spoke for many critics in her view that the denigration of the value of producing a baby and the high valuation of the penis by both sexes was a fallacy of Freud's theories.

Contemporary views of the psychology of women attempt to construct an understanding based on the study of female development and experience, not out of context and in isolation from male development, but also not based on considerations which start from the male as the basic model. In doing so, the special anatomical aspects of the female body and the implications of her being the bearer of children are certainly critical. With the widening of roles and responsibilities for women, reproductive potential and its defining role need reassessment as a central component in identity and self-esteem.

More recently, parenthood has been seen as providing experience for maturation for both parents (64). However, the potential for women's growth through motherhood has been stressed more consistently. For example, Benedek clearly believed that women have a better chance to achieve completion of their physical and emotional maturation through motherhood than if motherhood is not experienced (59). Bibring saw pregnancy as a developmental crisis with maturational potential (60). In her view, the gratifying experience of successful mothering established self-confidence. Later, Benedek spoke of parenthood as a developmental phase with genuine ego maturation in the parent in response to all levels of the child's growth. Erikson described "generativity" as a later stage to be achieved in adult development (55). It is, in fact, in regard to parenting that attention was first paid to the genuine continued development of an individual throughout adulthood.

Superego Development

Freud's observations on women's "sense of justice" and morality are well-known. He believed that women had little sense of justice because of the predominance of envy in their mental life (10). Freud was not stating that men's morality was actually better than woman's; from his own experience he had a low estimate of most people's morality (61). But this implication emerges from his descriptions. He said that "for women the level of what is ethically moral is different from what it is in men. Their superego is never so inexorable, so impersonal, so independent of its emotional origins as we require it to be in men . . . they are less ready to submit to the great exigencies of life . . . they are more often influenced in their judgements by feelings of affection or hostility—all these would be amply accounted for in the modification of the formation of their superego" (10, pp. 257-8). He considered the responsiveness to emotional demands of people close to them as a potential corruption of an abstract sense of fairness and justice.

The idea that moral reasoning and a sense of justice are best expressed by adherence to abstract principles is also expressed in the formulations of Kohlberg, who has developed a means of measuring moral development in which the highest stage is the most principled and abstract. Gilligan has criticized this approach as reflecting primarily male development and style (27).

Schafer (61), in a critique of Freud's psychology of women, refers to the quality of moral rigidity which characterizes men more than women. Schafer states that Freud was referring to the greater capacity for isolation of affect, which is seen in many men, and that the greater predominance of obsessive morality is founded on reaction formation against sadistic, aggressive tendencies and intense unconscious guilt and is therefore a poor model of morality. He further argues against the appropriateness of morality detached from the fear of loss of love, a characteristic of women which Freud described and thought of as a source of potential weakness. It is paradoxical to note that it is a widely held belief that women are the "guardians of civilized conduct and morality." Many have also thought that it is more important in the long run for the survival of humanity and humanistic values to have a less abstract and more responsive justice, although retaining objectivity and fairness. Schafer stresses the intrusion of patriarchal and evolutionary values into Freud's judgments, in which observed qualitative differences are referred to as differences in worth or maturity. This point of view is supported by Miller (25), Gilligan (27) and others.

There are also wide variations in superego development among individuals. However, those differences which may be characteristic of women as compared with men can be seen in the light of their complex antecedents and functions; they do not merely reflect "better" or "worse" styles.

IMPLICATIONS FOR TREATMENT

The judgment of "normality" obviously affects treatment approaches, goals and assessment of outcome. The often quoted study by Broverman et al. (62) indicated that men and women therapists reflected bias in their judgments about patients and saw as healthy for women what was felt to be dependent, weak, and not sufficiently assertive when applied to evaluations of men's mental health. This is an example of the intrusion of values into issues of health. Confounding what is merely different with that which is "sick" is another well-known fallacy (6). Although many would assert that a "good" therapist has his or her patients' goals in mind, rather than intruding the therapist's own values, in practice this is not always the case and judgments are subtly influenced by one's own point of view.

I will mention a few of the areas where therapeutic norms and practices have been influenced by changes in thinking about women. The expansion in the judgment of what is viewed as a "normal" life pattern has been considerable. Along with this has been an extension of what is considered appropriately "feminine." It is obvious that not all psychoanalysts or therapists share the same views or approaches. However, although there may not be full agreement theoretically, in practice there have been a number of widespread shifts.

Women are no longer expected to spend their entire time at home or with children, even when children are small. In most settings the mother is regarded as and in fact is the primary caretaker, so there is still great emphasis on "mother-child" interactions. However, increasing acknowledgment of the role of family factors and the importance of the father in the development of the child has contributed to changes in what are thought to be appropriate concerns and activities of fathers as well as mothers.

Goals for women include their own wishes for self-actualization, as well as reproductive goals. Most women do want to marry and have children, but it is not automatically assumed to be the only appropriate goal; nor is a treatment judged successful if its primary accomplishment is, like in the fairy tale, that the woman patient marries and lives happily ever after.

Some confusion exists for a "liberated" therapist as to how best to help a woman patient accomplish her goals. The legitimization of women's strivings for equality and access to professional positions has led some therapists to encourage competitiveness; others are exploring patterns which patients and therapists may define as more "feminine" or collaborative ones. Work as an important part of women's lives is recognized. In this therapists are reflecting a major societal shift, in that the number of women entering into the workforce has risen tremendously and continues to rise, so that over 50% of women are now doing paid work outside the home. Although much of this work is unfulfilling and undertaken essentially for economic reasons, increasing numbers of young women plan a career as part of their lives.

There have been changes in expectation of marital roles and styles. The dual-career family brings its own problems, challenges, compromises and strains (63). The therapist who wants to help patients in these life-styles must approach the problems with some openness. In focusing on where unconscious and past conflicts interfere with resolution of current issues, therapy is not necessarily different from therapy in the past, but the assumptions as to appropriate resolutions may have shifted. One clinical vignette may illustrate this: A child analyst was treating a little girl with nightmares. To comfort herself and create a feeling of protection, she slept with a stuffed snake. The interpretation that this was a penis-symbol which made her feel more powerful, like her fathers and brothers, may have been obvious. A therapist currently might, however, approach her sense of vulnerability and defectiveness without this symbolic object, and see this feeling of hopelessness as the primary problem.

The expression of a wider range of responses as appropriate for women forms part of contemporary psychotherapy and psychoanalysis, including more open recognition of anger and aggression. It is important to differentiate realistic anger at injustice, including how an individual woman responds to her life experience, from pathological or neurotic responses. Since women have not readily acknowledged their anger at many experiences, it is important to bring it into awareness without at the same time externalizing the difficulty so that one is simply blaming the environment.

It follows from what was discussed earlier that masochism, helplessness and inappropriate passivity are not seen as "normal" but as problems requiring treatment.

Transference issues remain central in psychoanalytic psychotherapy. However, it is important to differentiate a patient's bringing to her treatment the expectations, fantasies and responses to her therapist which arise from childhood relationships and need to be explored and understand before she can function freely as an adult, from the authority aspects of the doctor-patient or therapist-patient relationship which are assumed to be part of appropriate social interaction between a male therapist and a female patient and are therefore not analyzed or explored.

The interest in and increasing availability of women therapists, supervisors and teachers will undoubtedly continue to have some impact on women's experience in therapy. However, in many ways psychotherapy for women reflects the changing issues in psychotherapy for all patients and will continue to respond to societal changes. At the same time therapists will continue to pursue the goals of relief of pain and suffering and improved capacity for attaining fulfillment and creativity.

REFERENCES

1. Horney, K.: The flight from womanhood. *Int. J. of Psychoanalysis*, 7:324-339, 1926. Reprinted in Miller, J. *Psychoanalysis and Women*. New York: Brunner/Mazel, 1973.
2. Jones E.: Early female sexuality. *Int. J. of Psychoanalysis*, 6:263-273, 1935.
3. Thompson, C.: Some effects of the derogatory attitude towards female sexuality. *Psychiatry*, 7:257-96, 1944.
4. Zilboorg, G.: Masculine and feminine: Some biological and cultural aspects. *Psychiatry*, 7:257-96, 1944.
5. Freud, S.: Femininity, new introductory lectures (1933). In *Standard Edition of the Complete Works of Sigmund Freud*, J. Strachey (Ed.), London: Hogarth,
6. Notman, M., Nadelson, C., and Bennett, B.: Achievement conflict in women: Considerations. *Psychotherapy and Psychosomatics*, 29:203-213, 1978.
7. Moss, H. A.: Sex, age and state as determinants of mother-infant interaction. *Merrill-Palmer Quarterly*, 13:19-36, 1967.
8. Maccoby, E., and Jacklin, C. N.: *The Psychology of Sex Differences*. Stanford: Stanford University Press, 1974.
9. Parsons, J., and Ruble, D.: Is anatomy destiny? Biology and sex differences. In *Women and Sex Roles*, I. Frieze et al. (Eds.), New York: Norton, 1978.
10. Freud, S.: Some psychical consequences of the anatomical distinction between the sexes (1925). *Standard Edition of the Complete Psychological Works of Sigmund Freud*, Vol. 19, London: Hogarth, 1961.
11. Freud, S.: Female sexuality (1931) in Introductory Lectures, *Standard Edition of the Complete Psychological Works of Sigmund Freud*, Vol. 21, London: Hogarth, 1961.
12. Kleeman, M.: *Psychoanalysis of Children*, London: Hogarth, 1932.
13. Kestenberg, J.: Vicissitudes of female sexuality, *J. of Amer. Psychoanalytic Assoc.*, 4:453-75, 1956. Revised and republished in Kestenberg, J. *Children and Parents*, New York: Aronson, 1975.
14. Benedek, T.: *Psychosexual Functions in Women*, New York: Ronald Press, 1952.
15. Bonaparte, M.: *Female Sexuality*, New York: International Universities Press, 1953.
16. Deutsch, H.: *The Psychology of Women*. New York: Grune and Stratton. Volume I, 1944, Vol. II, 1945.
17. Benedek, T.: The psychology of pregnancy. In J. Anthony and T. Benedek (Eds.), *Parenthood*. Boston: Little, Brown, 1970.
18. Winnicott, D.: The mother-infant experience in mutuality. In J. Anthony and T. Benedek (Eds.), *Parenthood*, Boston: Little, Brown, 1970, pp. 246-255.
19. Brazelton, T.: *Infants and Mothers*, New York: Delacorte Press, 1969.
20. Mahler, M., Pine F., and Bergman, A.: *The Psychological Birth of the Human Infant*, New York: Basic Books, 1975.
21. Blum, H.: Masochism, the ego ideal and the psychology of women. *J. of Amer. Psychoanalytic Assoc.*, 24:5, 1976, 157-191.

22. Easser, R.: "Womanhood." Unpublished manuscript, prepared for Panel on Female Psychology, Amer. Psychoanalytic Assoc., 1975.
23. Clower, V.: Theoretic implications of current views of masturbation in latency girls. *J. of Amer. Psychoanalytic Assoc.*, 24:5, 1976, 109-125.
24. Chasseget-Smirgel, J.: Feminine guilt and the oedipus complex. In *Female Sexuality*, J. Chasseget-Smirgel (Ed.), Ann Arbor: University of Michigan Press, 1970, p. 114.
25. Miller, T.: *Towards a New Psychology of Women*. Boston: Beacon Press, 1976.
26. Stoller, R.: Primary femininity. *J. of Amer. Psychoanalytic Assoc.*, 24:5, 59-78, 1976.
27. Gilligan, C.: In a different voice: Women's conception of the self and morality. *Harvard Educational Review*, 4:4, 481-518.
28. Ruble, D.: Sex differences in personality and abilities. In *Women and Sex Roles: A Social Psychological Perspective*, I. Frieze et al. (Eds.), New York: Norton, 1978, pp. 45-68.
29. Stoller, R.: Overview, the impact of new advances in sex research on psychoanalytic theory, *Amer. J. of Psychiatry*, 132:241-251, 1973.
30. Money, J. and Erhardt, A.: *Man and Woman, Boy and Girl*. Baltimore: Johns Hopkins University Press, 1972.
31. Abelin, E.: Some further observations and comments on the earliest role of the father. *Int. J. Psychoanal.*, 56:293-302, 1975.
32. Hoffman, L. and Nye, F.: *Working Mothers*. San Francisco: Jossey-Bass, 1974.
33. Galenson, E.: Report of Panel on Early Infancy and Childhood. *J. Amer. Psychoanalytic Assoc.*, 24:2, 141-160, 1976.
34. Riviere, J.: On the genesis of psychical conflicts in early infancy. *Int. J. Psychoanal.*, 17:395-422, 1936.
35. Brunswick, R.: The pre-oedipal phase of the libido development. *Psychoanalytic Quarterly*, 9, 293-319, 1940.
36. Lampl de Groot, J. Problems of femininity. *Psychoanalytic Quarterly*, 2, 489-518, 1933.
37. Chodorow, N.: *The Reproduction of Mothering: Psychoanalysis and the Sociology of Gender*. Berkeley: University of California Press, 1978.
38. Williams, J.: The emergence of sex differences. In *Psychology of Women*, J. Williams (Ed.), New York: Norton, 1977, pp. 121-157.
39. Moss, R.: Sex, age and state as determinants of mother-infant interaction. In *Readings in the Psychology of Women*. J. Bardwick (Ed.), New York: Norton, 1977, pp. 121-157.
40. Will, J., Self, R., and Datan, N: Maternal behavior and perceived sex of infants. *Amer. J. Orthopsychiatry*, 46:1, 135-139, 1976.
41. Kleemen, J.: Freud's views on early female sexuality in the light of direct child observation. *J. Am. Psychoanalytic Assoc.*, 24:5, 3-27, 1976.
42. Galenson, E. and Roiphe, H.: Some suggested revisions concerning early female development, *J. Am. Psychoanalytic Assoc.*, 24:5, 29-57, 1976.
43. Lerner, H.: Parental mislabelling of female genitals as a determinant of penis envy and learning inhibitions in women. *J. Amer. Psychoanalytic Assoc.*, 24:5, 269-283, 1976.
44. Kohut, H.: *The Analysis of the Self*. New York: International Universities Press, 1968.
45. Jacobson, E.: The regulation of self-esteem. In *Depression and Human Existence*, E. J. Anthony and T. Benedek (Eds.), Boston: Little, Brown, 1975.
46. Mead, G.: *Mind, Self and Society*. Chicago: University of Chicago Press, 1934.
47. Bibring, E.: The mechanism of depression. In *Affective Disorders*, P. Greenacre (Ed.), New York: International Universities Press, 1953.
48. Weissman, M. and Paykel, E.: *The Depressed Woman*. Chicago: University of Chicago Press, 1974.
49. Zilbach, J., Notman, M., Nadelson, C., and Miller, J.: Reconsideration of Aggression and Self-esteem in Women. Paper presented at International Psychoanalytic Assoc., August 1, 1979, New York.
50. Kaplan, E.: Manifestations of aggression in latency and preadolescent girls. *Psychoanalytic Study of the Child*, 31:63-78, New Haven: Yale University Press, 1976.

51. Horner, M.: Toward an understanding of achievement-related conflicts in women. *J. Social Issues*, 28:157-175, 1972.
52. Weissman, M. and Klerman, G.: Sex differences and the epidemiology of depression. *Arch. Gen. Psychiat.*, 34:98-111, 1977.
53. Gove, W.: Sex differences in the epidemiology of mental disorder: Evidence and explanations. In *Gender and Disordered Behavior: Sex Differences in Psychopathology*. E. Gomberg and V. Franks (Eds.), New York: Brunner/Mazel, 1979, pp. 23-68.
54. Erikson, E. Womanhood and the innerspace. In *Identity, Youth and Crisis*. New York: Norton, 1968, pp. 261-294.
55. Erikson, E.: *Childhood and Society*, New York: Norton, 1950.
56. Gilligan, C. and Notman, M.: Midlife in women: On the integration of autonomy and care. Paper presented at American Sociological Assoc., March 1, 1977.
57. Notman, M. and Nadelson, C.: New views of femininity and reproduction. Paper presented at annual meeting of American Psychiatric Assoc., Chicago, May 1978.
58. Mead, M.: *Male and Female*. New York: William Morrow, 1949.
59. Benedek, T.: Parenthood as a developmental phase. *J. Amer. Psychoanalytic Assoc.*, 389-417, 1959.
60. Bibring, G.: Some considerations of the psychological process in pregnancy. *The Psychoanalytic Study of the Child*, 14:113-121, New York: International Universities Press, 1959.
61. Schafer, R.: Problems in Freud's psychology of women. *J. of Am. Psychoanalytic Assoc.*, 22:459-485, 1974.
62. Broverman, I., Broverman, D., et al.: Sex role stereotypes and clinical judgments of mental health. *J. of Consulting and Clinical Psychology*, 1970, 341-347.
63. Rapoport, R. and Rapoport, R.: *The Dual Career Family Re-examined*. New York: Harper and Row, 1976.

Chapter 3

Testing Analytic Hypotheses: Do Personality Attributes Predispose to Depression?

Gerald L. Klerman, M.D.

INTRODUCTION

Psychoanalysis has had major impact not only on psychiatric theory and clinical practice but also upon the general intellectual developments of twentieth century life. At the same time as its impact upon intellectual activities, the arts and humanities has increased steadily throughout the twentieth century, its scientific status has been surrounded by controversy. Within both psychiatry and related scientific fields such as psychology, biology and sociology, the debate continues as to whether or not psychoanalysis is scientific. What is meant by "scientific"? One interpretation—the set of answers given by Freud himself and his followers in the early decades of this century—was to claim scientific status by virtue of the fact that the explanatory concepts were naturalistic, materialistic, and deterministic. In that sense, psychoanalysis, like Darwin's biology and Copernicus' physics, represented a break with previous explanations of behavior that tended to be supernatural or idiosyncratic.

In recent decades, however, a new set of criteria for scientific disciplines has emerged from the philosophies of science such as those proposed by Kuhn and Polanyi. According to these criteria, the test of a scientific discipline is its capacity to generate hypotheses that are capable of being tested. More specifically, according to Polanyi, hypotheses must be capable of being tested by the process of being nullified. Can the propositions be disproven? Can they be quantified? Do they lend themselves to experimental designs in which specific factors are isolated and tested independently of each other or in combination?

According to this point of view, psychoanalysis has not yet established its scientific status. According to the late twentieth century criteria defining a science, psychoanalysis has not yet codified its propositions or proposed testable hypotheses. Furthermore, it has not developed quantitative measures for some of its key concepts, such as cathexis, ego functioning, etc.

My personal view is that there is nothing intrinsically unscientific about psychoanalytic theories and that many of them are potentially testable and even quantifiable. According to my view, psychoanalysis is not one theory but a collection of theories: developmental, psychopathological, and therapeutic. Part of what is necessary is the disaggregation of the corpus of psychoanalytic theories into discrete subtheories tied to specific propositions and the reformulation of these propositions into hypotheses capable of being tested and capable of being nullified.

There are a large number of clinical theories derived from psychoanalysis providing explanations for the psychogenesis of specific clinical disorders such as schizophrenia, depression, hysteria, and phobia. Using the criteria of the modern philosophy of science, the psychoanalytic formulations as to the psychogenesis of each of these discrete clinical disorders are themselves potentially testable. In order to accomplish this, what is needed is to take the formulations essentially derived from clinical experience and reformulate them or retest them into propositions which are of the form of a hypothesis: Y is a function of X ($y = f(x)$).

One such example is the psychoanalytic theory of the relationship between personality and depression. Thus, applied to depression, the formulation would be that the predisposition to clinical depression is a function of X, i.e., certain personality predispositions such as oral dependency, which have their origins in the early developmental experiences of the future adult depressive.

Not only must the psychoanalytic propositions be reformulated, but each of the components must then be operationally defined in ways that are capable of quantification. A major problem of psychoanalytic methodology is to develop quantitative means for measuring concepts such as ego strength, depth of regression, hysterical personality or attachment.

While these problems may be difficult, they are by no means insurmountable. Part of my goal in this chapter is to illustrate how the psychoanalytic concepts describing the personality traits of hostility, hysteria and dependency can be tested to determine their relationship to clinical depression.

PSYCHOANALYSIS AS HYPOTHESES-GENERATING AND HYPOTHESES-TESTING

Psychoanalysis has been very successful in hypothesis-generating, but the transition to hypothesis-testing has faltered. The nearly 100-year history of psychoanalysis has been a period of great ferment, particularly the early years which were a time of extraordinary discovery gleaned from clinical observation. Out of this early work grew theories to explain phenomena not readily apparent. Theories evolved of unconscious motivation, repression and anxiety and explanations were offered of the relationship between childhood experience and predisposition to later psychopathology. As a result of this brilliant early work, a corpus of hypotheses exists, many of which are very imaginative and creative; however, the transition to hypothesis-testing has been weak. Psychoanalysis has not developed a cadre of persons or a consensus as to appropriate methodology for testing these hypotheses.

Problems concerning the testing of these hypotheses apply not only to psychoanalysis as a theory about personality and psychopathology but also to psychoanalysis as a therapeutic methodology claiming treatment efficacy for character and personality disorders. This chapter will attempt to show that it is possible to scientifically test psychoanalytic concepts by choosing a specific set of hypotheses. The basic focus will be to examine psychoanalytic propositions using depression as a model problem and to evaluate scientifically generated evidence to answer the question: Do personality attributes predispose to depression?

RELATIONSHIP OF PERSONALITY TO DEPRESSIVE DISORDERS IN ADULTS

Efforts have been made to identify a single psychodynamic factor or mechanism as central and unique to the psychogenesis of depression. While these factors have received wide clinical emphasis, the research evidence supporting their etiological basis is still being developed. The two main psychoanalytic formulations of depression are that: 1) Early childhood experiences predispose to later adult depression. 2) Personality structures predispose to depression.

Early Childhood Experiences

Basic to psychoanalytic thinking is the belief that the most crucial etiological forces are those that operate in childhood. Regarding depression, emphasis on infancy and early childhood has focused on possible impairments of ego function and sensitivities to separation and loss that arise from the vicissitudes of the early mother-child relationship. Attempts to test this hypothesis have relied on direct observation of infants and young children, particularly those in institutions who develop the "anaclitic" depressions described by Spitz (1) and Bowlby (2). Another line of investigation has focused on the frequency of parental loss and kinds of psychic trauma in the childhood of depressives. While these studies indicate that, as a group, depressives seem to experience more parental loss from death, separation, or other causes than normal or other diagnostic groups, this factor alone does not seem sufficiently universal to account for all forms of depression. At the present time, these psychoanalytic hypotheses are primarily of great heuristic value, contributing to case formulation and guidance of psychotherapeutic practice, but additional research is necessary to test their veracity.

Personality Structures

Clinicians since the time of Hippocrates have noted that certain "temperaments" are related to depression, but only in the twentieth century, following the observations of Freud (3), Abraham (4), Rado (5), Bibring (6) and other psychoanalysts, have these relationships been explored in depth. It is widely believed that persons prone to depression are characterized by low self-esteem, strong superego, clinging and dependent interpersonal relations, and limited capacity for mature and enduring object relations. While these traits are common among depressives, no single personality trait, constellation, or type has been established as uniquely predisposed to depression. All humans, of whatever personality pattern, can and do become depressed under appropriate circumstances, although certain personality types—the oral-dependent, the obsessive-compulsive and the hysterical—may be at greater risk of depression than the antisocial, the paranoid or certain other types who utilize projection and other externalizing modes of defense. Psychodynamic formulations are concerned not only with ongoing dynamic conflicts, evident in guilt, reactions to loss, or hostility turned against the self, which may be involved in the manifest depressive episode, but also with features that may antedate the acute depressive episode and therefore may be regarded as etiological. Since these are rooted in personality, a major psychodynamic hypothesis focuses on the predisposition of certain personality types to depression. Personality can be related to depression in various ways.

Hostility related to depression

The role of hostile feelings in the psychodynamics of clinical depressive states remains a problematic issue in contemporary psychiatric thinking. Since the early decades of this century, classical psychoanalytic discussions, relying heavily upon the insights of Abraham (4), Freud (3) and Rado (5), have emphasized the importance of hostility in the psychodynamics of depression. In this view, inward-directed hostility, whether consciously or unconsciously turned against the self, is considered the sine qua non in the formation of depressive symptoms. This view has become standard teaching in many psychiatric centers.

Until recently, this dominant clinical teaching became the practical distillate of the classic psychodynamic theory of depression initially proposed by Abraham and Freud during the period of 1908 to 1921. In this classical view, the clinical features of adult depression result from retroflexion onto the self of the hostility directed at the lost object. Through incorporation, the self identifies with the lost object. The self is defended against the trauma of loss and, thus, avoids its psychic consequences. In depression, predisposition to this mechanism is postulated to have been determined by libidinal fixations in the late oral or early anal stages of development. Crucial to this formulation is the central role given to aggressive drives aroused by the ambivalence and dependency characteristic of the depressed person in his or her interpersonal and object relations (5, 7).

It is interesting to recall that Freud used a transformation (or alchemy) explanation for three clinical phenomena: conversion hysteria, anxiety and depression. Freud's earliest conception of the conversion mechanism in hysteria, developed about 1895, postulated that in the process of symptom formation, psychic energy that was not discharged was converted into a physical symptom of an hysterical nature, such as paralysis of limb or loss of vision. Freud proposed a similar transformation explanation of anxiety in his early toxicological theory: For many years he held that anxiety neurosis was one of the "actual neuroses," arising from biological causes, rather than a psychoneurosis arising from conflict. His initial formulation was that anxiety was the psychological manifestation of undischarged sexual libido, and not until 1923 did he formulate his signal theory of anxiety, in which he designated the role of anxiety as the initiator of defense processes. Freud's concept of depression as the transformation (retroflexion) of aggressive drives deriving from oral fixations persists into the present time as the dominant view in many clinical settings.

As Bibring (6), Rapaport (8) and Chodoff (9) have elucidated, the classical theory derives from an exclusively instinctual view of the genesis of emotions and from insufficient attention to modern views of ego functions. The classic theory of depression fails to classify depression as a primary affective state in its own right but, rather, relegates depression to a transmutation of transformation of another affect, hostility.

Testing analytic hypotheses about hostility and depression. Work by Gershon et al. (10) reported observations that in certain individuals depressive episodes were associated with manifest expressions of hostility-out as well as hostility-in and described the use of certain statistical methods for analyzing serial observations of individual patients followed longitudinally throughout the course of their depression. In their study, they focused on the recovery process as observed during hospitalization because this period lends itself more readily to direct clinical observation. They made repeated observations on a series of depressed women, attempting to identify changes in their depression symptoms and concomitant changes in the intensity and direction of their hostile feelings.

Specifically, Gershon et al. were interested in the following questions:

1) Is there a positive correlation of hostility-in with depression?
2) Is there a positive correlation of hostility-out with depressive affect?
3) Will different patterns of hostility-in and hostility-out be identified in different patients?

Clinically validated assessments of hostility and depression obtained independently from concurrent measurements of clinical symptoms were used repeatedly on the same person during the course of illness. Depression was measured using a modified form of the Hamilton Rating Scale for Depression (11) and clinical assessments of symptomatology were derived from psychiatric interviews. Hostility was measured using a modification of the three scales devised by Gottschalk and associates (12) based on the psychoanalytic technique of free association. The three scales were: the Hostility-Out, the Hostility-In, and the Ambivalent Hostility scales.

The results, using these scales, indicated that Hostility-In was related to depressive symptoms; however, no consistent relationship was found between Hostility-Out and depressive symptomatology. The authors hypothesized that there were two subgroups, as measured by the hostility and depression scales, distinguishable from each other statistically and clinically.

The findings indicated that these two patterns of hostility and depression obscured each other in the pooled correlations. In both patterns, high hostility-in was associated with clinical depression. However, in the pattern that was found in patients with hysterical personalities, hostility-out increased with deepening depression and subsided with improvement in depression. In the second pattern, which occurred in women with many obsessive features, there was either no demonstrable relation or a low negative relation of hostility-out to clinically evident affect.

It was the verbal expression of affect, rather than the clinical severity of the illness, which differentiated the two groups. Using the average depression scores as a quantitative index of the severity of the clinical depression, there was no difference between the two groups of patients. Therefore, it was the qualitative difference in symptoms and expression of hostility that distinguished them.

This study documented the classic formulation of the reciprocal relation of hostility and depression in certain patients, and also reported on the observation of an alternative pattern in which manifest hostility and depression coexist and are not negatively correlated. The findings, however, cannot automatically be generalized to the onset of depression. Discussions of the psychodynamics of depression are usually concerned with reconstructing the onset of the illness and delineating the childhood factors predisposing to adult psychopathology. In practice, however, data are rarely obtained directly during childhood or onset of illness. Most often, the patient is studied during the illness, and patterns observed during the recovery phase are extrapolated to earlier phases. In studying the process of recovery from depression, the authors were interested in the views of psychoanalytic writers who see the recovery process as the process of becoming ill in reverse. However, the processes may not be at all symmetrical, and one might do well to follow the suggestion of Abraham that manic-depressive patients should be studied during the interval between episodes in order to observe closely the onset of the episode.

It has been argued that the second group—those who manifested hostility-out—did not have deep "core" depressions and were not truly depressed, but were instead sad and unhappy as part of character neuroses or reactions to life circumstances. To argue that they are not truly depressed may be a useful mode of discourse, but it is a more restricted use of "depression" than is currently employed in most clinical settings. Most of these patients are generally called depressed in clinical settings. Moreover, and most pertinent for research, their psychodynamics are often discussed in terms of the "depression equals hostility turned inward" formulation.

In their discussion, Gershon et al. (10) avoided the metapsychological problems of the relationship of hostility as a feeling or impulse to aggression as a primary instinctual drive. The initial formulations concerning the role of hostility in depression anteceded the development of Freud's theory of the dual instincts of libido and aggression. The way in which hostility was defined and measured in this study was similar to the usage found in the hypotheses of Freud and Abraham, which were phrased in terms of hostility as a feeling-state.

In the classical psychoanalytic formulation of depression, the hypotheses connecting hostility and depression were relatively explicit and did not involve many intervening variables between hostility and depression. It may be that depressions are related to alterations of aggressive drives, but these drives are more complex than hostility as a feeling and beyond the methods of assessment currently available.

The presence of both high hostility-in and hostility-out in the same patient at the same time implies that hostility is not a unitary force with a fixed total quantity which can be turned either in or out. Instead, each type of hostility may have separate mechanisms both for its initiation and for its defensive alterations. One attractive possibility is that there is alteration in awareness of the depressed affect and that an expression of hostility drains off awareness of depression, as occurs in abreaction. Another possibility is that hostility-out, depression and hostility-in are all serving the same underlying purpose—Rado's "great despairing cry for love" (5). These interpretations are consistent with Bibring's (6) formulation that the underlying process in depression involves the vicissitudes of ego functioning and that the aggressive impulse is not necessarily the essential factor. Bibring's formulations are attractive for another reason: Among psychoanalytic theorists, his are the formulations which most readily allow multiple dispositions of aggressive impulses during the onset of and the recovery from severe depressive states.

The work by Gershon and his colleagues (10) questioned the universality of the relationship between inward-directed hostility and depression. The findings from this study confirmed the independence of depression from hostility. The data show alternative patterns: Both high and low intensities of manifest hostility occur, depending on the patient's personality patterns and the nature of his or her social relations. This research supports the desirability of rejecting the hostility-turned-against-itself mechanisms as universally necessary and primary in the pathogenesis of depression. These findings support the hypothesis that depressive affect is a primary ego state that serves important ego-adaptive functions.

Klerman and Gershon (13) also investigated the effects of imipramine upon hostility in depressed patients to test further the classic psychodynamic view postulating a reciprocal relationship between hostility and depression and suggesting that the turning of hostility away from the object world and onto the ego is a crucial mechanism in the psychogenesis of depressive episodes.

Based on clinical observations and research studies, it has been postulated that imipramine mobilizes hostility and that this mobilization underlies the drug's therapeutic psychodynamic action. Klerman and Gershon studied changes in women with depression to test this view. Three women, hospitalized for their depressions, were studied longitudinally before and during treatment with imipramine, and hostility directed inward and hostility directed outward were measured. No significant differences were found between the imipramine and pre-imipramine periods, despite significant clinical improvement during the drug treatment period. The authors suggest that further longitudinal studies of the effects of imipramine upon hostility are needed, before the "mobilization hypothesis" can be accepted or dismissed.

Hysteria related to depression

Lazare and Klerman (14) studied the role of hysterical personality features in the symptomatology and clinical course of depression. Although the hysterical personality has been discussed in many contexts, it still remains a subject of considerable controversy. Part of the difficulty stems from the lack of clear criteria with which to determine who shall be considered hysterical. The task of investigators would be simplified if hysterical symptoms, manifest hysterical personality traits, the unsuccessful resolution of the oedipal conflict, and the predominant use of repression as a defense mechanism always occurred simultaneously.

This is not the case, and we are left with at least four meanings of "hysterical," depending upon whether the point of reference is the symptom, the personality traits, the unsuccessful oedipal resolution or the defense of repression.

It was partially in reaction to this confusion in the meaning of hysteria that psychoanalysts began to observe variations in ego strength and associated personality processes in the hysterical personality. The terms "infantile hysteric," "primitive hysteric," "oral hysteric" and "hysterical psychosis" have evolved to describe these variations.

In their study, Lazare and Klerman attempted to define hysterical personality in a precise and measurable fashion so that only one aspect of the global concept of hysteria—manifest personality traits—was investigated. The hysterical personality was defined by the traits of demanding dependence, egocentricity, exhibitionism, fear of sexuality, lability of affect, sexual provocativeness and suggestibility. Using reliable and valid rating scales for these traits and the Hamilton Rating Scale for Depression (11), 43 percent of hospitalized depressed women were found to have predominant hysterical personality features.

The question then arises: "Do hysterical personality features predispose a woman to depression, or are they associated with a high incidence of depression?" The answer to that question was beyond the scope of this study, but further investigation of the relationship of depression to hysterical personality features in the general population will help to ascertain the answer.

However, the findings of the Lazare and Klerman (14) study suggest that hysterical personality features, whether or not they predispose to depression, influence the nature and course of the depressive illness. Depressed women with hysterical personality features exhibit a high incidence of hysterical symptoms. Furthermore, there is a reciprocal relationship between these symptoms and certain depressive symptoms, so that the hysterical patients appear less depressed. In other words, the hysterical symptoms protect the patient from or defend her against a more severe depression. This phenomenon was originally described by Janet (15) and later confirmed by hypnotic experiments (16).

This "protection" was also illustrated by Stengel (17), who found, in describing fugue states, that there was a depressive disorder in nearly every case he studied. He felt that the fugue protected the patient against a more severe depression, since the 12 patients in his study who made suicide attempts did so either before or after—but not during—the fugue. It is of interest that Breuer and Freud (18) made some of the earliest observations on the relationship of hysterical symptoms to the nonsexual affects, including depression:

> It was the rule for the emotional disturbance—apprehensiveness, anger, irritability, grief—to precede the appearance of the somatic symptom or to follow it immediately. . . . It is self-evident and is also sufficiently proved by our observations that the nonsexual affects of fright, anxiety, and anger lead to the development of hysterical phenomenon.

The high frequency of hysterical personality features among the depressed women in this study seems to belie the common teaching that all depressed patients are necessarily characterized by an anal-obsessive personality or by oral fixations. This formula emanates from the early work of Freud (3) and Abraham (4), as further developed by Rado (5) and others. Personality terms employed by these authors to discuss the depressed patient are: "orally frustrated," "obsessive character," "oral sadistic" and "receptive orality." On the other hand, Reich (19) observed that "one often finds depressive mechanisms" in the hysterical personality. He explained this by oral regression and qualified the character structure as no longer specifically hysterical. Marmor (20) noted that there was a close relationship between hysterical personality and certain types of depression as result of oral fixations which he felt were of basic importance in the genesis of the hysterical personality. Bibring (6), in questioning the usual formulations of premorbid character in depression, defined depression as an ego phenomenon "essentially independent of the vicissitudes of aggression as well as of oral drives." The findings of the Lazare and Klerman study were consistent with these views of Reich, Marmor, and Bibring.

In addition to these psychoanalytic studies, two recent empirical studies of depressed patients using factor analysis found patterns similar to the "hysterical depression" as described in this paper. Grinker and associates (21) described the group as having:

> . . . less than average depressed affect, guilt, or anxiety. In current behavior they are outstanding in their agitated, demanding, hypochondriac complaints, associated with psychosomatic symptoms. . . . The striking aspect of this pattern is the low loading on dismal and hopeless affect in contrast to the active irrational complaining attitudes (p. 220).

Friedman and associates (22) described a similar pattern:

> . . . a querulous, hypochondriacal type, self-preoccupied, de-
> manding and complaining, irritable with marked body conscious-
> ness and many physical complaints. . . . These patients utilize
> complaints to obtain attention. . . . (p. 507).

In spite of these observations, there continues to be disagreement as
to whether the hysterical personality features are common predispositions to depression. The source of the disagreement may not be in the
clinical phenomena but rather in the meaning of concepts. The crucial
question is: "Who shall be called depressed?" Some psychiatrists have
argued that the depressed patient with hysterical personality features
as described by this study is not suffering from a "true" depression.
They reason that the sine qua non of the "true" depression is the lowering of self-esteem with hostility turned on the self. If this is the issue,
then we must distinguish at least two types of depressive disorders.

This study supports the view that the "hysterical" depression mani-
fests different clinical features than does classical depression. However,
in clinical practice and research projects both groups are almost always
referred to as "depressions." They are often treated with similar psychotherapeutic maneuvers, and both groups often receive the same so-
matic treatments. It is hoped that the separation of the depressions into
meaningful groupings will facilitate psychodynamic and biochemical
studies.

A subsequent series of studies conducted by Lazare, Klerman, and
Armor (23, 24) explored the empirical basis of three personality types
frequently discussed in the psychoanalytic literature—oral, obsessive
and hysterical. More specifically, the trait patterns which historically
have been said to characterize each of the three personality types were
reexamined by means of factor analysis, and a self-rating form was
offered as a measure of these personality types.

The three personality types were defined by a total of 20 personality
traits which were obtained by a review of the literature. Ninety female
patients were measured for the 20 personality traits by means of a self-
rating form. The trait scores of the 90 patients were subjected to factor
analysis. There were three factors which accounted for 90 percent of the
common variance. Each of the factors resembled one of the personality
types. The obsessive personality was nearly identical to its factor while
the oral and hysterical personality corresponded to lesser degrees to
their factors. Of interest was the mixture of traits in the oral and hysterical factors so that each had traits of both personality types. These

studies represent a partial validation of the descriptive aspects of the psychoanalytic concepts of personality types and demonstrate the potential utility of psychological and mathematical techniques in the testing of a psychoanalytic concept.

Dependency related to depression

For over 50 years the role of dependency has dominated the discussion of the psychogenetic factors which predispose an individual to become clinically depressed. The theories that have attempted to explicate the relationship between dependency and depression have been based largely on the study of a single case or a few cases observed during the course of intensive psychotherapy. However, efforts to frame the relationship in the form of testable hypotheses applicable to larger populations have not been prominent.

Recently, however, Hirschfeld and colleagues (25, 26) reviewed the conceptual development of the interaction between dependency and depression, using as an intervening variable the self-esteem system of the individual who is subject to depression. As used in these studies, interpersonal dependency refers to a complex of thoughts, beliefs, feelings, and behaviors which revolve around the need to associate closely with, interact with and rely upon valued other people.

Their review of predominantly psychoanalytic and ethological theory regarding the personality attributes predisposing to depression suggests considerable consensus. Investigators of the psychodynamics of depression appear to agree that one quality which renders an individual vulnerable to depressive illness is related to continuing conflicts about dependency, coupled with a fragile self-esteem system. Based upon this review and an analysis of shared clinical experience, several important factors in the relationship between dependency and depression may be identified:

1) During the manifest state of depression, self-esteem is low. Although this statement is so widely accepted that it could almost be considered tautological, it is not essential for the diagnosis of depression and has not been extensively investigated empirically.

2) Depression-prone people have a chronically low level of self-esteem (i.e., quantity). This hypothesis stems more from the observations of the cognitive and behavioral theorists, and less so from the psychodynamic writers, who have emphasized the fragile nature of the self-esteem.

3) A fall in self-esteem marks the onset of clinical depression.

4) The nature (quality) of self-esteem is especially fragile in depression-prone people due to reliance on continual satisfaction of excessive interpersonal dependency needs to the relative exclusion of other determinants of self-esteem. When these needs are frustrated, as they are bound to be, the already low level of self-esteem, which is without significant other resources to shore it up, is further lowered, and clinical depression results.

The authors describe two important ways that the depressive's self-esteem system differs from that of normal personality. First, the depressive's interpersonal dependency needs are greater. The authors characterized these increased needs as a trait composed of thoughts, feelings, and behaviors, and labeled it "undue interpersonal dependency," following Chodoff. Individuals possessing higher amounts of this trait desire more support and approval from important others, are more anxious about being alone or being abandoned, have more fragile feelings, have low social self-confidence, have difficulty in making decisions on their own (note the distinction from the obsessional difficulty in decision-making due to ambivalence), lack confidence in their own judgment and are never able to get enough care and attention.

Such people may even feel quite good about themselves to the extent that they are able to bask in this externally derived approval. Loss of such support, however, either directly or indirectly, due to changes in the relationships with others on whom they are dependent, will lead to a fall in self-esteem and this contributes significantly to the onset of depression. Impairment of intrapsychic mechanisms for maintaining approval from others may also precipitate loss of support.

Second, the depressive's self-esteem even in the intermorbid state depends, to a great degree, on the satisfaction of interpersonal dependency needs, other self-esteem determinants being of relatively little importance. In other words, being successful in business or athletics, performing charitable deeds, improving one's appearance, or doing something well are not, in and of themselves, sufficient to maintain a reasonable level of self-esteem in such a person. This lack of diversity in the determinants of self-esteem renders it quite unstable and vulnerable. Thus, if approval and support from significant others are withdrawn, other resources are inadequate to shore up the self-esteem, and it will fall.

These hypotheses represent still tentative formulations of the relationships among interpersonal dependency, self-esteem, and depression. It is uncertain, however, whether or not this is the only route to the depressed state, even if it is a major one. Lowering of self-esteem is surely involved in the development of depression, but suppose the person's self-esteem rests on needs other than dependency. For example, there is the hard-driving businessman, quite free of excessive dependency, but whose sense of worth rests heavily on financial success. Suppose his business fails, perhaps even through his bad judgment. With his entire sense of integrity and value sharply balanced on the need for business success, would we not predict that he, just as the excessively dependent person, would become depressed? Common sense would suggest a simple "yes." Perhaps the depression would be less intense, perhaps qualitatively different, or even less likely to occur, but it seems unreasonable to suppose that a person who is not excessively dependent could not become depressed. Such an hypothesis follows from Bibring's formulation of the mechanism of depression. However, the literature on the subject, presumably reflecting clinical experience, seems to indicate that unmet dependency needs have a special potency in precipitating depression.

Based upon these descriptions of the depressive's personality, Hirschfeld et al. (25) made the following predictions about a population of documented clinically depressed patients, as compared with appropriate controls: If tested after recovery (that is, when symptom-free), self-esteem would be low, determinants of self-esteem would rest heavily in the receptive area, and undue interpersonal dependency scores would be high. In a population of adults without history of significant depression, it can be anticipated that those people who scored similarly to the recovered depressives would be much more likely to become depressed in the future than the others.

The proposed mechanism, with its corresponding set of hypotheses, probably does not account for all significant clinical depressions. For instance the "apathetic, anhedonic, empty" syndrome observed in individuals who have emerged from concentration camp experiences may not involve low self-esteem. However, the model is expected to have explanatory value for a major proportion of depressives. The issue of various diagnostic groupings within depression was avoided because the theoretical literature on the depressive personality has included little nosologic information. However, current research evidence has strongly suggested the existence of different affective entities. In light of this evidence the authors anticipate that the model will be most applicable to depressives categorized as neurotic, reactive, unipolar or situational.

Hirschfeld et al. (25) summarized their work as follows:

. . . we have reviewed and described a mechanism of depression that involves undue interpersonal dependency and fragile self-esteem. In essence, the depression-prone person has excessive interpersonal dependency wishes on which his self-esteem system relies. Should dependency be frustrated, self-esteem will fall and clinical depression will develop. We have suggested a list of hypotheses corresponding to the model, as well as techniques to test these hypotheses. We believe that this formulation accounts for the psychological elements in a major subset of all depressions. We are aware that these psychological factors must articulate with various genetic, biological, and environmental ones to produce the complex of affective disorders (pp. 386-7).

A subsequent study by Hirschfeld et al. (26) attempted to elucidate empirically aspects of the relationship between personality, especially undue interpersonal dependency, and depression. A review of existing self-report inventories revealed none that adequately assessed interpersonal dependency. Therefore, a new 48-item self-report inventory that assessed interpersonal dependency in adults was developed, using large samples of both psychiatric patients and normals, and it was cross-validated on two additional samples. This assessment device attempted to scale three major psychometric components of this complex: 1) emotional reliance on another person, 2) lack of self-confidence, and 3) assertion of autonomy.

There are several possible theoretical sources of interpersonal dependency, including a psychoanalytic explanation. The authors make an effort to link the scales of their interpersonal dependency measure to basic theoretical formulations emphasizing attachment and dependency. Their inventory represents one empirical approach to explaining how these qualities relate to the adult personality.

CONCLUSIONS

The research described in this chapter has attempted to investigate associations between certain personality patterns defined by manifest traits—hostile, hysterical, and dependent—and the psychodynamic processes underlying depression. The purpose was to identify homogeneous groups of variables that reflect some underlying psychological process. This group of studies successfully demonstrates that psychoanalytic theory can be validated by nonanalytic means, but difficult questions remain as a challenge to future research.

The implicit psychoanalytic theory of behavior has not been fully systematized, and there is no doubt that the logical distance from underlying assumptions to specific hypothesis is long and complicated. Furthermore, the development and execution of appropriate methodological mechanisms, including experimental designs and measurement techniques, are equally arduous. Only limited attempts have been made to generate and test psychoanalytic hypotheses in settings other than the psychoanalytic therapy situation. A scientific theory that depends on only one method of data-gathering has limited generalizability; one cannot judge the extent to which the theory applies to psychological phenomena in general, as well as to the methods of psychoanalysis.

Clinical psychoanalysis has been a brilliant exercise in hypothesis generation. However, hypothesis generation is only one-half of the activities of a scientific discipline; the other half is hypothesis-testing. Whereas hypothesis generation is a creative, almost artistic, process encompassing the free play of ideas and experience, hypothesis-testing requires more discipline, rigor and systemization. The failure of psychoanalysis to generate a cadre of investigators—disciplined and systematic in their methods, conversant with modern statistics and techniques from experimental psychology and versed in the tenets of the new philosophy of science—has been to the detriment not only of psychoanalysis but of clinical fields in general. There is the serious danger that if the brilliant insights generated by the psychoanalytic pioneers of the first half of the century are not systematically tested by empirical and experimental methods, the field will fall into continual disrepute and disregard and psychoanalysis will become a historical artifact.

REFERENCES

1. Spitz, R. A.: Anaclitic depression. The Psychoanalytic Study of the Child, Vol. 2, New York: International Universities Press, 1946.
2. Bowlby, J.: *Attachment*. New York: Basic Books, 1969.
3. Freud, S.: Mourning and melancholia. *Standard Edition*, Vol. 14, London: Hogarth Press, 1917.
4. Abraham, K.: *Selected Papers of Karl Abraham, M.D.* London: Hogarth Press, 1927.
5. Rado, S.: The problem of melancholia. *International Journal of Psycho-Analysis*, 9, 420-438, 1928.
6. Bibring, E.: Mechanism of depression. In *Affective Disorders*. P. Greenacre (Ed.), New York: International Universities Press, 1953.
7. Cohen, M. B., Blake, G., Cohen, R. A., Fromm-Reichmann, F., and Weigert, E. V.: An intensive study of twelve cases of manic-depressive psychosis. *Psychiatry*, 17, 103-138, 154.
8. Rapaport, D.: Edward Bibring's theory of depression. In *Collected Papers of David Rapaport*. M. Gill (Ed.), New York: Basic Books, 1967.

9. Chodoff, P.: The core problem in depression: Interpersonal aspects. In *Science and Psychoanalysis*, Vol. 17, J. Masserman (Ed.), New York: Grune and Stratton, 1970.
10. Gershon, E. S., Cromer, M., and Klerman, G. L.: Hostility and depression. *Psychiatry*, 31, 224-235, 1968.
11. Hamilton, M.: A rating scale for depression. *Journal of Neurology, Neurosurgery and Psychiatry*, 23, 56-62, 1960.
12. Gottschalk, L. A., Gleser, G. C., and Springer, K.: Three hostility scales applicable to verbal samples. *Arch. Gen. Psychiatry*, 9, 254-279, 1963.
13. Klerman, G. L., and Gershon, E. S.: Imipramine effects upon hostility in depression. *J. Nerv. Ment. Dis.*, 150, 127-132, 1970.
14. Lazare, A., and Klerman, G. L.: Hysteria and depression: The frequency and significance of hysterical personality features in hospitalized depressed women. *Amer. J. Psychiatry*, 124 (Supplement), 48-56, 1968.
15. Janet, P.: *The Major Symptoms of Hysteria*. New York: Macmillan, 1907, pp. 277-316.
16. Seitz, P. F.: Experiments in the substitution of symptoms by hypnosis. *Psychosomatic Medicine*, 15, 405-424, 1953.
17. Stengel, E.: Further studies on pathological wanderings. *Journal of Mental Science*, 89, 224-241, 1943.
18. Breuer, J. and Freud, S.: *Studies on Hysteria*. New York: Basic Books, 1957.
19. Reich, W.: *Character-Analysis*. New York: Orgone Institute Press, 189-193, 1945.
20. Marmor, J.: Orality in the hysterical personality. *J. Amer. Psychoanalytic Assoc.* 1, 656-671, 1953.
21. Grinker, R. R., Sr., Miller, J., Sabshin, M., Nunn, R., and Nunnally, J. C.: *The Phenomena of Depression*. New York: Paul B. Hoeber (Harper & Row), 1961.
22. Friedman, A. S., Cowitz, B., Cohen, H. W., and Granick, S.: Syndromes and themes of psychotic depression. *Arch. Gen. Psychiatry*, 9, 504-509, 1953.
23. Lazare, A., Klerman, G. L., and Armor, D. J.: Oral, obsessive, and hysterical personality patterns: An investigation of psychoanalytic concepts by means of factor analysis. *Arch. Gen. Psychiatry*, 14, 624-630, 1966.
24. Lazare, A., Klerman, G. L., and Armor, D. J.: Oral, obsessive and hysterical personality patterns. *Journal of Psychiatric Research*, 7, 275-290, 1970.
25. Hirschfeld, R. M., Klerman, G. L., Chodoff, P., Korchin, S., and Barrett, J.: Dependency—self-esteem—clinical depression. *J. Amer. Acad. Psychoanalysis*, 4, 373-388, 1976.
26. Hirschfeld, R. M., Klerman, G. L., Gough, H. F., Barrett, J., Korchin, S. J., and Chodoff, P.: A measure of interpersonal dependency. *Journal of Personality Assessment*, 41, 610-618, 1977.

Chapter 4

Some Psychoanalytic Contributions to the Understanding and Treatment of Patients with Primitive Personalities

Stephen B. Bernstein, M.D.

INTRODUCTION

The area of the primitive personality disturbances lies between the neuroses and the psychoses. Over the past 30 years these patients have been the focus of increasing attention and investigation. A large psychiatric literature has arisen in an attempt to describe and more clearly understand this group of patients. In this effort psychoanalytically based methods of observation and understanding have been effective in gathering clinical data and generating conceptual models to facilitate understanding and develop treatment strategies in work with these patients.

The work of Otto Kernberg, especially in the area of the borderline patient (and narcissistic personality disorders), and that of Heinz Kohut, in the area of the narcissistic personality disorders, are examples of evolving, comprehensive systems or models for the understanding and

Supported in part by NIMH, Psychiatry Education Branch, Grant No. MH 08377-15.

treatment of types of primitive patients. Although the elegant, complicated, and often contrasting work of these two men is at the forefront of current psychoanalytic knowledge in this clinical area, it owes a debt to work done by many psychoanalytic clinicians and researchers who have treated and studied these patients and contributed to the literature.

It is the purpose of this chapter to describe the history, development, and current state of clinical and theoretical psychoanalytic contributions in relation to patients with primitive personalities. Special emphasis will be placed on clarifying the complex concepts of both Kernberg and Kohut through explanations of their ideas and by the use of clinical examples.

We will begin with the question of why it was originally necessary to define the group of primitive patients. We will then review briefly the early literature on the borderline patient. These patients were not initially differentiated (and Kernberg still does not fully differentiate them) from the more recently described narcissistic personality disorders. This early literature also produced descriptions of subgroups of patients such as the "false self" patients and the "as if" personalities.

Margaret Mahler's crucial descriptions of the separation-individuation process in child development, especially during the "rapprochement subphase," with its important influence on object relations theory and its use in Kernberg's work, will be discussed. Next, Kernberg's ideas, based on an elaboration of the psychoanalytic structural model integrated with current object relations theory, will be explained and clarified through clinical examples. This will include Kernberg's use of the "structural interview" to assess both descriptive and structural diagnostic features. In addition, Kernberg's application of objects relations theory, his concepts of the borderline's defenses and "pathology of internalized object relations," and his method of treatment will be explored.

Kohut's "psychology of the self" will next be discussed, especially in relation to his concept of the "self," the development of the self, self-object transferences and examples of these, fragmentation of the self, and the concept of "transmuting internalization." Kernberg's views and those of Kohut will then be compared and contrasted.

Finally, examples of some other current contributions to the theory and research with these patients will be presented, together with an attempt to enumerate present and future questions. A brief restatement and summary of Kernberg's and Kohut's formulation will end the chapter.

THE NEED TO DEFINE PRIMITIVE PATIENT GROUPS

Investigation of the "borderland" of patients (between neurosis and psychosis) was thought necessary to more clearly define neurotic patients suitable for analysis, to clearly differentiate borderline from schizophrenic patients for therapeutic, prognostic and research purposes, and also to define those patients who would respond to the then newly developed psychotropic medications.

Initial awareness of the borderline group of patients and its early demarcation began in an effort to explain why certain seemingly "neurotic" patients, who were thought to be analyzable, had shown greatly more chaos and regression than expected and at times psychotic manifestations during an attempt at psychoanalytic treatment (1, 2). They had been unable to form a collaborative working relationship or "therapeutic alliance" with their analyst, wherein they could both experience past longings, wishes, and feelings, and also step back from these to examine them at some distance. The analytic technique, which by relative frustration deprived patients of the efficiency of their past defenses, was experienced as too frustrating. Instead of being able to contain feelings and yearnings and increasingly focus them in the encapsulated analytic relationship, they experienced a reactivation of past experiences of loss and abandonment. There was a resultant increased demand for support and sustenance from the analyst, and an increased regression and acting-out of their wishes in their environment. They experienced an intensified sense of aloneness and abandonment and showed a relative incapacity for self-regulation of soothing, sustenance, and self-esteem. These patients came in contact with basic unregulated, destructive feelings directed toward the analyst or the environment and more frequently acted out toward themselves. The clearest and most systematic elaboration of these patients has come from Kernberg (3-15), drawing on the work of Klein (16-22), Jacobson (23-26), Fairbairn (27-30), Guntrip (31, 32), and Winnicott (33-39).

Subsequent writers, such as Adler and Buie (40-50), Meissner (51-55), and a great many others (56, 57), have elaborated, clarified, synthesized and contributed newer observations. The slightly more recent interest in the narcissistic character disorders has been spurred by Kohut's contributions (58-62) and those of his colleagues, Gedo (63-66), Goldberg (63), P. and A. Ornstein (67-69), and M. Tolpin (70), as well as other writers. Modell's (71-75) work in this area has also been quite important.

Besides these investigators working with patients at the "border" of neurosis and analyzability, there were those working with patients at the "border" of psychosis. Such writers wondered why certain "schizophrenic" patients had surprising and uncharacteristic "remissions," in addition to better abilities to relate to others, to function, and to show little deterioration compared to more usual schizophrenic patients. These patients also did not respond as markedly to the then (late 1950s) newly developed psychotropic medications. Early attempts to describe such confusing patients used the terms latent psychosis (76), psychotic personality structure, ambulatory schizophrenia (77-78), and pseudoneurotic schizophrenia (79-81). Still other authors described borderline patients using the terms psychotic character (82, 83), borderline personality organization (3-15), borderline syndrome (84), borderline states (1, 2), borderline patients (85), "as if" personality (86), and the "false self" (31, 37).

DIFFICULTIES WITH THE DISEASE MODEL

Some confusion in the early attempts to define the primitive personality area has come from efforts to apply a disease model to either stable or transient psychological interpersonal or behavioral reactions to life experiences or stresses. The disease model attempts to describe categories with little overlap and few borders. This is related to the fact that diseases of the body tissues generally do not overlap but cause discrete tissue damage due to the interruption of nervous impulses or blood flow. Interruption of nerves often causes specific damage in a predictable, non-overlapping area. Such a pathophysiological approach has been ineffective in the psychological sphere and has left patients with the more fluid psychological responses to life experiences "around the borders."

THE EARLY BORDERLINE LITERATURE

Freud's elaboration of the structural model in the 1920s in *The Ego and the Id* (87) and *Inhibitions, Symptoms, and Anxiety* (88) paved the way for the developmental and structural theories of character formation. Here anxiety was seen as the ego's response to danger. The capacity to deal with such anxiety resulted from the developing relationship between the child and its mother. Freud's student, Reich (89), explored the development of defensive structures which protect against infantile anxieties. Reich pointed to stable patterns of defense and of interpersonal relationships, which become a coherent character structure over time. These could be seen in adult relationships or in the therapeutic situation. Understanding of character formation paved the way for an eventual fuller understanding of borderline character pathology.

In 1938 Adolph Stern (90, 91) presented one of the early clinical descriptions of borderline patients and proposed clinical formulations which have subsequently been supported by the literature. He described the borderline symptoms of poor reality-testing, use of projection, feelings of inferiority, masochism and difficulty expressing hostility. Such persons showed a sensitivity to therapeutic interpretations, which were experienced as injuries and which the patient felt threatened his relationship with the therapist. Self-esteem depended on approval from the loved object. Such patients seemed to be more interested in the analyst's love than in therapeutic work. Stern postulated these symptoms as resulting from early deprivation in the infant-mother relationship.

Stern's ideas about the relationship between the mother's level of anxiety and that of the infant interestingly antedates Winnicott's important and often quoted concepts of the "holding environment" and "good enough mothering," as well as Bion's (1962) less well-known but quite moving concept of "containment," as described by Grinberg (92): ". . . when the infant feels very acute anxiety (for example, fear of dying), he needs to project it into a container (his mother) capable of holding it and giving it back in such a way that the anxiety is lessened. If the mother fails to metabolize this anxiety and even deprives it of its specific quality (fear of dying), the infant will receive back a 'nameless dread' which he cannot tolerate."

The later attempt to find such a container and metabolizer of anxiety with whom to share pain and anxiety is what brings many patients to treatment. An example of this childhood experience revived in an ongoing psychotherapy was stated by a patient as follows:

> I can't stand the pain and emptiness I feel right now. But I feel that if you could share the feelings with me, experience and feel them, they would seem less to me. Maybe sharing the feelings with you would make them go away a little.

Knight's (1, 2) early, influential papers attempted to differentiate borderline patients from analyzable neurotics. This was necessary since the former, although seemingly normal or neurotic, at times could develop psychotic symptoms in psychiatric treatment. Knight described borderline states which seemed more transient than the borderline personality organization later described by Kernberg. Knight's patients showed apparently neurotic symptoms but also impaired ego functions, and at times a lack of boundaries between fantasy and reality. On interview there was thought-blocking, odd word usage, inappropriate affect, and suspiciousness. Knight distinguished between the autoplastic or ego-alien symptom complexes, where the ego was fending off symptoms and in which there was a favorable prognosis, and the alloplastic or ego-syntonic illnesses, where the ego itself was distorted.

Early Descriptions of Borderline Subgroups

The "false self"

Other writers focused on careful clinical descriptions of what may be specific types or subgroups of borderline patients. Guntrip's (31, 32) description of the "false self" phenomena (schizoid), which is related to Winnicott's (33-39) formulations, concerns withdrawn, introverted, quiet, shy, uncommunicative, detached, and shut-in patients, who seem cold and unmoved as a defense against their underlying needs and fears of people. If their defenses are penetrated, they reveal a secret, vulnerable, very needy, fear-ridden, infantile self, showing up in dream and fantasy world and hidden from the surface self, the "false self" which the world sees. The true self is so far shut away that when they find someone to depend on, they cannot feel or get in touch with that person. This limits the capacity to love, to feel understanding, warmth, and personal concern for others. They are only able to be aware of the dreaded sense of isolation within. Guntrip quotes Winnicott referring to the "true self" of the infant in an unnurturing environment as being "put into cold storage with a secret hope of rebirth" in a better environment later on, while a "false self" is developed on the conscious surface. An example of this "false self" experience was stated by a patient in treatment as follows:

> I feel that I have a "personality in reserve." There's a part inside me that never gets out. It's scared and I hate it sometimes. It's my real self, the real me, and I keep it far apart from the rest of me so I won't go crazy. It's as if I'm another person trapped inside myself. Sometimes I talk to it but I don't want you to know it because it's too sad. That part inside me can be hurt very easily. Things are always better if people see a side of me that I like, or that I like them to see.

"As if" personality

Another specific configuration of borderline patient was elaborated by Helene Deutsch (86) in her pioneering and elegant description of the "as if" personality. She described a type of patient whose life seems externally to run along "as if" it were complete. But such people lack genuineness, warmth and expression of emotions, which is noticeable to others. They also seem to be without a sense of inner experience. True empathic relationships with others are not possible, and instead of normal relatedness there is something similar to the child's imitativeness and identification with their environment, a mimicry. There is "a passive attitude to the environment with a highly plastic readiness to pick up signals from the outer world and to mold one's self and one's behavior accordingly. The identification with what other people are thinking and feeling is the expression of this passive plasticity and renders the person capable of the greatest fidelity and the basest perfidy" (86, p. 265). Also there is an "automaton like" suggestibility, and evidence of extreme passivity. The extreme need to comply and obey leads to the "chameleon-like" characteristics so excellently described by Deutsch. An example of this "as if" quality was stated by a patient as follows:

> I go out of my way to please people and then I feel protected. It's like I am creating a play in which I play many characters. I am performing for people and I try to do and be whatever will please them. I try to figure out what people want, and I try to behave that way. I don't have a very good picture of what I am. It's more like I am what I think people want me to be.

MAHLER'S CONTRIBUTIONS

Margaret Mahler's (93-99) extremely important contributions to the understanding of the developmental defects possibly present in the borderline conditions stem from extensive observation of infants and children with their mother, especially during a specific part (the rapprochement subphase) of the separation-individuation process.

Mahler describes several subphases of early infant and child separation-individuation. The earliest stage is one of *symbiosis* during the first five to eight months. During this time the human infant is interdependent with his or her mother, relying on her for self-preservation. The infant has not differentiated an enduring internal image of himself or herself (self-representation) as different from an enduring internal image of his or her mother (object representation). In the earliest forms of separation the infant begins to experience some internal indication of longing for the mother when she is absent for brief periods of time, or "separation anxiety." There is a wish for the comforting and soothing return to symbiotic closeness in which the mother is experienced as a part of the infant.

During the next subphase, eight to 16 months, with the infant's beginning to walk and enjoying the capacity for self-propulsion, there is the beginning of an experience of independence and separation. The toddler alternates between independent motile exploration and a return for "refueling" to the soothing protection of the mother.

During the next or *rapprochement* subphase, 16 to 25 months, there is an increased sense of vulnerable separateness and a decrease in the sense of the mother's omnipotent presence. There is also a feeling of being alone in the absence of the mother, with some increase in separation anxiety. There is both a wish to be reunited with the mother and a fear of being engulfed. The mother is experienced at times as a positive caretaking separate object and at times as a negative abandoning object. Resolution of the rapprochement subphase with mastery of the separation-individuation process leads to the child's and later the adult's being able to have both negative and positive intrapsychic representations of himself and others. The capacity to master the rapprochement subphase, to separate from the mother, to tolerate and integrate positive and negative self experiences and positive and negative object experiences leads to the subsequent "capacity for ambivalence." The ability to retain both positive and negative images of others (objects) even while separated from them leads to the capacity for "object constancy."

Defects in the rapprochement subphase of separation-individuation lead to an inability to tolerate ambivalent experiences and see an object as whole and constant. Although Mahler does not tie this separation-individuation defect to any specific borderline characteristics, others have felt that borderline patients continue into adulthood with enmeshed "symbiotic" relationships. An example of such separation difficulties in adulthood is illustrated by the following:

A 28-year-old male patient was accompanied to his psychiatric hospital admission by his wife and mother. In the waiting room he looked depressed and sat with his head down on his mother's lap, while his wife sat close to him, holding his hands and stroking his back. When it was time for him to go to the ward, these three people did not want to leave one another and were only separated with great difficulty. During his hospitalization he called his mother four times a day and his wife on several other occasions. When he was called by his family, there were usually three or four other people on the phone extensions at home. At meetings with the staff, at which the family sat extremely close together, when questions were asked of the patient, they were frequently answered by his wife or mother. On one occasion, when a staff member asked the patient to tell his wife how depressed he was, he said, "Oh she already knows, we're so close. It's almost like she can read my mind." His wife nodded in agreement.

KERNBERG'S CONTRIBUTIONS

Kernberg's (3-15) comprehensive and useful contributions to the spectrum of diagnosis, treatment and prognosis of the borderline disorders stress the concept of a "structural diagnosis," a description of stable intrapsychic personality structures based on an elaboration of object relations theory. The "structural diagnosis" is established through a specific "structural interview" focused on an understanding of the general nature of the patient's symptomatology, object relations and defensive operations, as well as of the interaction between the patient and others in his or her life and between the patient and the interviewer. Kernberg points out that reliance on descriptive characteristics alone may cause confusion in diagnosis since certain symptoms generally seen in borderline patients, such as anger, depression or impulsivity, may not be seen in some of these patients but may be seen in neurotic and at times psychotic patients. He feels that the diagnosis of borderline personality organization can be "enriched" and made more powerful by the addition of the structural approach to previous descriptive methods.

Diagnosis

The structural diagnosis of the borderline personality organization adds to the descriptive diagnosis specific assessment of: identity diffusion, defensive operations related to splitting and derived from pathological internalized object relations, maintenance of reality-testing, and poor superego integration.

Descriptive diagnosis

Descriptive symptoms of the borderline patient are basically neurotic-like symptoms which, because of their nature, bizarreness, primitiveness, intensity or limitation of the patient's life, lead the clinician to feel the patient's character structure is more primitive than neurotic. Similarly, transient, psychotic-like symptoms in a patient without a clear psychotic diagnosis should lead the clinician to consider the borderline category. Kernberg sees some neurotic-like symptoms as "presumptive" of the borderline patient:

1) diffuse or chronic anxiety;

2) a cluster of two or more neurotic symptoms (polysymptomatic neurosis) such as: multiple restricting phobias; obsessive-compulsive symptoms which have become part of the patient's life and do not cause much conflict; chronic multiple or bizarre conversion symptoms; dissociative reactions such as fugue states or alterations of consciousness; hypochondriasis, if combined with paranoid trends or any other neurotic symptom;

3) sexual deviations with several perverse trends (polymorphous perverse sexual trends) related to unstable interpersonal relationships.

An example (from my own experience) of polymorphous perverse sexual trends is the following:

A 27-year-old borderline woman with a history of intermittent and indiscriminate lesbianism had married a man who was a homosexual, feeling that this was the only type of man with whom she could live. At a time when he was more actively involved with homosexual partners, she found the only way she could be involved with him was to participate in his homosexual love affairs. Later, at a time of some withdrawal of her husband from her, she also began having a desire to sexually molest her two young daughters.

4) classical prepsychotic personality structures such as the paranoid personality, schizoid personality or hypomanic personality;

5) impulse neuroses and addictions, which are pleasurable during the episode although guilt may follow and exist between episodes, e.g., drug addictions, and some forms of psychogenic obesity and kleptomania;

6) "lower level" character disorders where there is less reaction formation and where the personality is invaded by chaotic and primitive impulse discharge mechanisms. Here Kernberg includes infantile personalities, narcissistic personalities, "as if" personalities, and antisocial personalities.

Structural diagnosis

Kernberg's basic understanding of the borderline personality organization is based upon elaborations of the structural model. Here the structures (id, ego and superego) are seen as a group of relatively stable mental processes which focus and modulate intrapsychic functions. Genetic, constitutional, biochemical, familial, psychodynamic and psychosocial ideologic factors bear upon personality development and formation. These are reflected in the intrapsychic structures and their internalized object relations, which become apparent to the clinician during a structural interview.

Kernberg's "structural analysis" requires an understanding of the object relations theory which he has elaborated, based on important contributions by Klein, Fairbairn, Jacobson, and Mahler, among others. Understanding the relationship of the intrapsychic structures (ego, id, superego) and the nature of internalized object relations leads to an assessment of whether a patient functions on a neurotic, borderline or psychotic level.

Object Relations Theory

Kernberg feels that there are two early and essential tasks which must be accomplished for the developing infant. These are: 1) the differentiation of self from other (the differentiation of self-images from object images) present in borderline but not psychotics; and 2) the ability to integrate and interrelate positively felt or loving and negatively felt or aggressive images of oneself and of others (which leads to the capacity for ambivalence). By self-image is meant an experience of the self at a particular time, which may involve the experience of one's body or inner mental state. Such an experience of one's self is contructed from sensations, emotions, and thoughts. This image of the self may be conscious or unconscious and may be realistic or unrealistic. The self-image is more transient than the more enduring self-representation, which is built by the ego out of many self-images presented to the ego over time. In a parallel fashion, one may speak of object images (as opposed to the more enduring object representations) as the more transient perceptions gained directly or indirectly of others.

In the optimal infant-mother situation, gratification and pleasurable experiences are provided for the infant's needs. From this arises an experience in the infant of feeling fused with the mother. The mother is experienced as being part of the infant's self (without self-other differentiation). The experience of basic trust in this relationship and the gratifying feelings it produces lead to the trusting, fertile soil of strong ego development. From this gratifying experience arises a feeling of something being good inside the self and good experiences being possible in the future.

The natural frustration and resultant anxiety which also occur in infancy are experienced as "bad," leading to an experience of a negative internal image. Although both positive/gratifying and negative/frustrating self- and other images occur, in the "good enough mother" situation the positive ones predominate. If, however, there is a predominance of frustration and negative experiences, early aggressiveness results. In the psychotic patient, the experience has been so painful, unsoothing, and frustrating, that in order to feel relief it was necessary for the infant to defend against frustration by reuniting the positive self-images and the positive object images. This results in the psychotic lack of self- and object differentiation.

In the borderline patient, however, there has been less early frustration, but enough to cause early aggression and the creation of a more easily stressed structure. It is more easily fatigued by aggressive pressures in response to frustration. Under stress it may distort its boundaries (where it stops and others start) or distort perceptions of internal and external reality. Children with such difficulties are threatened by their aggression and frustration, and experience this as potentially destructive to themselves and especially to others whom they need. The conflict and anxiety which result from the presence of both positive and negative images about themselves and others is defended against by the defensive separation of the positive and negative self- and object images, called "splitting." This is the major defensive operation of the child who may become borderline.

Splitting is a carry-over into later life, in the borderline, of the lack of integration of "good and bad" images normally seen in early childhood. Splitting is associated with other defensive operations, such as denial, primitive idealization, omnipotence, projection, and projective identification, which tend to reinforce the splitting defense. The ego is protected against unbearable conflicts between love and hatred at the cost of its growing integration. Kernberg points out that as a result of these defensive operations: 1) There is faulty development of an integrated self-concept and overdependence on others in order to gain stability over time (syndrome of identity diffusion); 2) a polarization of good and bad self- and object images makes interpersonal relationships difficult; 3) superego formation and its relationship to ego formation is skewed because it reflects the extremes of both good ideal images and sadistic images; and 4) there are difficulties with the level of empathy possible because of a difficulty in separation between the self and others and a difficulty acknowledging others as independent. People are seen as either positive or negative, good or bad, as parts but not as whole or total persons (part rather than whole objects). Such people are experienced as changing from good to bad and bad to good, as not constant or whole. They cannot, therefore, be experienced as totally separate or having their own personality. Resultant ego defects lead to difficulty in anxiety tolerance, impulse control and the ability to sublimate. The ego is less solid and more easily stressed than in the neurotic patient. It cannot easily modulate the pressures of underlying instincts and drives and smooth these out to the less extreme derivatives seen in the neurotic patient.

Borderline Manifestations

Manifestations of the borderline personality organization and its related faulty object relations ("the pathology of internalized object relations") are described below.

Identity diffusion

Because of the lack of a stable and encompassing experience or picture of one's self and others, there is a lack of identity cohesion and, instead, a defensive self-experience of identity diffusion. Subjectively, this is experienced as chronic emptiness, with shallow, constricted and contradictory perceptions of oneself and of others. There are contradictions between the patient's beliefs and behavior. He cannot describe cohesively his or others' internal or external experiences. He does not feel defined or separate enough to put himself in another's place and test out what the other is feeling (lack of empathy). Likewise, the defensiveness of such a patient's self-experience and his or her experience of others makes the interviewer unable to empathize with the patient. There is no sense of a whole person in contact with the interviewer. Instead, the patient experiences himself and others as split apart, separate poles of contradictory and opposed "good and bad" feelings and attributes. The patient's descriptions of both himself and of others lack cohesiveness and leave the interviewer unable to get a clear, whole picture of the other person being described.

Splitting and related defensive operations

In contrast to the neurotic's use of repression and other high level defensive operations, such as reaction formation, isolation, undoing and intellectualization, the borderline patient avoids conflict and anxiety by the use of primitive defensive operations related to the mechanism of splitting. This avoidance of conflict, however, is at the expense of weakening ego functioning.

a) *Splitting*. Splitting, the separation of others to "all good" and "all bad" poles, may be observed during an interview with a patient or in the environment a patient creates around himself. An example which occurred on a psychiatric unit is as follows:

> A 26-year-old woman was noted by the hospital staff to wait impatiently and with great expectations for interviews with her male psychiatric resident, whom she saw as "caring, understanding, and wonderful, and the most sensitive man I ever met." The rest of the staff had little contact with her. She kept away from them, saw them as intruders and as incompetents. She did not participate in ward activity and waited only to see her evaluator. When she saw him she talked about how helpful he was and how much better she was feeling because of his help. However, when on rare occasions she talked to nurses and other staff, she conveyed a sense of helplessness and hopelessness and talked about her suicidal preoccupations.

b) *Primitive Idealization*. This serves to reinforce the splitting operation by creating powerful positive images of an ideal or omnipotent person which defend against the unstated powerful "all bad" figures. In the previous example, the psychiatric resident represented the patient's primitive idealization, which protected against the devalued nursing staff. An example of such idealization was stated by a patient in therapy as follows:

> Nobody understands me like you do. You're so understanding, so helpful. I get the feeling when I sit with you that you can make me better. I've never had this feeling before, the sense of calm, the sense that you know exactly what I'm thinking. It's like a powerful force that you exert and I know it helps me every time I sit and talk with you.

c) *Primitive projection and projective identification*. In primitive projection the impulse, attributed to an outside object, is not able to sufficiently remove anxiety, as it is in the neurotic mechanism of projection. The patient continues to experience the feeling (e.g., anger), even though it is experienced as coming from the other person. Fear of the person onto whom the impulse is projected necessitates in the patient the need to control the external object. The need to control the feared object, therefore, induces the patient to act in certain ways, so as to attempt to induce reactions in the other object, reactions that the patient feels will help him control the other person. In order to rid himself of the unacceptable feeling, the patient increasingly accuses the other of having it, tries to control him and by this may actually stir up such feelings in others. The patient's hostile onslaught on his therapist may be an attempt to stimulate counteraggression in the therapist in a sadistic attempt to control him:

> A patient took up many therapy hours accusing his therapist of being angry at him, disliking him, and wanting to hurt him. The therapist noted anger in the patient, but he disowned and denied any feelings of anger. The therapist noted that when he would tell the patient he was not angry, the patient would more frantically insist that he was angry and not to be trusted. He noted that over a period of time, as his statements that he was not angry at the patient were met by increased accusations, he did indeed begin to feel some annoyance with the patient and his mounting accusations and demands.

d) *Denial*. Denial serves to reinforce the splitting. Since people have many and opposing qualities, seeing them as one-sided, all good or all bad, requires a denial of the other realistic qualities of the person:

> A 34-year-old female borderline patient was admitted to a psychiatric inpatient unit, after being transferred from the Intensive Care unit. She had entered the hospital after a massive overdose of sleeping medication in a severe suicide attempt, which produced coma and near death, subsequent to learning of an affair which her husband had had. In an interview soon after her transfer, the patient stated that her suicide attempt was probably an accident and that she really no longer had any suicidal preoccupations. She stated that she had forgiven her husband for his unfaithfulness, that her overdose had not been severe, and that, even in the face of her treatment on the Intensive Care unit, her suicide attempt "just happened" and would never happen again. The patient stated that she was no longer depressed, even though she appeared clinically depressed, and that she had absolutely no concerns or problems. She said that her overdose was merely a response to a transient situation which had no meaning, and that there had been no previous problems in her life. She looked forward to returning to her "wonderful" family and her "happy marriage."

e) *Omnipotence and devaluation.* Here, instead of idealizing one person and devaluing another, idealization is of oneself in relation to a devalued other, again in the service of splitting. An example of both omnipotence and devaluation occurred in a female patient, newly admitted to a psychiatric ward. She soon became argumentative and told the nurses:

> I'm probably the healthiest person around here. I'm not used to this kind of treatment where I come from. Besides, this unit is a pigsty. Why are all these nurses walking around the floor? Couldn't they find something better to do? What are all these unmarried nurses doing around here anyway? Why don't they get married and have children like the rest of us? This whole place doesn't help me. The other patients are crazy, and I don't want to associate with them.

Other Considerations

Reality-testing

The borderline patient maintains his ability to test reality more firmly than the psychotic patient. This is manifest by the absence of hallucinations and delusions, the lack of bizarre or inappropriate behavior, affects, or thoughts, and some capacity to allow others to empathize with his thoughts and feelings. The borderline identity diffusion and primitive defenses can lead to lapses in reality-testing less pervasive than those of psychotic patients but quite different from those of neurotics.

Nonspecific manifestations of ego weakness

These are so-called "soft" signs of ego weakness which, although useful, are not as specifically related to the borderline diagnosis as other previously mentioned characteristics. These are a lack of anxiety tolerance (the capacity to tolerate increased anxiety without new symptom formation or regressive behavior); a lack of impulse control; and a lack of specific avenues for sublimation.

Superego functioning

Borderline patients often show distortion of superego formation, characterized by early unmodulated aggressive, sadistic and at times idealized fantasies and retained parental images. There are often harsh,

excessive guilt feelings and/or depressive states. Severe superego pathology may also be manifest by mistreatment or exploitation of others
and difficulty adhering to ethical and moral principles. Kernberg feels
that superego functioning is a less specific structural indicator of borderline pathology, but that prognostically it and the level of object relations are the two best structural indicators of the capacity for intensive
psychotherapy.

Developmental Considerations

Infantile or primitive aggression in borderline patients invades all levels of development and leads to weakening of the ego and the lack of
capacity to integrate good and bad self- and object images. Sadism or
hostility intrude at levels where they should be modified and modulated.
Oedipal rivalry becomes a terrifying death struggle and usually con-
tainable levels of anxiety become linked with a sense of annihilation.
Such a threat is heightened by the confusing and changing images of
mother and father. In addition, seemingly higher level issues are colored
by earlier unmodified needs and fantasies. Kernberg illustrates this by
stating that the penis may have the pregenital meaning of a "feeding,
withholding, or attacking" mother, and the vagina may become a "hungry feeding or aggressive mouth."

The Structural Interview

In order to elicit the data necessary for differentiation of the borderline
patient from the neurotic and psychotic patient, Kernberg (15) suggests
a specific type of "structual interview," which emphasizes techniques
to activate the patient's symptoms and conflicts, especially those which
emerge in the interaction between the interviewer and the patient.
Through the use of clarification, confrontation, and interpretation, the
patient's "predominant defensive or structural organization" is elicited.
The interviewer tries to focus on and heighten the patient's conflict,
in order to mildly stress the patient's defenses and observe the effects
of this on his identity sense, defensive operations, and capacity for
reality-testing. In *clarification*, the interviewer tries to have the patient
elaborate on unclear or contradictory information and asks for an understanding of information which may be conscious or preconscious. In
a slightly more challenging way, the interviewer uses *confrontation* to
elicit information about areas which may be more conflictual or contradictory. Drawing upon the patient's history, as well as the here-and-

now of the interview, the therapist asks the patient about contradictions, defenses, or any lack of awareness in certain reality situations. The patient's capacity to have some distance on this interaction, without further regression, is noted and is important. Also, the interviewer's increased capacity to be more empathically in tune with the patient after such a confrontation reflects an increase in the patient's social awareness, as well as in his reality-testing.

By the use of *interpretation*, the material produced in confrontation is linked to the possible manifestation of defensive and other operations in the relationship with the interviewer. Although confrontation has brought together contradictions observed in the interview, the interpretation asks the patient to try to link the here-and-now with underlying, causal, unconscious or preconscious relationships. The confrontation highlights the underlying anxieties and conflicts which the therapist has observed in the interview. In the interpretation one may suggest that these anxieties come, for example, from an underlying anger at the interviewer because of the patient's feeling that he is being intruded upon. In the *transference interpretation*, the patient is asked to see that the underlying anger is a reenactment in the interview situation of a situation from the patient's past, i.e., from the relationship with his parents.

Kernberg suggests that there are different responses to the structural interview in neurotic, borderline, and psychotic patients, because of the differences in their defenses, identity sense and capacity for reality-testing. Borderline patients with an ability for reality-testing tend to show reorganization and improvement in functioning during this interview. They can respond empathically to the interviewer's questions and help the interviewer understand conflicting ideas or seeming contradictions. They are able to use insights and have some distance on the contradictions in their life situation, although the emptiness and chaos of their life and their defective object relations are apparent. Psychotic patients with difficulty in reality-testing may show further lessening of reality-testing. Neurotic patients show a greater sense of themselves than borderlines and allow the interviewer to have a greater sense of empathy with their conflicts. They show none of the emptiness and confusion in their social relations and interpersonal situations which are evident in the borderline patients.

Treatment

In general, Kernberg suggests a modified psychoanalytically-oriented psychotherapy, the modifications being necessitated by the borderline patient's evidence of ego weakness, proneness to transference psychosis, and tendency to act out instinctual conflicts. The process of working-through is different with borderline patients than with neurotics because the acting-out of the borderline tends to gratify pathological instinctual needs. Supportive psychotherapy, which reinforces defenses and builds up adaptive living patterns, although preventing regression and transference psychosis, does not lead in the long run to much improvement. There is, instead, a building up of negative transference which, when not worked with in the treatment, tends to be acted out, sometimes dangerously, outside of the therapeutic relationship.

Generally Kernberg's modifications of psychoanalytic technique involve:

> 1) elaboration of the manifest and latent negative transference and "deflection" of this direct negative transference away from the relationship between the therapist and patient, as well as exploration of the configurations in the patient's outside relationships;
>
> 2) interpretation of the pathological defenses which contribute to the patient's ego weakness, decreased reality-testing, and affect the negative transference;
>
> 3) structuring and limit-setting in the therapeutic situation, in order to decrease acting-out of the transference within the therapy hour itself. In neurotic patients such acting-out is a repetition of the past and can be worked through. In borderline patients, it tends to gratify instinctual needs and is less easily worked through by interpretation. Limit-setting tends to give the patient distance from his or her emotions and limits the gratification of the instinctual needs;
>
> 4) utilization of structuring outside the therapy hours, such as day hospitalization, if acting-out of the transference endangers the patient and the treatment;
>
> 5) use and protection of the positive transference to support the treatment; and
>
> 6) support of expression of more mature and appropriate sexuality to free it from its pregenitally aggressive determinants.

Premature, full-blown transference manifestations may be activated, immediately, in the initial transference of the borderline patient. Since the borderline defenses against the often negative transference are ego-weakening and cause the severe regression of the patient, their consistent interpretation is crucial. Ego-weakening leads to decreased self-observation (therapeutic alliance). The patient may feel overwhelmed by the feelings and thoughts which are stirred up. Use of projective identification may lead to chaos in the treatment and the stirring up of countertransference responses. The patient experiences fear and distrust of the therapist and attempts to control the therapist by aggressive or controlling means. It is through constant attention to the latent negative transference that increased capacity for self-observation and alliance formation is built. This leads to a decrease in the pressure of the negative transference and a lightening of the countertransference load of the therapist.

In borderline patients a "transference psychosis" may occur, with transient loss of reality-testing and the appearance of some delusional material during therapy hours. This may not seem to affect the patient's outside life, unlike the transference psychosis in psychotic patients. Kernberg suggests that many such reactions in borderline patients can be worked through by interpretation and limit-setting in the therapeutic hour and do not require hospitalization, although at times this may prove necessary.

The countertransference reactions stimulated by borderline patients may be related to partial reactivations of early ego identifications and early defensive mechanisms in the therapist. Such responses may come close to duplicating the early reactions which the patient experienced and so may be useful to the therapist. They may also threaten the treatment. The reemergence of chronic recurrent countertransference reactions over time, stimulated by treatment of such patients, may be manifest by the exacerbation of previously abandoned neurotic character traits in relationship to a specific patient, such as withdrawal or over-involvement in an unrealistic treatment situation.

To Kernberg it is clear that the borderline defensive operations defend against the emergence of primitive, predominantly negative transferences. These defenses, although tending to decrease anxiety, lead to identity diffusion, difficulties in object relations, poor reality-testing, and inability to form a therapeutic alliance. Effective treatment can only come about through the consistent interpretation of the patient's need to use these defensive operations and to compartmentalize different sections of his or her personality. Kernberg stresses that to accomplish this one does not try to make the unconscious conscious, because repression is not one of the major defenses of the borderline. Instead, one brings together and integrates various split-off segments of the patient's personality, in order to facilitate their integration.

We will now move on to explore Kohut's views regarding narcissistic personalities. Kernberg's ideas in this area will be compared and contrasted with Kohut's.

KOHUT'S CONTRIBUTION

For Kohut (58-62) patients with narcissistic personality disorders are not treatable by classical psychoanalytic technique because of specific developmental and other defects which predate the defects characteristic of the neuroses. Because of early empathic failures in the infant-mother relationship, the narcissistic expression of archaic (primitive) grandiosity through parental admiration of the child's exhibitionistic expressions of grandiosity (mirroring), as well as idealization of the parents, is impeded. A blockage of narcissistic (self-love) maturation results, affecting later areas of self-esteem and self-worth. This leads to impediments in the areas of ambition, ideals, and creativity. Such persons develop defenses of denial, disavowal, shame, and disgust, which help them deal with their narcissistic vulnerabilities. They often show outward manifestations of grandiosity, arrogance, coldness or inordinate self-sufficiency, on the one hand, or withdrawal, shyness, decreased self-esteem, and hypochondriasis, on the other hand.

Persons with narcissistic personality disorders have object relations in which they try to have others fill the void of their unmet needs to be admired (mirrored) by or to admire (idealize) someone else. Optimally, in childhood, the need to idealize, when sufficiently gratified, causes a modification of this into mature ego ideals. The need to be admired (mirrored) as the expression of archaic grandiosity, if satisfied, produces a modification of this into normal self-esteem and ambition. Insufficient parental responses to these needs cause their blockage and a lack of modification from their archaic roots, while correct responses lead to a less vulnerable "cohesive" self. The concept of the "self"—how it develops, how we experience it, how it affects our functioning and relations with others and how it may be helped to mature—is the focus of Kohut's work, his "psychology of the self" or "self psychology."

Development of the Self

The unimpeded development of the "self" dates from the second year of life. Optimally, the self develops through a generally empathic relationship between infant and mother and results in the child's developing a sense of having independent initiative and perceptions, which are integrated with his ambitions and ideas and with an experience of a unity of mind and body. This cohesive psychic configuration, in connection with individual talents that the individual develops, forms the central core of personality (59). The normal process of "self"-development, beginning in infancy, is related not to the parents' intellectual childrearing beliefs but, instead, to the integration and cohesiveness of their own selves. If the normal process of self-development is blocked, it must be reactivated and remediated in the therapeutic situation.

In the process of self-formation and strengthening of the cohesive self during development (and during therapeutic efforts), relative defects in one of the components of the self may be compensated for by a stronger development of the other. Kohut feels that the child has "two chances" in his or her formation of a cohesive self and the severe disturbances of the self result only if there is a failure of both of these components. Specifically, the two chances relate to fulfillment of the *mirroring* and *idealizing* needs. In the case of a young boy, merging or mirroring is accomplished by the maternal self-object, while idealization is responded to later by the father. This process varies in different children; it may be more complicated in some children than in others. If there is a failure of the mirroring or idealizing pole, this may be compensated for or remedied by a more adequate experience at the other pole. In the treatment of patients showing evidence of early failures in self-development, the specific transference manifestations may show which unmet needs have been blocked in their maturational progression and need remediation.

The Cohesive Self

The narcissistic patient, unlike the borderline or schizophrenic patient, has a "cohesive self." Existence of a cohesive self means that the patient has attained fairly stable psychic structures (which maintain psychic stability), stable and fairly realistic relationships with others, and relatively modulated self-esteem, even under stress. Such patients are not threatened by an irreversible disintegration or fragmentation of their psychic selves or of their relationships with others. They can establish stable transferences, allowing therapeutic reactivation of the manifestations of their unmet grandiosity and self-esteem issues without unlimited regression. Establishment of such stable narcissistic transferences (selfobject transferences) is a reliable sign that the patient has a narcissistic personality disorder and is not psychotic or borderline. Kohut believes, therefore, that narcissistic patients have achieved a level of development higher than the borderline syndromes.

This idea is in contrast to Kernberg's position that the narcissistic personality disorders are a subtype of borderline patient. Although Kernberg has added an important contribution to this area of study, his work derives from his theories of borderline patients and will be discussed here only in contrast to Kohut ideas. The application of Kohut's ideas to the understanding of borderline patients has just begun to be explored (49) and may provide theoretical advances in the future.

The Selfobject Transferences

Patients with narcissistic personality disorders have major difficulties in maintaining self-esteem. Although on the surface they may appear similar to neurotics, such patients may show signs, on the one hand, of haughty grandiosity, coldness, contempt, inordinate self-sufficiency, or on the other hand, shyness, sensitivity, and feelings of inferiority. In addition, both of these types may coexist. When such patients enter psychoanalysis, they do not establish classical transference neuroses, as do patients with the "structural" neuroses. Kohut feels that when such patients are treated with a classical technique, one that does not recognize their "self pathology," results are not satisfactory. What does occur with these patients, however, is the reactivation of certain types of transferences—the mirror transference and the idealizing transference—representing the revival of specific unmet narcissistic needs. The recognition of these transferences, which are pathognomonic for the narcissistic personality disorder, makes psychoanalytic treatment possible.

The idealizing and mirror transferences are the result of the reactivation of specific arrested needs for gratification of unmet infantile needs related to the development of the self. The lack of appropriate gratification of these needs led to the failure of development and maturation of narcissism (i.e., self-love, self-esteem, self-worth) through the appropriate expression of and reaction to the child's grandiosity and need to idealize. These defects are recognized as needing correction before resolution of subsequent pre-oedipal and oedipal object-directed developmental steps are possible.

Kohut postulates that in early childhood there are separate parallel developmental lines of narcissism (self-love) and object love. Narcissistic maturation depends on a foundation of early empathic parental responses to two specific needs. First, there is the need to express grandiosity and to have this archaic grandiose self enjoyed (mirrored) by the parents. If this is responded to empathically and appropriately, normal self-esteem and ambition develop. Second, there is the archaic need to idealize the parents (idealized parent imago), which if handled correctly and empathically by the parents leads to the development of healthy ego ideals. Massive parental deficiencies in handling these two needs lead to arrested ideals and ambitions and vulnerability in the area of self-esteem. Archaic versions of these persist and are manifest and defended against by the symptoms of the narcissistic personality disorder. These symptoms of arrogance or shyness are defenses against the unmet grandiosity. Under stress there are also symptoms of shame, withdrawal, depression, hypochondriasis and intense (narcissistic) rage.

Such people have difficulty with mutuality and often enter relationships under the burden of emotional pain and decreased self-esteem. They attempt to use their relationships with others to fulfill the needs and functions not fulfilled in childhood and experienced as absent. If this occurs in the relationship, the defects in the self are temporarily filled in, with resultant decrease in pain and stabilizing of self-esteem. The person who has supplied the "absent" function is experienced as a part of the self. Such an object is called a "selfobject." The selfobject relationship corresponds to the selfobject experiences in childhood where the child's sense of greatness and power, on the one hand, and ability to look up to and merge with a person of soothing calmness and omnipotence, on the other, are confirmed. The former or mirroring selfobject and the latter or idealized selfobject are reactivated later in life in psychoanalytic treatment in the mirror (selfobject) transferences and the idealizing (selfobject) transference.

Clinical Examples—Selfobject transference

Kohut describes *three variations of the mirror type* of selfobject transference. These variations are along a continuum from the most archaic *merger transference*, to the intermediate *alter-ego* or *twinship transference*, to the most mature or *"mirror transference in the narrower sense."* As pointed out by Adler (49), "they seem to be along a continuum from symbiosis to separation." In the mirror transferences, the analyst seems to serve a function of the optimal mother, supplying a function to the patient which he experiences as lacking in himself.

In the *merger transference*, the analyst is seen as *an extension* of the patient's archaic greatness and exhibitionism. In the *alter-ego* or *twinship transference*, the analyst is experienced as a *separate bearer* of the patient's own repressed perfection. In the *mirror transference in the narrower sense*, the analyst confirms or echoes the patient's greatness and is a *silent approver* of his exhibitionistic manifestations. Through the reactivation of these transference states, there is also the necessary revival of the unmet, grandiose needs (grandiose self). The transferences mobilize and maintain the analytic and working-through process by the elaboration of the grandiose fantasies and wishes which are derived from the grandiose self, so that these can eventually be tamed.

An example of a *merger transference* was expressed by a patient as follows:

> I want to keep you close to me all the time as if you were inside of me, looking out. It would be like the two of us were one and we didn't have separate minds. We could talk our own special language. Just the two of us together as one.

The *alter-ego* or *twinship transference,* in which the analyst is experienced as the bearer of the patient's own repressed perfection, was expressed by a patient as follows:

> You are very much like me. We have a lot of the same kinds of qualities. We have both accomplished a great deal. You have this really super and powerful position and can influence a lot of people's lives. Sometimes I see that I have the same kind of situation: power over people, the ability to get instant recognition. Sometimes I like to compare your office to mine and to compare my car to yours. There are a lot of similarities.

In the *mirror transference in the narrower sense* the patient experiences the analyst as even more separate. But there is the need to have the analyst, either through silence or in some other way, confirm the patient's fantasies of his own greatness and to approve manifestations of his exhibitionism.

> An example cited by Gedo (65) relates the mirror transference of a young male patient who had the fantasy that he could become a serious operatic singer despite his lack of musical training and no intention of acquiring this. During analytic hours, he would attempt to see if he had become an operatic singer by attempting to sing an operatic aria during the analytic hour. The patient could not carry a tune but still demanded some confirmation of the excellence of his performance.

Although a seemingly extreme example, Gedo's case description demonstrates that mirroring confirmatory requests made by patients may vary along a continuum from the need for the analyst's silent, uninterrupted listening, on one end, to the desire for unrealistic confirmations, on the other. Most mirror transferences, however, are less extreme and at times may even go unnoticed, as the analyst silently listens to the patient's productions and the patient feels empathically soothed and admired. This experience was lucidly expressed by a patient as follows:

> I wish you would see me as some kind of art that you would admire. I could grow and develop and see you watching me. I don't want you to see anything bad inside me, no ugliness, but only good things. Sometimes I imagine that I see a twinkle in your eye made just for me. I always wanted to be special to someone, to be a super-person to them. I want you to see me as something growing, in transformation.

In the *idealizing transference*, the need is for the patient to use the analyst as the supplier of a powerful, perfect, idealized person with whom the patient can merge and, through such a union, complete a part of himself previously experienced as deficient. This need was expressed by a patient as follows:

> In my fantasies, you are always there and you behave perfectly. You are powerful and strong and you want to help me. You are looking after me. I respect you enormously and you give me respect. You are very strong and powerful and, because you want to help me, I become more important. When I feel that way, I feel calm and secure.

Mobilization of the narcissistic patient's infantile unmet needs through the above-mentioned selfobject transferences is the driving force behind the analysis and modulation of these needs. But these transferences are defended against by defensive maneuvers which require long and careful analysis. Systematic analysis of such resistances to the manifestations of these transferences leads eventually to their elaboration and potential working-through. In addition, since the selfobject transferences supply needed functions the patient felt lacking in himself, there tends to be an improvement in ego functioning because of an increase in self-cohesiveness. The selfobject bond revives the time of soothing contentment when the child felt united with the mother and experienced a sense of firmness and cohesion in his own internal environment or self.

Fragmentation of the Self

The self of the child is optimally established by the empathic, appropriate, or "good enough" parental responses to the child's grandiose expressions, which are empathically responded to by mirroring or by the parents' unconsciously allowing themselves to be idealized. Empathic failures to the child's needs can be corrected by "in-tune" corrective responses which reestablish the needed narcissistic equilibrium. But chronic empathic failures can lead to longstanding injury. Since the infant's needs, which require empathic "in-tuneness" by the mother, are experienced by the infant as a part of himself or herself (selfobject), lacks in this area are experienced by the infant as a loss of part of the self. While the narcissistic patient has a cohesive self and can tolerate some empathic lacks, added stress may cause a temporary "fragmentation of the self."

With neurotic patients, anxieties relate to specific danger situations. However, with the narcissistic patient, anxieties relate to awareness of some disintegration or fragmentation in the cohesiveness of the self. Such indication of a partial dissolution of the self shows the vulnerability of such patients. An intense and pervasive anxiety indicates a degree of disintegration or fragmentation and may be manifest by moderate to severe loss of initiative, severe decrease in self-esteem, or feelings of emptiness or meaninglessness. Such an experience of fragmentation may also be manifest by hypochondriacal symptoms or a sense that various parts of the body are not connected. Fragmentation of the self may result from a separation from an important person, frustration over meaningful events, or transient empathic failures on the part of the analyst. Such an experience was expressed by a patient as follows:

> After you said that, a strange feeling came over me. I feel as if there is a cloud around my head and my body feels different. It's as if I feel my arms or legs will shoot up in the air and that my head is not connected to my body. It's an upsetting feeling, like I'm all disconnected from myself. I feel like I am falling apart, and that I can't get myself back together again.

Such a sense of fragmentation may be transient, and the selfobject transference may be reinstated by the appropriate empathic responses on the part of the analyst. This interaction may be similar to the transiently unempathic, but then corrected, responses of the "optimal" mother, as opposed to the chronic, long-term, unempathic "lack of in-tuneness" responses of the "less than optimal" mother.

Countertransference

The analyst must pay close attention to the demands or burdens placed on him by the patient's archaic wishes. The analytic capacity for empathic listening and responses often reflects the analyst's own state of self-development. The analyst must realize that the patient's needs to idealize or be mirrored must not be met by reality-testing, but instead are phase-appropriate responses related to early blocked "normal" development of the grandiose self. If these are accepted as in need of expression, such demands may be elaborated, worked through and modified. The analyst must not prove to the patient that his or her desires are unrealistic, but instead show that they were quite appropriate at an earlier time, and that they have been revived in the transference. In this accepting environment, the patient will allow himself to express grandiose and idealizing fantasies, which will eventually lead to the modification and maturation of the grandiosity (integration of the grandiose self) and the production of a more realistic psychic structure, which will transform such wishes into mature derivatives. Questioning or harsh confrontation of such grandiose needs drives them underground. Asking the patient to step back and use his "observing ego" or actively helping him to "form an alliance" tends to disrupt the selfobject transference by asking for a separation of the patient and analyst. Such requests for an alliance, which are experienced as abandonments, may also lead to transient fragmentation of the cohesive self.

Transmuting Internalization

Therapeutically, it is the reactivation of unmet needs in the analytic situation (activation of the grandiose self seen through the mirror and idealizing selfobject transferences) which opens the door to narcissistic maturation. The enfeebled self is opened up for a new experience of appropriate and empathically in-tune responses by the analyst, experienced as the merged, need-fulfilling selfobject.

Structural growth, in the optimal childhood situation or in the analytic situation, happens via the process of psychological structure formation, which Kohut has called *transmuting internalization*. In this process, the analyst continues the work blocked during development. The analyst, responding empathically to the patient's mirroring and idealizing needs, occasionally and inevitably has minor empathic failures. These may lead to the patient's transient self-fragmentation. In the analytic process, the so-called cure occurs by "filling in the defects" in the self-structure through working-through of the selfobject transference and through transmuting internalization.

Transmuting internalization in the analytic relationship reflects the optimal process of structure formation in the child-mother relationship. Here the archaic idealization and mirroring needs are fulfilled in the early selfobject mother-child relationship, with the child gaining an experience of soothing equilibrium as his needs for merger with a perfect powerful figure are satisfied. However, optimally transient imperfections in the mother's responses to the child's needs occur. These disappointments are, however, short-lived, and the child's equilibrium is soon reestablished. If the mother's empathic failures are transient, and not chronic, the child gradually begins to modify his limitless expectations and temper his confidence in his mother's perfection. The withdrawal of such expectations from the mother allows the child to lay down, instead, small segments of an inner sense of tempered expectations. Once such a structure is established, the child can fulfill some of the mother's functions in the maintenance of the soothing, stabilizing, sustaining, narcissistic balance.

Chronic failures of maternal empathy, on the other hand, lead to an inability to limit expectations of maternal perfection and a failure of transmuting internalization. Instead, there is the continuing psychic expectation and wish for absolute perfection in the selfobject and the continued quest for mirroring. Internal equilibrium may then require external, behavioral means, such as defensive sexuality, drug use, alcohol intake or various types of exhibitionistic or idealizing behaviors. Optimally, in the analytic situation, the patient's occasionally frustrated quest for gratification causes small degrees of withdrawal of his yearnings from the selfobject through the process of transmuting internalization. The patient comes to realize that the object of his need-fulfilling desires is unrealistic, unavailable, or imperfect. Part of the investment in the external object is therefore withdrawn into the self, thereby strengthening the internal structures.

COMPARISON OF KERNBERG'S AND KOHUT'S VIEWS (100-102)

Kernberg sees the narcissistic personality disorders as a subtype of the borderline personality organization, with similar diagnostic, therapeutic and prognostic considerations. Both groups have underlying issues of primitive rage and envy, as well as defenses centering around splitting, reinforced by projection, especially projective identification, primitive idealization, omnipotent control, narcissistic withdrawal and devaluation. The narcissistic personality disorders are differentiated from the broader category of borderline patients because the former have an integrated, although still highly pathological, grandiosity, which through a sense of specialness and early fantasies of power, wealth and beauty has compensated for difficulties in self-esteem. This has helped the young child deal with frustrations and early failures of the mother, through the maintenance of ideal, giving, loving fantasies of the mother. Such grandiosity (the grandiose self) defends against a full elaboration of the otherwise borderline personality structures and defenses, which, however, still exist. For Kernberg, as opposed to Kohut, the grandiose self is a pathological structure which defends against underlying primitive rage and envy.

Kohut, in contrast, differentiates the borderline patient from the narcissistic personality disorders through the existence of a cohesive self in the latter. Diagnosis of the narcissistic personality disorder patient is related to the existence and evolution of specific types of transferences, specifically, the idealizing and mirroring transferences, in which the analyst is not treated as an autonomous independent object by the patient but as an aspect of the patient himself. The grandiose self postulated by Kohut is not pathological but is caused by a fixation of an archaic "normal" primitive self, a blockage in the evolution of the normal infantile narcissism and self-esteem.

Etiologically, Kernberg feels problems for such patients center around early underlying conflicts around oral rage and envy, related to severely pathologically-integrated object relations at a pre-oedipal, especially oral, level. This contrasts with Kohut's formulations concerning the unmet, idealizing and mirroring needs for empathically in-tune parental responses to the evolving narcissistic needs of the child. Again, developmentally, Kernberg differs from Kohut, feeling that the development of narcissism and object relations (love of the self as opposed to love of others) cannot be separated and are intertwined. One cannot study the problems of narcissism without studying the problems of object relations and vice versa. However, for Kohut there are separate, independent, and parallel lines of development of narcissism and object relations in childhood; this means that the patient's relationship to himself (narcissism) can be studied somewhat independently of his relations to others (object relations).

Kernberg's view of the narcissistic transferences is also different from that of Kohut. For Kernberg the narcissistic patient denies the independent autonomous existence of the analyst as a human being. He also denies his dependence on the analyst. These manifestations are the result of a rigid defense against primitive pathological object relations centered around narcissistic rage and envy, as well as fear and guilt because of this rage. There is, however, also a longing for a loving relationship with the analyst who would be destroyed by the hatred which the patient has been defending against. Differentially the borderline patient has a clinging dependency while the narcissistic patient has the absence of the ability to depend on the analyst. Idealization of the analyst therefore represents a defense against the emergence of oral rage and envy and also the paranoid fears which are projected onto the analyst. Idealization also may function as a defense against basic feelings of emptiness, loneliness, and longings for love, as well as against guilt over aggression. For Kohut the idealizing and mirror transferences are not defensive but are the result of unresolved early infantile strivings which have been blocked and need to be revived and worked through.

Both Kernberg and Kohut feel the grandiose self must be activated and the narcissistic transferences must be analyzed before oedipal material can be cohesively manifest and worked through. But the narcissistic transferences serve a defensive function (against rage and envy) for Kernberg, while for Kohut they serve a developmental function and provide an opportunity to complete the unfinished business of the maturation of infantile narcissism. Both Kernberg and Kohut agree that there must be the establishment of a full narcissistic transference and reactivation of the grandiose self. For Kohut this leads to the completion of a normal process that had been arrested and facilitates the growth of primitive narcissism into mature narcissism. For Kernberg it leads to the modification of a pathological narcissism.

A central technical divergence of the two authors resides in how they view the analysis of aggression. Since Kernberg sees envy and rage as underlying the pathological difficulties, he suggests the analysis of both libido and aggression but seems to see aggression as paramount. Kohut, on the other hand, also acknowledges the libidinal and aggressive drives, but seems to regard the aggression as reactive and therefore emphasizes it less. These distinctions make Kernberg feel that Kohut's approach may gratify the loving or positive aspects of the transference and hinder the full development of the transference, especially the negative transference aspects. Because the negative transference is not delved into and focused on, there may be a continuation of the patient's unconscious fear of his envy and rage, which may hinder the working-through process in relationship to the pathological grandiose self. Kohut feels the analyst must tolerate and allow the idealization and mirror transferences, which he sees as paramount. Kernberg feels that there must be a systematic analysis of both the positive and negative aspects of the patient's transference from a neutral position, in order to better activate the narcissistic transference. He feels that when the transferences, especially the positive transferences, are not seen as defensive against the underlying envy and rage, and when the negative transference is not interpreted, the patient increasingly comes to fear his own destructiveness.

Although synthesis, if possible, of Kohut's and Kernberg's work is far beyond the scope of this chapter, it is important to note that the work of both authors, although well described in various publications, must be considered still at the stage of growth and development. Perhaps the appearance of both these theories at a similar time may add to a stimulating and mutually competitive examination. This may lead to further understanding of primitive patients. Both authors are pioneers in a previously confusing and at times therapeutically unsatisfying area of theory and treatment. They are attempting, from different vantage points and frames of reference, to extend the psychoanalytic framework into the understanding and treatment of patients with whom such work was previously confusing and often unsuccessful. Attempts to find common denominators or reduce their work to common basic ingredients would be simplistic and detract from the tension and progress fostered by their often opposing points of view. A time of continuing great exploration seems to be at hand in this area, based upon the structural and object relations positions of Kernberg, the child observation work of Mahler, and the "psychology of the self" described by Kohut. Application of these frameworks to clinical treatment and the presentation of treatment results may lead to exciting feedback, related to the applicability and clinical usefulness of such formulations. Too early closure, certainty, and deification of any point of view at this time can only impede progress. Instead, the psychoanalytic framework presents a dynamic, progressive movement toward the fuller understanding of previously confusing patients, because of the open attention to opposing viewpoints, new frames of reference, and the open discussion of theoretical and clinical data in a rigorous and yet flexible manner.

OTHER CONTRIBUTIONS

The theoretical and clinical formulations so far mentioned have been broadened and expanded by numerous psychoanalytic writers covering a wide field of observation. The work of Adler and Buie is an example of this broadening and deepening of previous concepts, the bridging of gaps in areas faintly understood, and the integration and extension of concepts, especially regarding the borderline patient.

Adding to Kernberg's earlier description of the borderline patient, Adler described the intense and persistent types of devaluation of the therapist by such patients in the psychotherapy situation (40). Such devaluations may be motivated by:

> 1) rage because of the patient's unsatisfied, unrealistic expectations;
> 2) the need to protect against wishes for nurturance and closeness, which are experienced as terrifying because of their anticipated disappointment;
> 3) defense against envy of the therapist;
> 4) the need to protect against projected anger, where the devaluation makes the therapist less threatening.
> 5) the need to protect against low self-esteem, by placing the patient's defect on the therapist;
> 6) transference manifestation in which the patient identifies with the devaluing parent, and treats the therapist as he himself felt treated as a child.

Adler stresses that the therapist's consistent, empathic, nonretaliatory work with the patient's hopelessness, rage and devaluation allows the pathological defenses to gradually be given up. The patient can then begin to identify with the therapist's mature ego capacities and eventually experience the therapist as a good object (40).

In the face of the patient's devaluating onslaught, the therapist's countertransference responses may be manifest in various ways. Especially in the younger, less experienced therapist, feelings may be stimulated of guilt, anger, worthlessness, shame, envy, or hopelessness. Withdrawal, as a result of these feelings, may be manifest by the therapist's inattentiveness, daydreaming, feelings of defensiveness, boredom, relative passivity, or anger. The therapist may try to prove his omnipotence and love of the patient in order to show that he is not helpless or he may respond to the devaluation by angry attacks—either subtle teasing or overt hostility. Lastly, the therapist may decrease the tension of the angry attacks on himself by interpreting the patient's anger as masking loving feelings which the patient cannot tolerate. Although this may be true, it is also a way by which the therapist avoids the patient's rage.

Adler proposes ways of dealing with these countertransference responses by increased self-observation, increased theoretical understanding of such patients, and the use of careful formulation of the patient's
conflicts, defenses and transferences. These efforts help the therapist
gain some distance on the patient's expressed rage and personal assaults
(40).

Strong reactions of helplessness and frustration may occur also in
inpatient staff members working with borderline patients. The staff may
feel increasingly ineffective as the patient seems regressed, helpless,
hopeless and self-destructive. Such "helplessness in the helpers" may
stimulate anger and result in punitive action against the patient, ration-
alized as "limit-setting" (41).

The psychiatric inpatient unit staff, as the recipient of the patient's
anger and devaluation, must struggle with their own retaliatory rage
and use empathic, nonpunitive limit-setting to decrease regression and
allow the patient to experience the staff as neither destroyed by his anger
nor stirred to retribution or abandonment by it. Adler explains the effect
of the patient's projected identification and splitting on the inpatient
staff and shows how their appropriate responses may lead to the patient's therapeutic growth (42).

Adler has also described how unresolved developmental issues in the
patient evolve during psychotherapy and may require the added support
of inpatient hospitalization. At times the therapist's countertransference
difficulties may have, in part, led to the need for hospitalization or these
may become manifest while the patient is hospitalized. Here the staff's
countertransference responses may either encourage patient regression
or, if such responses are used as signals, further the evaluation of the
patient-therapist interaction and foster its improvement (43).

Adler and Buie have discussed the uses of confrontation in the psychotherapy of borderline patients to overcome the avoidance defenses
which protect them from pain in relation to the intense issues of their
daily life and which also affect the transference (44, 45). This is also
extremely important when the patient is unaware of motivations which
may influence his existence and put him in real danger. Conversely,
such patients are intensely vulnerable to adverse effects from confrontation because of the fragility of their defensive structure, the power of
their wishes and impulses, and the tenuousness of the working relationship with their therapist. The therapist must be careful in evaluating
the patient's capacity to tolerate confrontation, especially when the confrontation may be a response to the countertransference responses
evoked by such patients. Such misuses of confrontation may occur when

the patient's regression, demandingness, or devaluation stirs responses in the therapist. Such a reaction, for example, might cause the therapist to confront the patient with his need to give up his infantile wishes. The therapist may also misuse confrontation as a defense against the patient's rage or in order to keep the therapy quiet, controlled and less stressful.

In a very important contribution, Adler and Buie, drawing on the work of Piaget, Fraiberg and A. M. Sandler, attempt to delineate an important underlying developmental defect related to the borderline patient's experience of intense, painful aloneness (46). They describe the borderline's relative or total inability to remember positive images or fantasies of "sustaining people in the patient's present or past life" or, conversely, the experience of being "overwhelmed by negative memories and images of these people." Developmentally, the child goes from a state of being able to recognize an object when present (recognition memory) to a more mature stage of being able to evoke the memory of objects not present (evocative memory). Borderline patients do not have a stable capacity for object permanence which is related to the development of solid evocative memory capacity. Under the stress of their anger, they may regress to the stage of recognition memory experienced by them as the loss of the therapist even in his presence, with a resultant intensification of their feelings of aloneness and abandonment. Such a defect may relate to early empathic parental failures during the rapprochement subphase of separation-individualization as postulated by Mahler. Adler and Buie discuss treatment implications of this formulation, such as the need for the therapist's availability or for the use of "transitional objects" during times of the patient's transient loss of evocative memory.

Adler also has questioned the existence of a therapeutic alliance in the therapy of borderline patients or patients with narcissistic personality disorders (48). Instead, there exist sustaining selfobject transferences rather than a real working collaboration. Although different from Kohut's view, this and other contributions by Adler have expanded the usefulness of Kohut's concepts into the borderline realm.

Further, Adler extends Kohut's ideas to the neurotic realm where therapeutic alliances exist, by describing the "silent selfobject transferences" which serve as the backdrop of analytic work with neurotic patients (49). The mature therapeutic alliance is in part the result of the resolution of the selfobject transferences. Only the precursors of the alliance are, therefore, present in the primitive patients. The full, stable, mature and autonomous therapeutic alliance is only present after the working-through of much of the selfobject transferences. Resolution of the selfobject transferences necessitates the patient's ability to feel separate from the therapist and acknowledge the therapist's real and separate qualities. Before this, the patient's demands to know about the therapist's "real" life may signal a fragmentation of the selfobject transference and may be the patient's attempt to regain through information what he feels is currently missing in the therapeutic relationship.

Finally, Adler describes a continuum between the borderline patient and the narcissistic personality disorders, related to more or less firmness of the cohesive self, stability of selfobject transferences, and the greater or lesser capacity for the patient to tolerate mature aloneness. These three capacities allow a patient to be placed along the continuum from borderline regression at the lower end to stable narcissistic personality disorders at the upper end (50).

In addition to the previously mentioned theoretical and clinical applications of psychoanalytic concepts to work with primitive patients, attempts have been made to apply such ideas to more objective and statistically based research. Although not presented as representative of the entire field, one such project is that being pursued by the Tufts Workshop on the Primitive Personality. Here clinical investigations are underway using the concept of the "sustaining fantasy." The sustaining fantasy is defined as a compensatory mechanism used at times of lowered self-esteem or other psychic stress to ease painful affective reactions. Through the creation in fantasy of a sustaining or ideal situation or one counter to the situation which stimulated the experience of injury, a sense of satisfaction and decreased frustration is produced, with a resultant restoration of self-esteem and a return to an emotional equilibrium (103, 104).

Sustaining fantasies are characteristic of a specific patient and contain consistent, familiar, repetitive and cohesive themes, content and structure over time. This consistency differentiates them from more fleeting daydreams or fantasies. They are subject to change and development according to age, stage of life, and levels of ego capacity or regression. Sustaining fantasies have the quality of being "old reliable friends" which one calls forth to help comfort or sustain oneself. Clinically, these fantasies may be elicited by asking a patient, "When you feel hurt or upset by someone or something, do you ever have some thought or idea or personal story that you think about to make yourself better?"

This sustaining fantasy research project is investigating both the capacity to effectively use sustaining fantasies to regulate self-esteem and the loss of this capacity during times of stress and regression, which is similar to the loss of "evocative memory capacity" as described by Adler and Buie (47). The sustaining fantasy material is obtained by the use of a questionnaire composed of fantasies of varying levels of maturity or primitiveness. It is seen as a potential means to clarify and objectify:

> 1) diagnostic categories, especially in the area of primitive patients (borderline, narcissistic);
> 2) regression or therapeutic progress in such patients as they lose or regain the capacity to use sustaining evocative memory functions;
> 3) developmental levels of a patient's ego capacities for social and work functioning;
> 4) indications for various treatment modalities, such as insight-oriented psychotherapy or hospitalization.

In addition, an exciting possibility would be that objective data gained from such research might aid psychoanalytic theory formulation and clinical practice.

CONCLUSIONS

In the preceding sections we have reviewed the central dynamic and psychoanalytic themes, theories and observations concerning the category of primitive patients. But what has been mentioned is only a small part of this total literature. We must now reflect on what areas of confusion still exist and what questions must be asked in the future.

One area of confusion is related to the unclear and overlapping nature of psychiatric diagnosis. Names used for such diagnoses are often too specific, too general, too idiosyncratic or too literary. Also, the referent to which the name refers may not be clear. Examples are that:

> 1) "borderline" relates to a spatial point on the "border" of two areas;
> 2) narcissism originally referred to an ancient myth and more recently to the concept of the "self" and issues of self-esteem;
> 3) schizophrenia refers to a splitting;
> 4) and hysteria referred originally to the uterus.

Such terms have no solid focus or point of reference but require rapid semantic and conceptual shifts when discussing or comparing patients with different diagnoses.

Confusions also relate to the diverse viewpoints of different observers. Some clinicians focus on symptoms, others on descriptions of behavior

or interpersonal relations, while still others look at the dynamic manifestations of intrapsychic structure and therapeutic transference responses. Still other difficulties are caused by the highly complex
vocabulary and writing styles by which some observations are conveyed.

Some specific questions which arise from the conflicts in the current
literature and which must be addressed in the future are as follows:
How can we integrate the enormous contributions of Kernberg and
Kohut into a model which would more fully explain and strengthen our
understanding of primitive patients? Is such an integration of the structural and the self-psychology approaches useful? Will new knowledge
come through their integration or through the building of new models?
Is there an advantage to not integrating these theories but allowing them
to serve as opposite poles, similar to the paradoxes of ancient mythology
which served through their conflictual nature to push thought in new
directions?

Future research, helped by the more recent descriptive work of Gunderson and co-workers (105, 106), will probably focus in two directions:
1) the continued search for unifying characteristics which underlie the
different diagnostic categories of primitive patients and perhaps point
to a continuity, and 2) the delineation of subgroups of primitive patients,
which might allow greater understanding of the internal underlying
qualities of each subgroup and the possible interrelation of subgroups.
For diagnostic, therapeutic, and evaluative reasons it is necessary to
know if borderline and narcissistic categories are discrete and separate
entities or points on a continuum and how they can be differentiated
from neurotic patients, on the one hand, and psychotic patients, on the
other.

SUMMARY

Patients with a borderline personality organization are described by
Otto Kernberg as having diffuse, intense, and multiple neurotic-type
symptoms which are pervasive and limiting to their functioning and
relations with others. They use specific "lower level" defenses (splitting,
projection, projective identification, denial, primitive idealization, and
devaluation) to defend against underlying feelings of primitive rage and
envy. Under stress they may present transient psychotic manifestations.
Patients with narcissistic personality disorders, according to Kernberg,
have a borderline personality organization but have somewhat less vulnerability to regression, because of the presence of a useful, although
still pathological, sense of specialness and power (the pathological gran-

diose self) which is not present in the wider group of borderline patients. This sense of specialness compensates for their poor self-esteem and self-concept and allows for a seeming better adaptation and higher level of ego functioning despite their otherwise primitive defenses.

For Heinz Kohut, the narcissistic personality disorder patient is quite different from the borderline patient. In his view, they frequently function on a higher and less chaotic level and can tolerate a greater degree of stress and frustration without major regression. They are also able to establish a stable psychoanalytic relationship in which they manifest specific psychoanalytic transference reactions (the selfobject transferences) centering around idealization and a desire to be admired (mirrored). Their symptoms of arrogance, coldness or inordinate self-sufficiency on the one hand, or shyness and feelings of inferiority on the other, are reactions to early unempathic interactions and unmet needs, for admiration and to idealize the parents. Such unmet needs have caused a blockage in the normal modulation and maturation of grandiose and narcissistic strivings. These frustrated strivings continue in their grandiose fantasies which are defended against by shame, humiliation and either arrogant or shy external characterological manifestations. The dammed up and unexpressed grandiosity can be reactivated in the proper psychoanalytic situation to form specific transferences in which the analyst comes to function in a way experienced by the patient as fulfilling this early unmet need or function (a selfobject). The resultant selfobject transferences relate to the patient's need to idealize the analyst (the idealizing transference) or his desire to be admired (the mirror transferences). Proper analytic response allows these transferences to evolve, be interpreted and worked through with resultant modification and maturation of the blocked but normal grandiose strivings. Resolution of the idealizing transference transforms idealization into normal self-assertiveness and devotion to ideals, while the mirror transferences are transformed into ambitions and creativity. For Kohut, the narcissistic character disorders, unlike borderline patients, have developed a cohesive and stable psychic structure (the cohesive self). This protects them from the disintegration of their ego functions and the irreversible disruption of their fairly stable although primitive sense of self and their need-fulfilling relations with others.

REFERENCES

1. Knight, R. P.: Borderline states (1953). In *Psychoanalytic Psychiatry and Psychology*. R. P. Knight and C. R. Friedman (Eds.), New York: International Universities Press, 1954, pp. 97-109.

2. Knight, R. P.: Management and psychotherapy of the borderline schizophrenic patient (1953). In *Psychoanalytic Psychiatry and Psychology*. R. P. Knight and C. R. Friedman (Eds.), New York: International Universities Press, 1954, pp. 110-122.

3. Kernberg, O.: Structural derivatives of object relationships. *Int. J. Psychoanal.*, 47:236-253, 1966.

4. Kernberg, O.: Borderline personality organization. *J. Am. Psychoanal. Assoc.*, 15:641-685, 1967.

5. Kernberg, O., Coyne, L., Horwitz, L., et al.: The application of facet theory and the technique of multidimensional scalogram analysis to the quantitative date (1968). In "Psychotherapy and psychoanalysis: Final report of The Menninger Foundation's Psychotherapy Research Project," by Kernberg, O., Burstein, E., Coyne, L., et al. *Bull. Menninger Clin.*, 1972, pp. 87-178.

6. Kernberg, O.: The treatment of patients with borderline personality organization. *Int. J. Psychoanal.*, 49:600-618, 1968.

7. Kernberg, O.: A psychoanalytic classification of character pathology. *J. Am. Psychoanal. Assoc.*, 18:800-822, 1970.

8. Kernberg, O.: Early ego integration and object relations. *Ann. N.Y. Acad. Sci.*, 193:233-247, 1972.

9. Kernberg, O., et al.: Psychotherapy and psychoanalysis: Final report of The Menninger Foundation's psychotherapy research project. *Bull. Menninger Clin.*, 36 (1/2), 1972.

10. Kernberg, O.: Contrasting viewpoints regarding the nature and psychoanalytic treatment of narcissistic personalities: a preliminary communication. *J. Am. Psychoanal. Assoc.*, 22:255-267, 1974.

11. Kernberg, O.: *Borderline Conditions and Pathological Narcissism*. New York: Jason Aronson, 1975.

12. Kernberg, O.: Transference and countertransference in the treatment of borderline patients. Strecker Monograph Series, XII; Also in: *Journal of the National Association of Private Psychiatric Hospitals*, 7:14-24, 1975.

13. Kernberg, O.: *Object-Relations Theory and Clinical Psychoanalysis*. New York: Jason Aronson, 1976.

14. Kernberg, O.: Technical considerations in the treatment of borderline personality organization. *J. Am. Psychoanal. Assoc.*, 24:795-829, 1976.

15. Kernberg, O.: The structural diagnosis of borderline personality organization. In *Borderline Personality Disorders*. P. Hartocollis (Ed.), New York: International Universities Press, 1977, pp. 87-121.

16. Klein, M.: *The Psycho-Analysis of Children* (1932). New York: Delacorte, 1975.

17. Klein, M.: Notes on some schizoid mechanisms. *Int. J. Psychoanal.* 27:99-110, 1946.

18. Klein, M.: A contribution to the psychogenesis of manic-depressive states (1935). In *Love, Guilt, and Reparation and Other Works*. New York: Delacorte, 1975, pp. 262-289.

19. Klein, M.: Mourning and its relation to manic-depressive states (1940). In *Contributions to Psycho-Analysis 1921-1945*. London: Hogarth Press, 1948, pp. 311-338.

20. Klein, M.: The oedipus complex in the light of early anxieties: General theoretical summary (1945). In *Contributions to Psycho-Analysis 1921-1945*. London: Hogarth Press, 1948, pp. 377-390.

21. Klein, M.: *Envy and Gratitude: And Other Works by Melanie Klein*. New York: Delacorte, 1975.

22. Segal, M.: *Introduction to the Work of Melanie Klein*. New York: Basic Books, 1964.

23. Jacobson, E.: Contribution to the Metapsychology of cyclothymic depression. In *Affective Disorders*. P. Greenacre (Ed.), New York: International Universities Press, 1953, pp. 49-83.

24. Jacobson, E.: Contribution to the metapsychology of psychotic identifications. *J. Am. Psychoanal. Assoc.*, 2:239-262, 1954.

25. Jacobson, E.: Denial and repression. *J. Am. Psychoanal. Assoc.*, 5:61-92, 1957.

26. Jacobson, E.: *The Self and the Object World*. New York: International Universities Press, 1964.
27. Fairbairn, W. R. D.: Schizoid factors in the personality (1940). In *An Object-Relations Theory of the Personality*. New York: Basic Books, 1952, pp. 3-27.
28. Fairbairn, W. R. D.: A revised psychopathology of the psychoses and psychoneuroses (1941). In *An Object-Relations Theory of the Personality*. New York: Basic Books, 1952, pp. 28-58.
29. Fairbairn, W. R. D.: Endopsychic structure considered in terms of object-relationships (1944). In *An Object-Relations Theory of the Personality*. New York: Basic Books, 1952, pp. 82-136.
30. Fairbairn, W. R. D.: A synopsis of the development of the author's views regarding the structure of the personality (1951). In *An Object-Relations Theory of the Personality*. New York: Basic Books, 1952, pp. 162-179.
31. Guntrip, H.: *Schizoid Phenomena, Object Relations and the Self*. New York: International Universities Press, 1968, pp. 275-309.
32. Guntrip, H.: *Psychoanalytic Theory, Therapy, and the Self*. New York: Basic Books, 1971.
33. Winnicott, D.: Primitive emotional development. *Int. J. Psychoanal*. 26:137-143, 1945.
34. Winnicott, D.: Hate in the countertransference. *Int. J. Psychoanal*. 30:69-74, 1949. Also in *Collected Papers*, New York: Basic Books, 1958, pp. 194-203.
35. Winnicott, D.: Transitional objects and transitional phenomena (1953). In *Playing and Reality*. New York: Basic Books, 1971, pp. 1-25.
36. Winnicott, D.: The capacity to be alone (1958). In *The Maturational Processes and the Facilitating Environment*. New York: International Universities Press, 1965.
37. Winnicott, D.: Ego distortion in terms of true and false self (1960). In *The Maturational Processes and the Facilitating Environment*. New York: International Universities Press, 1965, pp. 140-152.
38. Winnicott, D.: The development of the capacity for concern. *Bull. Menninger Clin*., 27:167-176, 1963.
39. Winnicott, D.: The use of an object. *Int. J. Psychoanal*., 50:711-716, 1969.
40. Adler, G.: Valuing and devaluing in the psychotherapeutic process. *Arch. Gen. Psychiatry*, 22:454-461, 1970.
41. Adler, G.: Helplessness in the helpers. *Br. J. Med. Psychol*., 45:315-326, 1972.
42. Adler, G.: Hospital treatment of borderline patients. *Am. J. Psychiatry*, 130:31-36, 1973.
43. Adler, G.: Hospital management of borderline patients and its relationship to psychotherapy. In *Borderline Personality Disorders, the Concept, the Syndrome, the Patient*. P. Hartocollis (Ed.), New York: International Universities Press, 1977, pp. 307-323.
44. Buie, D. H., Jr., and Adler, G.: The uses of confrontation with borderline patients. *Int. J. Psychoanal. Psychother*., 1:90-108, 1972.
45. Adler, G., and Buie, D. H., Jr.: The misuses of confrontation with borderline patients. *Int. J. Psychoanal. Psychother*., 1:109-120, 1972.
46. Adler, G., and Buie, D. H., Jr.: Aloneness and borderline psychopathology: the possible relevance of child development issues. *Int. J. Psychoanal*., 60:83-96, Part I, 1979.
47. Buie, D. H., and Adler, G.: Definitive treatment of the borderline patient. I. Theoretical considerations of the primary sector of borderline psychopathology. II. Phases of treatment of primary and secondary sectors of borderline psychopathology, 1979 (submitted for publication).
48. Adler, G.: The myth of the alliance with borderline patients. *Am. J. Psychiatry*, 136:5, 642-645, 1979.
49. Adler, G.: Transference, real relationship, and alliance. *Int. J. Psychoanal*., 61:547-558, 1980.
50. Adler, G.: The Borderline-Narcissistic Personality Continuum. Presented at the American Psychiatric Association meeting, Chicago, May, 1979.

51. Meissner, W. W.: Notes on identification. I. Origins in Freud. *Psychoanal Q.*, 39:563-589, 1970.
52. Meissner, W. W.: Notes on identification. II. Clarification of related concepts. *Psychoanal Q.*, 40:277-302, 1971.
53. Meissner, W. W.: Notes on identification. III. The concept of identification. *Psychoanal Q.*, 41:224-260, 1972.
54. Meissner, W. W.: Theoretical assumptions of concepts of the borderline personality. *J. Am. Psychoanal. Assoc.*, 26:559-598, 1978.
55. Meissner, W. W.: Internalization and object relations. *J. Am. Psychoanal. Assoc.*, 22:345-360, 1979.
56. Main, T. F.: The ailment. *Br. J. Med. Psychol.*, 30:129-145, 1957.
57. Zetzel, E. R.: A developmental approach to the borderline patient. *Am. J. Psychiatry*, 127:867-871, 1971.
58. Kohut, H.: The psychoanalytic treatment of narcissistic personality disorders. *Psychoanalytic Study of the Child* 23:86-113. New York: International Universities Press, 1968.
59. Kohut, H.: *The Analysis of the Self.* New York: International Universities Press, 1971.
60. Kohut, H.: Thoughts on narcissism and narcissistic rage. *Psychoanalytic Study of the Child* 27:360-400. New York: International Universities Press, 1972.
61. Kohut, H.: *The Restoration of the Self.* New York: International Universities Press, 1977.
62. Kohut, H., and Wolf, E. S.: The disorders of the self and their treatment: An outline. *Int. J. Psychoanal.*, 59:413-425, 1978.
63. Gedo, J. E., and Goldberg, A.: *Models of the Mind: A Psychoanalytic Theory.* Chicago: University of Chicago Press, 1973.
64. Gedo, J. E.: Forms of idealization in the analytic transference. *J. Am. Psychoanal. Assoc.*, 23:485-505, 1975.
65. Gedo, J. E.: Notes on the psychoanalytic management of archaic transferences. *J. Am. Psychoanal. Assoc.*, 25:787-803, 1977.
66. Gedo, J. E.: Theories of object relations: A metapsychological assessment. *J. Am. Psychoanal. Assoc.*, 27:2, 361-373, 1979.
67. Ornstein, P.: On narcissism: Beyond the introduction, highlights of Henry Kohut's contributions to the psychoanalytic treatment of narcissistic personality disorders. *Annual of Psychoanalysis* 2:127-149, New York: International Universities Press, 1974.
68. Ornstein, P.: A discussion of the paper by Otto Kernberg on "Further contributions to the treatment of narcissistic personalities." *Int. J. Psychoanal.*, 55:241-247, 1974.
69. Ornstein, P., and Ornstein, A.: On the interpretive process in psychoanalysis. In *Frontiers of Psychoanalytic Technique*, R. Langs (Ed.), New York: Jason Aronson, 1975.
70. Tolpin, M.: On the beginnings of a cohesive self: An application of the concept of transmuting internalization to the study of the transitional object and signal anxiety. *Psychoanalytic Study of the Child*, New York: International Universities Press, 26:316-352, 1971.
71. Modell, A. H.: Denial and the sense of separateness. *J. Am. Psychoanal. Assoc.*, 9:533-547, 1961.
72. Modell, A. H.: Primitive object relationships and the predisposition to schizophrenia. *Int. J. Psychoanal.*, 44:282-292, 1963.
73. Modell, A. H.: *Object Love and Reality.* New York: International Universities Press, 1968.
74. Modell, A. H.: A narcissistic defense against affects and the illusion of self-sufficiency. *Int. J. Psychoanal.*, 56:275-282, 1975.
75. Modell, A. H.: "The Holding Environment" and the therapeutic action of psychoanalysis. *J. Am. Psychoanal. Assoc.*, 24:2, 285-307, 1976.
76. Bychowski, G.: The problem of latent psychosis. *J. Am. Psychoanal. Assoc.*, 1:484-503, 1953.
77. Zilboorg, G.: Ambulatory schizophrenias. *Psychiatry*, 4:149-155, 1941.

78. Zilboorg, G.: Further observations on ambulatory schizophrenia. *Am. J. Orthopsychiatry*, 27:677-682, 1957.
79. Hoch, P. H., and Polatin, P.: Pseudoneurotic forms of schizophrenia. *Psychiatric Quarterly*, 23:248-276, 1949.
80. Hoch, P. H., and Cattell, J. P.: The diagnosis of pseudoneurotic schizophrenia. *Psychiatric Quarterly*, 33:17-43, 1959.
81. Hoch, P., Cattell, J. P., Strahl, M., et al.: The course and outcome of pseudoneurotic schizophrenia. *Am. J. Psychiatry*, 119:106-115, 1962.
82. Frosch, J.: The psychotic character: Clinical psychiatric considerations. *Psychiatric Quarterly*, 38:81-96, 1964.
83. Frosch, J.: Psychoanalytic considerations of the psychotic character. *J. Am. Psychoanal. Assoc.*, 18:24-50, 1970.
84. Grinker, R. R., Sr., Werble, B., and Drye, R. C.: *The Borderline Syndrome*. New York: Basic Books, 1968.
85. Schmideberg, M.: The treatment of psychopaths and borderline patients. *Am. J. Psychother.*, 1, 1947.
86. Deutsch, H.: Some forms of emotional disturbance and their relationship to schizophrenia. In *Neuroses and Character Types*. New York: International Universities Press, 1965, pp. 262-281.
87. Freud, S.: The ego and the id (1923). *Standard Edition*, 19:13-66, London: Hogarth Press, 1961.
88. Freud, S.: Inhibitions, symptoms and anxiety (1926). *Standard Edition*, 20:87-174, London: Hogarth Press, 1961.
89. Reich, W.: *Character Analysis*. New York: Orgone Institute Press, 1945.
90. Stern, A.: Psychoanalytic investigation of and therapy in the borderline group of neuroses. *Psychiatric Quarterly*, 7:467-489, 1938.
91. Stern, A.: Psychoanalytic therapy in the borderline neuroses. *Psychiatric Quarterly*, 14:190-198, 1945.
92. Grinberg, L.: On acting out and its role in the psychoanalytic process. *Int. J. Psychoanal.*, 49:171-178, 1968.
93. Mahler, M. S.: Thoughts about development and individuation. *Psychoanalytic Study of the Child*, 18:304-324, New York: International Universities Press, 1963.
94. Mahler, M. S.: *On Human Symbiosis and the Vicissitudes of Individuation. Vol. I: Infantile Psychosis*. New York: International Universities Press, 1968.
95. Mahler, M. S.: A study of the separation-individuation process: And its possible application to borderline phenomena in the psychoanalytic situation. *Psychoanalytic Study of the Child*, 26:403-424, New York: International Universities Press, 1971.
96. Mahler, M. S.: On the first three subphases of the separation-individuation process. *Int. J. Psychoanal.*, 53:333-338, 1972.
97. Mahler, M. S.: Rapprochement subphase of the separation-individuation process. *Psychoanal. Q.*, 41:487-506, 1972.
98. Mahler, M. S.: Symbiosis and individuation: The psychological birth of the human infant. *Psychoanalytic Study of the Child* 29:89-106, New Haven: Yale University Press, 1974.
99. Mahler, M. S., Pine, F., and Bergman, A.: *The Psychological Birth of the Human Infant*, New York: Basic Books, 1975.
100. Blanck, G., and Blanck, R.: *Ego Psychology: Theory and Practice*. New York and London: Columbia University Press, 1974, pp. 74-88.
101. Spruiell, V.: Theories of the treatment of narcissistic personalities. *J. Am. Psychoanal Assoc.*, 22:2, 268-278, 1974.
102. Wylie, H. W., Jr.: Threads in the fabric of a narcissistic disorder. *J. Am. Psychoanal. Assoc.*, 22:2, 310-328, 1974.
103. Bernstein, S., Myerson, P., Heijn, C., Jampel, R., Zelin, M., Adler, G., Buie, D., and Rizzuto, A. M.: The Sustaining Fantasy: Clinical Applications. (In Preparation)

104. Zelin, M., Jampel, R., Myerson, P., Bernstein, S., Heijn, C., Rizzuto, A. M., Buie, D., and Adler, G.: Sustaining Fantasies: An Objective Evaluation. (In Preparation)
105. Gunderson, J. G., and Singer, M.: Defining borderline patients: An overview. *Am. J. Psychiatry*, 132:1-10, 1975.
106. Gunderson, J. G., Carpenter, W., and Strauss, J.: Borderline and schizophrenic patients: A comparative study. *Am. J. Psychiatry* 132:1257-1264, 1975.

Chapter 5

Psychoanalysis: A Basis for Child Psychotherapy

Eveoleen N. Rexford, M.D.

Perhaps no psychiatric case study over the past 60 years has been scrutinized from so many points of view by so many people—students and teachers alike—as "Analysis of a Phobia in a Five-year-old Boy" (1), the story of Little Hans. He was the first son of two early adherents of Sigmund Freud, and his father, a physician, had kept the Professor informed of the little boy's progress. The parents "had agreed that in bringing up their first child, they would use no more coercion that might be absolutely necessary for maintaining good behavior. And, as the child developed into a cheerful, good-natured and lively little boy, the experiment of letting him grow up and express himself without being intimidated went on satisfactorily." When the boy showed symptoms of anxiety at age four and three quarters, the father was immediately in touch with Freud and there ensued a course of systematic child therapy which was carried out by the father and supervised by Freud.

The report of the findings, illuminating certain aspects of Freud's evolving theories and clinical techniques and corroborating others, became one of the cornerstones of Freud's remarkable series of case his-

118

tories. The first developmental reports of the three-year-old boy had begun to reach Freud in 1906, while the actual outbreak of the phobia took place in 1908. From January through May of that year, the physician-father-therapist carried out the analysis. Freud published the case history in 1909. There are earlier references to Hans in Freud's writings and the small group interested in psychoanalysis rapidly became familiar with the boy and with the vicissitudes of his emotional development.

Hans' father reported to Freud that the boy had suddenly become afraid to go out on the street for his daily walk because, as he finally stated, he was afraid a horse would bite him. The fright was obvious and he could not be cajoled out of it. It spread to fears of horses falling down, of heavy-laden carts and vans and other horse-related objects. His distress was so extreme that his routine and that of the household were disrupted and it threatened to extend to more and more objects and possibilities. He slept and ate poorly and within a few days was a quite different-appearing child from his lively, inquisitive young self. Freud suggested that such a phobia at Hans' age was perhaps the most common infantile neurotic ailment and one more frequent during pre-school years than many had suspected. Our clinical experiences over the past 65 years have confirmed Freud's views.

There are many vantage points from which one can discuss Little Hans: A favorite approach in student and candidate seminars is to de-lineate all of the ways "we would do it differently today." For instance, the Professor's statement that only the boy's father, a physician with whom the youngster had an excellent relationship, could have carried out the therapy has provided to generations of struggling young psychoanalysts welcome proof that Freud clearly could be wrong. A point of view relevant to the topic of this discourse is the study of Little Hans' contribution to the evolution of child psychotherapy, both the familiar type and the less frequently performed child psychoanalysis.

PRINCIPLES OF CHILD PSYCHOTHERAPY

Freud's study illustrates principles which may not be easy to teach didactically; yet if they are not accorded a significant role in a specific course of child psychotherapy, notable progress does not attend one's efforts. I will leave it to the reader to decide where they are crucial as well in the psychotherapy of adults. The first is the obvious respect Freud shows for his patient once-removed. Freud's repeated remarks of approval regarding the boy's growing scientific curiosity and the pertinence of his reasoning, the footnote, "Well done, little Hans!, I could wish for no better understanding of psychoanalysis from any grown-up," and his defense of Hans in the face of apparent intellectual deterioration are merely articulations of an attitude one senses from the beginning of the case history. The therapeutic climate would be inauspicious indeed if it were colored by the adult's feeling "Oh, he is just a child" or by his careless reaction to the comments or behaviors of a youngster "because they are so childish."

But, what do we mean by respect when we are thinking of a therapeutic couple consisting of an erudite experienced adult and a child of three going on four? First, perhaps, is an attitude assuming that each is a person, each different, one perhaps strange or inexplicable to the other; perhaps the two are at cross-purposes for at least a time. But the therapist within this frame of reference takes seriously what he hears of a child's troubles, he assumes there are reasons for the youngster's behavior, he does not take it for granted that the guardians know all and understand all about the child and so the child himself has little to contribute. In short, he sees the little patient as a unique individual, worthy of his careful attention. Only with considerable experience does one come to realize how infrequently a small child is accorded this kind of respect.

Such a framework does not preclude a therapist's making egregious mistakes, missing obvious cues, or jumping to outlandish conclusions. But the child—far more than the adult patient—will, if an atmosphere of respect obtains, give the therapist another chance, perhaps several. I remember an eight-year-old boy I saw years ago at the Judge Baker Guidance Center who met one of my daring and sophisticated "I wonder" interpretations with a shake of his head and a patient, "That's a crazy idea, Dr. Rexie. Now I know why they call you people here crazies. But we can do better than that!" Indeed we could, and later did, but the boy was willing to stay by me, assuming I would come to my senses in time. I listened more sensitively and my "wonders" became more sensible and helpful to him. One day he looked up angrily from his painting and burst out, "Why is it that when I get mad at what you say, it always makes me feel better afterwards?" and stamped out. The next week he was back, sunnily recounting recent events at school. Toward the end of the hour, he looked up from his drawing and remarked, "Feelings are funny, aren't they? I tell myself you don't like me or you wouldn't say such things but you never really cheat on me. Now, my music teacher is different. She only says nice things but she never really listens to me! Feelings are funny."

The issue of respect for one's child patient can be conceptualized and phrased in different ways. For instance, one can speak of supporting a child's narcissism by avoiding unnecessary affronts to his self-esteem. If he* comes to you for an evaluation at his parent's request or at the order of a court, it may be difficult indeed for him to confess all of his misdeeds the first time he sees you. Even if he does not have dramatic information to transmit, he may be ashamed and certainly will be apprehensive about the visit. We are not apt to think of how powerful and overwhelming we can seem to a child, even when we are being our most charming! But to force a youngster to choose between what may seem to him defiance or submission does not start a diagnostic encounter off on a fortunate note.

The same principle holds in choosing what to say and how to say it to a boy or girl. "Are you afraid of me?" may seem more like an invasion of a person's privacy than, "I wonder if perhaps you're a little scared here today?" or "Perhaps it's a bit scary to come to see a strange doctor?" "Moving in on" a child can be a pervasive and persistent attitude, far from therapeutic, usually an unconscious mode of intervention on the part of the therapist—and often a reaction to his or her own anxiety. If it persists without change after discussions in supervision, such a stance may suggest that one is not really suited for child work or, perhaps even more likely, that the adult therapist can use a period of psychotherapy himself. Seeing children therapeutically can stir up many ghosts, some from way back in the nursery. Such an occurrence is no cause for shame or embarrassment as long as one seeks to work out the underlying problems. It is likely that any psychiatrist working seriously with children should have psychotherapy or even psychoanalysis himself. Children can be uncanny in their skill at touching our most highly charged conflicts and assaulting our most valued defenses.

I recall vividly a self-possessed, intelligent boy of 11 who gave me succinct, clipped answers to questions the first two times he came to see me at the Judge Baker Guidance Center. He volunteered little, sitting very quietly while I waited for some spontaneous comment from him. During the third diagnostic hour, I saw that his anxiety was mounting, but my remarks and then my suggestions for checkers or drawing fell on seemingly deaf ears. I was puzzled. He had been referred by his pediatrician because of facial tics and nothing in the known history indicated a generally inhibited behavior or a serious, dangerous secret.

---

*To avoid awkwardness in wording, I use the pronoun "he" to designate either a boy or a girl.

I sensed that Bob wanted to like me, perhaps wanted my help, but every approach I made he skillfully parried.

Suddenly he wiggled in his chair, grasped the arms firmly, took a deep breath and ordered me, "All right. Bring on your Judge. Stop stalling!" It then developed that he had assumed, because of the name of the clinic, that he would have to encounter the Judge and he thought I was prolonging the agony by my delay. His delinquency was a private and relatively minor one but he dreaded quite naturally the confrontation with the authority of the law. From his point of view, he could either refuse to talk with me or submit to the threat. The working climate was not promising until his self-confidence and strength permitted him to bring the issue to the fore and let me clear up the misunderstanding. The power we grown-ups possess in therapy was illustrated so clearly by this boy's concern and by his courage that I have never forgotten the lesson he taught me that day. Incidentally, he later shared with me his confusion about sexual activities in a fantasy about elephants which ended with a triumphant, "I knew that it didn't make sense for elephants—and not for people either!" With our continued exploration of his sexual fantasies, Bob's tics disappeared. He was one of my most enjoyable young patients.

Another fundamental principle of child psychotherapy is illustrated repeatedly in the case history of Little Hans, namely, attention to the developmental process and the child's place within it. Hans observed and felt and made something of his experiences according to the psychological and intellectual equipment he had available at a certain period. It was as though he told himself from time to time, "So, that is what it was all about!" Sexual allusions or observations of animal or human behavior with a sexual connotation may provoke a vague excitement or apprehension in a young child at the time, but he or she may later become quite anxious and distressed or contrarily exhilarated when subsequent feelings or experiences enable him to connect the earlier happenings to current preoccupations. The biological elements of life—particularly regarding his body and that of others—are very interesting to a young child; how it is made and how it works, you recall, were sources of inquiry and interest to Little Hans even at age three. The case history shows how he interpreted observations and feelings in the light of his own fantasies and his intellectual and psychological makeup at the moment.

This principle of attention to developmental process has a very direct influence upon psychotherapy. If the therapist proceeds on the assumption of an adult understanding because a young child appears to agree with his formulations, the treatment course may soon be marked by confusion, anxiety and a need on the child's part to retreat. You will recall that Little Hans had his own theories of anatomy and physiology, particularly of intercourse and childbirth. Until the child could express his own thoughts and attain some distance from them, he was not ready to assimilate his father's corrective information. The formulations of emotional development we use, postulating a complex interaction of constitutional givens and experience, are among the most dynamic conceptualizations within psychoanalytic theory. Developmental theory is being continually elaborated and profitably used in today's clinical work. Development viewed in this light is a phasic process, one involving all aspects of functioning—cognitive and physical as well as emotional.

Hans' reaction to his father's eager questioning and "putting the boy right" about his sexual theories illustrates another analytic concept about how the young—and older—mind operates. Hans made his resistance quite clear in his lively, voluble descriptions of the fantastic events which he used to explain the advent of his little sister, Hanna. Since he was not ready to give up his private ideas, those of his father probably made him anxious at this time. His fantasy productions, about which he swore the counterpart of "It's true, what I say. Cross my heart and hope to die," quite defeated the father, and, as Freud remarked, "The analysis began to be obscure and uncertain." The boy was not expressing his own ideas and the father was both pushing him and still adhering to the stork fable. Freud's advice "not to try to understand everything all at once but to give an unbiased attention to each point that arises and to wait further developments" has been proved wise by generations of child therapists.

The therapeutic situation with Little Hans was indeed a unique one, but the essence of it is now well-known to us from thousands of child therapy cases carried out during the years since Hans and his father, with the Professor in the background, embarked upon their pioneering journey. The therapist setting out to come to know and to understand his young patient, respectful of the child, his individuality and his developmental characteristics, able to let or to find ways for the child to express his own thoughts in some modality, and willing to wait patiently while the child does so is a somewhat idealized but nonetheless familiar figure to us. The clinician, who sets up a series of hypotheses to be informally tested and frequently altered about the young person's difficulties, the direction of his growth processes and the aids to his progress or the blocks to his development, is experiencing the stuff of child therapy as we have known it and taught it for decades.

But, you may well say, Little Hans' treatment was surely an atypical process; if it is to be labeled, it was really a child psychoanalysis. What can you say about child psychotherapy? Is it, too, based on the same principles as child analysis? Was Little Hans a pioneer in child psychotherapy as well as child analysis? Let me admit at once that we have had many controversies over the years about the differences between child analysis and child psychotherapy. Pragmatically, the analytic supervisors accent what they consider crucial for the analytic process and the child psychiatric supervisor stresses the character and limits of psychotherapy.

DISTINCTIONS BETWEEN PSYCHOTHERAPY AND PSYCHOANALYSIS WITH CHILDREN

There are presently a number of schools and types of child psychotherapy, many of which are derivatives of child analysis or child guidance. Others derive from psychological counseling or educational techniques. The type which I call child psychoanalytic psychotherapy is based upon an understanding of the nature and development of the personality of the child from the psychoanalytic point of view; in the assessment processes, we seek to identify sources and characteristics of the problems which brought the child for evaluation and of the assets with which he can be helped to overcome them. The child's capacity to relate to another person, the state of his various ego functions, his physical growth and intellectual equipment, his resources in play, friends and interests in the outside world—all of these give us information about the kind of young person with whom we are dealing. The family, neighborhood and school setting require a careful evaluation. Of course, the problems, the procedures, the conceptualizations will vary with the age and developmental phase of the youngster.

In child psychoanalysis, we seek to achieve a resolution of unconscious conflicts and a rearrangement of the various structures of the mind so that the child's development can proceed without hindrance, undistorted by concentrations upon earlier periods of life, anxieties and powerful fantasies. The unconscious conflicts are patiently and systematically brought into the child's awareness and traced to their origins by way of the feelings and defenses which protected the child from the painful and frightening affects of those conflicts. In a setting where a nonjudgmental adult sets limits only as these are necessary to protect the child and the analyst and to preserve the progress of the treatment, a child, through his behavior, verbalizations and fantasy productions, expresses his thoughts and feelings while the analyst tries to follow the lines of ideation and emotion to sources in the child's earlier life. Because the child analyst is a relatively neutral figure who does not interject his own ideas, he becomes more readily the object of transference sentiments, that is, the recipient of feelings and fantasies which are or were directed at the parents. There is ample time for child and analyst to develop a style of interaction so that an object relation may appear and change and transference elements may appear, be worked through and understood.

Although the aim of child psychotherapy is basically similar to that of child analysis—that is, to help remove the roadblocks to the child's progressive development so that the forces of growth can take over—the goals of child psychotherapy cannot be as ambitious as those of child analysis. There are many reasons to decide initially on psychotherapy rather than analysis: Perhaps the time of a skilled therapist is not available; perhaps the child's guardian is unable to invest the money for treatment four or five times a week for an indefinite period; perhaps the diagnostician believes the forces of progressive development can be set in motion with less time and effort; or perhaps there are doubts that the child can tolerate the long, often painful task of analysis. The therapist may in time consider changing to psychoanalysis. He may find that his initial assessment suggested a more recent slowing-down of growth than the course of therapy indicates, or the child's mastery of earlier developmental tasks may prove to be more tenuous than originally thought. The child's defenses may prove so rigid that what is accomplished one week appears undone in next week's hour. Equally troubling would be a young patient's persisting demands for immediate gratification and a relationship constantly invaded by narcissistic needs. More frequent interviews with the child—two or three times a week rather than one—can be instituted to see if the therapeutic relationship becomes more vital and supports systematic work with the defenses and affects related to the one or two principal conflicts chosen for concentration. If very little progress is made over a reasonable period of time or, to the contrary, the child develops more severe symptoms of regression to and fixation in much earlier phases, exploration of the possibilities of psychoanalysis or, at any rate, an evaluation by a child analyst may be helpful.

DIAGNOSTIC ASSESSMENT

A significant portion of a child's psychoanalysis or a psychoanalytic psychotherapy process is the evaluation study. Before one is in a position to recommend therapy, what kind of therapy, what areas the treatment should cover and how it should be set up, one needs information about the child's personality, his behavior, his assets and his problems; we need data about his birth and development, his physical status and health history, his school experiences and achievements and problems. An understanding of the emotional climate of the home, of the personalities and interests of parents, along with information about the family's methods of child-rearing, the extended family, the neighborhood in which he lives, and how family members negotiate their differences with one another and with the outside world, tells us something of how the child is growing, the nature of the influences upon him, and the resources available to facilitate his development. A synthesis of these data from different sources provides the framework for assessing the child, recommending his care and setting a treatment structure. Some predictive judgment should be included.

The outline of a diagnostic study has become well standardized over the years but the creativity and usefulness of different studies vary with skills of the interviewers and the capacity of the child and family to convey facts and the meaning of them about themselves. The familiar diagnostic format can be abridged and shortened, depending upon circumstances and the skills of the clinicians involved. It is a useful process in many consultations, analogous to the invaluable medical history, even though the study may be greatly abbreviated on the ward or in the agency office. It trains the clinician to think figuratively and logically about the child, his family and the clinical situation.

The child mental health units of the 1960s and '70s have given far less weight to evaluation studies. Even clinicians of the child psychiatric facilities have placed less emphasis upon them. Some type of appraisal is usually carried out before a child is accepted to a program, however, and the governmentally mandated projects require an assessment study, so that professional custom has not died out. Along with the returning interest in individual psychotherapy for children in some community mental health centers, a more systematic assessment has become fairly common. The pediatrician and neurologist are more apt to contribute, especially when learning problems and/or multiple physical handicaps are present. The need for careful assessment before acting has been accepted by a growing number of child mental health workers because it promotes better care and a far more effective use of staff and family time.

Anna Freud's Developmental Profile

The other factor stimulating the renewed interest in the diagnostic assessment process is the publication of a number of books and papers concerning Anna Freud's Developmental Profile (2). Despite its complexity and its primary function as a research instrument, the Profile has engendered a great deal of discussion of the diagnostic appraisal of children and led many in the child field to reconsider the previous trend towards minimal assessment activity.

The quintessence of a psychoanalytic approach to the diagnostic study of children, the Profile was worked out at the Hampstead Clinic in London after a meticulous examination of a number of child psychoanalyses and developmental studies. It maps the lines of development of a child and their interrelationships with one another and the child's milieu; it also provides a highly sophisticated structure which identifies sources of strength and weakness, congruities and incongruities in the course of the child's development, areas of conflict, adaptive and defensive modes, and superego course. In recent years, the Profile has been extended to the study of adolescents and adults and to the examination of specific emotional illness.

The Profile is in truth a research instrument: Considerable time, effort and knowledge go into learning how to construct a particular child's Profile and how to use the data so arranged. The construction of a Profile at intervals during a child analysis provides the therapist with detailed information regarding the child's status, his progress or lack of it and the impact of traumatic events and developmental pressures upon him. While the Profile is used principally in a research, postgraduate, or teaching situation, the continuing studies and many publications regarding it enable an interested child therapist to add crucial insights to his understanding of the intricacies of growth and to heighten his assessment acumen and grasp of therapeutic techniques. Portions and modifications of the Profile are utilized in a few settings outside of frank research projects and it is possible that, in different forms, the Profile will become a regular modality in sophisticated child psychiatric facilities in the future.

THE PROCESS OF PSYCHOANALYSIS AND PSYCHOANALYTIC PSYCHOTHERAPY

The child psychiatrist trained in psychoanalytic psychotherapy or the child psychoanalyst proceeds in psychotherapy much as he would if his patient were an adult. The young patient's mode of communication until adolescence usually involves some forms of play; the content and form of the play provide the therapist with information about his patient as well as a means for exchange. He observes carefully, learns what he can of the child's conflicts, notes the development of transference elements, studies the patterns of the child's relating to him, becomes familiar with the child's cognitive and interactive style, and watches the ebb and flow of instinctual pressures and ways of dealing with them. But he does not pick up and work with the details and depths of all these phenomena; rather, he chooses the most pertinent theme or themes and works with those. There is always value in sensing more about a patient than one uses overtly; if, for instance, one notes repetitive symbolic material in drawings or motor play, one may not call it to the child's attention or explore its meaning at that point, but the knowledge that it is there can guide one in the therapeutic discussions of feelings, defenses, and behavior.

When eight-year-old Billy, who does poorly in school although he does well enough on I.Q. tests, comes to our waiting room, we go out to meet him, introduce ourselves and ask him to come into our office. We make some comment about worries or troubles and suggest that perhaps we can together find out what the difficulty is and how to deal with it. There are not too many play materials around the office, but these are usually attractive to a youngster his age. The play materials are designed to elicit his ideas and fantasies and help set the stage for the work together. The therapist remarks that boys and girls may find it a little strange to talk about themselves with a doctor they do not know (even if she is a talking doctor, not one who gives needles) and so they may find it more comfortable to draw or play checkers or make model cars while the two talk and get acquainted. (I have always objected to the appellation "play therapy" for the psychotherapy we carry out—the play is a means to an end, not an end in itself.) A variety of activities can occur from child to child, depending upon the child's interests and the therapist's. For instance, one of my friends was deft at molding clay figures and much of the discussion and fantasy exchanges within her therapy hours with children was accompanied by preparing and manipulating small clay figures. The child usually takes the lead in choosing and pursuing one type of play.

A very passive and frightened boy of 12, who had developed enuresis when he was about to enter junior high school, demonstrated no enthusiasm in the early sessions with me except in playing with toy soldiers. One day, I bought him a set of the Queen's Own at F.A.O. Schwartz and we spent most of our weekly sessions for nearly a year on war games. We acquired an expensive cache of toy soldiers and a very useful understanding of Jim's fears and dreams, his grandiose and sadistic fantasies, and his conviction that he would be and should be severely punished for these. Much of this material came up in the "impersonal" interactions of the war games and in our discussions of the character and problems of specific soldiers.

We discussed aggression in the minutest detail, while our concentration on war games often took me to the encyclopedia for information he demanded about specific armies, battles and leaders. For instance, he was fascinated by the issues of bravery and cowardice in "the ordinary soldier in battle." For days at a time, an infantry private would be the focus of the battle movements which we tried out preparation, the actual fighting, and the aftermath in a series of different actions. He would tell me of the young man's worries and fears of injury and death; sometimes the soldier was an unexpected hero and I would hear of the ambition for achievement and heroism which lurked in the shy young man's breast. Sometimes the hero died and received a brilliant funeral. Sometimes he could not carry out his duties well and felt guilty and ostracized after the battle.

In time, leadership became a focus and the hero a dashing young officer. The possibilities were numerous for presentation and playing out the hostile wishes and fears warring within Jim. The psychopathic soldier who killed because he loved to strike and wound and maim others gradually came into the picture. The acceptability of ambition and actions and the differentiation between wishes and acts became themes we discussed at great length, with some references to his own life, his predicaments and his opportunities.

However, we never strayed far from the toy soldiers and the scenes of battle. My role was that of the benign, supportive adult: I set the stage, I gave Jim permission to play war games, I clarified the issues and occasionally asked questions. More often, I nodded or spoke, underlining the issues presented graphically in the war games. My trips to the encyclopedia served the purpose of strengthening Jim's intellectual defenses—we learned a great deal about history, biography and human nature.

His learning and character set were illustrated by his persisting use of the war games, but we accomplished a good deal of forward motion as Jim stepped into early puberty. His enuresis had cleared up during the second month of treatment. By the end of the school year, some ten months after our work began, his very manner as he walked confidently into my office bespoke the struggles he had won with his fears of his own feelings, his direction toward an exciting future rather than a secure but babyish past, his lessened preoccupation with bloodthirsty fantasies, and an impression that there might be something to be said for becoming a six-foot-tall man. Since he was entering puberty early and came from a family of tall, sturdy men, he had become a bit complacent about his growing manhood.

COMPONENTS OF CHILD PSYCHOTHERAPY

What are the components of a "good" child psychotherapy case? First is surely a relationship with an interested adult who wants to understand and be helpful—one who is relatively benign but not indulgent, firm when necessary but not frightened by a show of anger, an adult who is honest with the child and can say "no" without guilt. Second is the opportunity offered for a transfer of certain feelings from parent to the therapist and the eventual discussion of them in a relatively calm atmosphere.

A third aspect is the manifestation and discussion of the characteristic behavior style of the boy or girl: How does he deal with the doctor? How does he handle his own wishes and feelings? How does he go about being a person? What does one learn about the child's ego defenses? Does he seem hindered by his typical ego responses? If he is angry with the therapist, does he start finding ways of telling the therapist how clever he thinks she is? If he has said or done something he regards as questionable, does he begin to behave like a younger child or turn to inappropriate modes of play? Along with the child's ego functioning, we observe the affects that appear to be related to specific ego mechanisms and defenses. Sadness, anger, anxiety—when do they appear, in relation to what? How are they dealt with? Can he talk with the therapist?

Fourth in our list we can place the data which emerge about key conflicts. Is a lively blonde girl conflicted about whether she should try to be like mother, a vivacious, bright, somewhat assertive woman, or like her favorite aunt, a soft, rather indolent person who seems nonetheless often to get her own way? Does this question then cover over deeper troubling problems of identification in the prepubertal girl who not only worries about what kind of woman she wants to be, but also about whether she wants to be a woman at all or whether she really wants to grow up? Indirect evidence of contradictory wishes about aggressiveness—Are there daydreams about blood running in the gutters? Whose blood is it and how was it let?—can emerge in stories written about a school play, the painting of a sunset, or a confused recital of a poem read for English class.

There are many opportunities to note the state of the young patient's superego. How strict is his conscience? What activities or thoughts seem to arouse guilt? Is the boy's conscience readily seduced? How much does a girl identify with her mother's overconscientious ways?

And then, what does the child do with the therapist? How does he seem to use the relationship? Can he put memories and fantasies together for himself once the therapist has started the process of speaking of patterns of behavior or connections between past and present, home and office, school and home? How does he assimilate and integrate new information about himself? Does he come to realize when he no longer needs the therapist? Can he leave and say goodbye, acknowledging regret or pain but still eager for going on without the treatment? Does he see his parents and siblings and teachers more clearly? Does he grant the adults the right to be occasionally wrong or weak or tired?

How one puts together what one is learning and how and when one offers one's ideas to the young patient is a function of patient and therapist interaction unique in each instance. There are many ways in which too rigid defenses or infantile character traits can be modulated and any one takes time and patience from both members of the therapeutic couple. Everything does not need to be spelled out, but sometimes one has to repeat a finding or a conjecture in multiple ways and from many points of view before the child can absorb it and alter his defensive stance or attitude accordingly.

What brings about change? Why is a certain psychotherapy effective? Among the most potent elements are the value of a relationship that "clicks," the organizing and enriching force of identification with the therapist, the clarification of confused and confusing observations and experiences, facts which acquire positive meaning when given by a trusted adult in terms and doses the child can absorb, and changes in rigid defenses. Underlying all is the freeing up of developmental forces so that progress can take place.

I do not know, for instance, precisely why Jim's enuresis cleared up so quickly in the once-weekly psychotherapy. Since I did not have him in analysis, I did not obtain the specific fantasy and affect material that could answer that question definitively. My impression was that, in the emotional climate of the therapy, he was playing out his conflicts upon the table with his soldiers, struggling to master them and not to settle for any infantile solutions. Early on I was able to point out the mixed feelings of his military characters and the ubiquity of ambivalence. We could work, too, on his strict and very demanding superego as we talked of the court-martial of one young soldier who ran away and others who blundered.

Jim and I did not work directly with his warm feeling for me or with his intense love for his mother. Jim had led us at once to the theme of aggression and made such definite headway that I decided that he might very well deal effectively with whatever problems his affection for his mother and admiration for his father might be causing him or might produce in the future. I was quite confident that Jim and his parents would return if new troubles arose and I viewed myself in the light of a general practitioner who treated the symptoms which were uppermost without finding it necessary to deal with every possible problem one could foresee in the future. The boy's impending puberty would release forces likely to carry him further along and I thought our work had started him well on the way. So it proved to be.

A few years ago, a young woman came up to me at a community planning meeting and introduced herself with a smile, realizing full well that I did not recognize her. As we talked, it turned out that she had been a psychotherapy patient during my early years in child psychiatry, one with whom my effectiveness had seemed very limited. But apparently more had gone on than I knew, largely, I think, through identification with her able mother, which became more acceptable because of her contact with another professional woman. Perhaps she split her mixed feelings between us! She had become a competent professional woman, which I would never have expected. I recalled the sullen, withdrawn, underachieving and not very attractive child of nine or ten. Much had happened to her besides her therapy, but she and her parents felt something had been loosened up and set free in the treatment to enable her to use resources we did not know were there.

Child psychoanalytic psychotherapy has become less popular and less well carried out in general with the development of the community mental health centers. There are suggestions that, after a decade or so, the child mental health workers are becoming more interested in such treatment of individual children and seek out supervision from experienced child psychotherapists. Occasionally, one of our consumers calls attention to the value of this approach: A few years ago, a woman of 30 visited a mental health center asking for "some talking with the doctor" for her seven-year-old son, Bob. She did not know exactly what it was that she wanted, but he was rambunctious, unhappy and failing in school. She could not do a thing with him. Several years before, a neighbor had brought her boy to this clinic and he talked to a doctor every week for a year. She did not know what the talks were about but they fixed up that James and that was what she wanted for her Bobby.

PSYCHOANALYSIS AND CHILD PSYCHIATRY

I have devoted a large portion of this essay to child psychoanalytic psychotherapy because it is a major descendant of psychoanalytic theory and of child psychoanalysis and because it is a major modality for the psychiatric treatment of children. I would like now to broaden the focus to consider briefly the contributions of psychoanalysis to child psychiatry in general and to the various activities carried out today within that widening field.

American child psychiatry had emerged by 1950 as a confluence of the principles and practices of child guidance and those of child psychoanalysis. World War I had convinced many American psychiatrists and neurologists of the significant role of childhood experiences in adult mental disorders and a group eager to apply mental hygiene principles to children with emotional disturbances joined with child advocates to establish child guidance clinics. The leadership was medical as well as psychiatric, the staff consisted of members from several disciplines organized as a team, and the study of the child attended to physical, psychological, and intellectual characteristics, as well as information about his family. Consultations with family and referring agency were based upon the conclusions from these data. The emphasis on the child himself, upon what William Healy called his "own story," was unique in professional practice. The conversational, hortatory and informational interviews of the child guidance format helped to promote the growth of many boys and girls in the decades after the first World War. Nevertheless, they were still regarded as secondary to the advice and instruction given to the parents and to the consultations with the pediatrician, clergyman or teacher who was in frequent contact with the child. These child guidance techniques, however, were not effective with many children referred to the increasing number of children's clinics. Indeed, by 1926, Douglas Thom, in his report to the Board of the Habit Clinic in Boston, stated that on the basis of five years of experience, they had learned that a substantial group of boys and girls did not respond to the Habit Clinic methods; he thought these children suffered from such difficulties as severe neuroses, character disorders, and serious learning problems. This is the group that made up the great majority of referrals to child psychiatric clinics and private offices by the 1950s and 1960s.

During the mid-1930s, a modest number of the American psychiatrists obtaining psychoanalytic training in Europe came to Vienna to work with Anna Freud and her colleagues. Very exciting applications of psychoanalytic techniques to the treatment of schoolchildren prepared a generation of teachers and consultants to American child care agencies of all types. Marian Putnam, Edith Jackson, Helen Ross, Lydia Dawes, Mary O'Neil Hawkins and Maxwell Gitelson were joined a decade or so later by the European child analysts fleeing the Nazis. They included Marianne Kris, Beata Rank, Edith Buxbaum, Erik Erikson, and Peter Blos. Formal child psychoanalysis was introduced, but it was also modified in a melding of child guidance techniques with the modalities of child analysis. The proportions of each approach varied according to the proclivities of the teachers, the setting and the nature of the child's dysfunctions. In some instances, the individual therapy resembled the analytic method more closely; in others, child guidance techniques appeared most prominent. The number of younger child psychiatrists who sought psychoanalytic training and the continuing presence of many child analyst supervisors promoted the evolution of a psychoanalytic psychotherapy suited to the more chronic, internalized and severe emotional disturbances to which Thom referred in 1926. These children did not respond to environmental manipulations, exhortations or friendly relationships. Within the child psychiatric clinics of the 1940s and 1950s, psychotherapy was a major mode of therapy.

Consultation has constituted a cardinal function of child psychiatric facilities since the early child guidance days. The community mental centers and particularly their child units rely heavily on the consultative process to families, social agencies, schools, courts and community groups. Whatever specific knowledge of individual children and their families may be required in these activities, the area of group process and interaction takes a special prominence. For many, consultations to a group of probation officers or the board of a Head Start program appear far from the realm of psychoanalytic concerns; however, one of the most valuable skills consultants may possess for these community encounters is a comprehension of unconscious factors and particularly of the manifestations of transference and countertransference. A very effective community psychiatrist, who is an analyst maintaining a regular half-time practice in psychoanalysis, frequently tells his colleagues and students that he needs his analytic activity for his community work. He needs it to keep alert to what is happening in the complex group interactions in which he is so frequently engaged, to what is going on within himself and the others in transference and countertransference reactions and in the rapid emergence of powerful but often destructive emotions, which can overwhelm a group if not quickly identified and dealt with. Certain consultants have a flair for this kind of sensing and acting spontaneously upon it in community groups, but the majority of us do not. Psychoanalytic understanding can make available tools to keep the group interactions in unconscious as well as conscious areas in a manageable form, without a mention of "jargon" or a taint of "doing therapy on us."

Another field for child psychiatry specialization is that of working as a staff member in different departments of a hospital or in teaching programs of different specialties. This psychiatrist's function is not that of a consultant, but rather that of a collaborator who brings his skills and knowledge to the common assessing and healing tasks. If part of his professional equipment is a thorough knowledge of interpersonal relationships, of the nuances of interactions among staff, the patient and his relatives, and of the impact of clinical and teaching experiences upon the personnel of the unit, he can bring far more than factual expertise or practical advice to the group. He is demonstrating aspects of the art of medicine, an area neglected today in medical education. Crisis situations such as the admission of a seriously battered child or the terminal state of illness of a child long a patient on a pediatric service throw into relief the gaps in contemporary professional training and the values of support and psychological first-aid to the young doctor, nurse and attendant. As in the psychotherapy of a child, the liaison psychiatrist will not take up all he has learned about the child, his family or the staff members, but he will pick a focus most helpful and meaningful to the patient and the staff.

Group and family therapies are prominent modes of treatment in centers and in private offices. Much of the pioneering work after World War II in group therapy with children was very directly linked to psychoanalysis and carried a strong analytic orientation. A number of varieties of group practice resembling educational or recreational techniques more closely have emerged so that the earlier ties to psychoanalysis are attenuated. Family therapy from its beginning was less influenced by the clinical theories and techniques of psychoanalytic psychotherapy. There is at present a proliferation of schools of family therapy and a strong predilection to regard work with the family the method of choice for children with emotional disturbances.

Specialization in neurological disorders, genetic counseling and drug therapy are carried out by certain child psychiatrists with little attention to the psychodynamic situation within the family or to the developmental history of the child. Other clinicians find that understanding the emotional climate of the home and viewing the child and his parents within the framework of psychoanalytic understanding add immeasurably to their search for significant ways of potentiating the value of the drugs or the information they offer.

The educational responsibilities of the child psychiatrist have multiplied. From the times of the early child guidance clinics, child psychiatrists and their colleagues assumed teaching tasks with social workers, teachers, pediatricians and others. Today, they have expanded their didactic activities to other groups working with children and families — sometimes in organized seminars or workshops, often in teaching conferences.

The child psychiatrist with a psychoanalytic orientation brings to these myriad teaching assignments a conceptual framework for understanding the child patient and his family. The intricate interactions of these patients with their social milieu, the added burden of racial and economic discrimination, and the resources offered by the neighborhood or nearby agencies can be integrated with the history of the individual child and the characteristics of the emotional climate of the home. Along with our growing sensitivity to the significance of the inner-city culture to child development has come attention to the role of middle- and upper-class society in the development of the child in the suburbs and affluent city areas.

Community mental health centers and, indeed, other helping agencies undertook their tasks in the 1960s with intense concentration upon social and economic forces as the major cause of emotional and mental problems. Many other staff members and students selected techniques which sought to improve the situation in which the child was living and being reared. It was natural, therefore, that they turned from individual therapy and didactic methods about individual and emotional development until clinical experience taught them that there is an inner as well as outer life and that helping techniques often have to take both into account. There have been cogent reasons for the popularity of the belief that mental disturbances are caused almost exclusively by poverty and racial and class discrimination. It is possible that we are going to witness another shift in the attitudes regarding the development of children—toward family relationships and different modes of promoting children's growth.

There has been a cyclic pattern to the focus of attention in child psychiatric facilities since their institution in the second decade of the twentieth century. But each shift from the emphasis upon the outer world to the inner and again to the external environment has brought with it insights and techniques from the prior phase. Probably the focus was never as exclusive as historians suggest when they characterize each phase. Many child psychiatrists do not know that Miss Freud's Vienna seminar group of the 1930s carried responsibilities in the municipal child guidance clinic there, or that classic cases of child analysis studied now for decades in psychoanalytic institutes involve children from the slums, victims of as much poverty, discrimination and crime as are contemporary inner-city children.

SUMMARY

Psychoanalysis provided a conceptual and technical foundation for child psychotherapy in the various combinations of child psychoanalysis and child guidance techniques which evolved in the 1930s and '40s in American clinics and child care agencies. Psychoanalytic child psychotherapy has proved to be an admirably flexible approach to the assessment, study, and treatment of children with internalized neurotic problems and serious developmental lags, one geared to the diminution of the hindrances to the child's progressive development. For the child from an harassed background, whether in the suburbs or inner-city, a period of work to stabilize the family or at least decrease the intensity of successive crises will often make it possible to focus upon the child's own growth and the inner hindrances to it and to apply the techniques of psychoanalytic psychotherapy with effectiveness despite the family disorders.

The consultant or liaison psychiatrist provides other clinicians with a deeper understanding of human development, interpersonal relationships and unconscious processes. He can work with an awareness of transference and countertransference processes among relatives, staff members and other children, adding depth to his assessment of crisis situations and to his suggestions of solutions for the problems brought to his attention. He can bring an educational function to his collaborations with other child caretakers which goes beyond the surface manifestations and the adaptive and defensive operations of the participants in the child care situation.

Many activities coming under the rubric of "biological" do not appear to rely so heavily upon an understanding of family interactions and child personality; specialists in these areas may regard psychotherapy as useless and dynamic understanding as unnecessary. Certainly, many child psychiatric functions can be carried out, and are indeed, without the attention to subjective and interactive factors in patient, family and staff which a psychoanalytic orientation encourages. It is a question whether scant attention to a whole order of phenomena related to the emotional life and personality development of a child patient represents an ideal approach to the care of the whole child. Psychotherapists have been reproached for years for their lack of interest in the physical condition of their child patients; such neglect appears out of date.

The human being is a highly complex, constantly changing, yet basically conservative, organism. The child, because of the very nature of childhood, is difficult at best to evaluate. It is even more difficult to predict his future development. Families alter, neighborhoods change, the vicissitudes of life and society cannot be foretold. We are seeking to understand very complicated phenomena. We need conceptual and technical tools to help us do that, and then we need to act upon our understanding. Psychoanalytic theory gives us the most comprehensive conceptualizations available to us today; it is undergoing a steady process of review and revision, adding to our capacity to use it fruitfully. Among clinicians, there are degrees of psychoanalytic sophistication, from that derived from psychoanalytic education to that gained in residency training and in earlier or other formal educational programs. The integration of these concepts into the body of medical and psychiatric theories and the formation of a personal style of using them as part of one's armamentarium while carrying out a broad range of activities constitute a course of continuous education for child psychiatrists.

REFERENCES

1. Freud, S.: Analysis of a phobia in a five-year-old boy (1909). *Standard Edition*, 10:1-149, London: Hogarth Press, 1955.
2. Freud, A.: Assessment of childhood disturbances. *Psychoanalytic Study of the Child*, 17, 149-158, New York: International Universities Press, 1962.

Chapter 6

Psychoanalytic
Group Psychotherapy

Max Day, M.D.

DEFINITION

Psychoanalytic group psychotherapy is based on psychoanalytic understanding of the unconscious motivating forces and the executive functions of the personality, as an individual and in the group setting; at the same time, psychoanalytic group psychotherapy is founded in the group dynamics implicit in a group interactive setting. The general guideline for the interaction as being "spontaneous but appropriate" elicits individual libidinal and aggressive impulses, on the one hand, and socially modulated ego techniques and superego values, on the other. Through this interaction, deepening relationships with the leader and the other members develop; these relationships are then studied for their realistic and unrealistic sources in the present and past. By means of universalizing, confrontation, clarification, and occasionally, the interpretation of unconscious material, the leader helps the members develop identifications with himself and one another. Many of the group dynamic concepts are couched in terms of the psychoanalysis of the individual, since the group psychoanalytic approach is primarily based in psychoanalytic understanding.

There is a broad spectrum of psychoanalytic group therapies, distinguished from one another by the degree to which the focus is on the individual in the group or on the group as a whole. At one extreme is the Tavistock type group (Bion (1) and others) who treat the group as a unit psychoanalytically. At the other end are Wolf and Schwartz (2), Durkin and Glatzer (3), and others, who treat the individual psychoanalytically in the group setting. Their main focus is on the psychodynamics of the individual. Foulkes and Anthony (4) occupy an intermediate position in that they treat a given group of patients for a period of time and then disband the therapy group, accomplishing whatever they can in that time with that group of people. The approach in this paper occupies another kind of intermediate position in the sense that the attention is focused on group and individual dynamics, depending on the most pressing issue of the moment.

The dynamic setting necessary for group therapy to take place and the free exchange of intimate feelings and ideas of a positive and negative nature are mutually supporting and build, preserve and recover the integrity of the group. Within that context a therapeutic alliance takes place at the group level. The patient's need for closeness leads to identification with the leader, identification with the other members of the group, regression, projection and acting-out, all of which could unbalance the therapy group. These forces are counterbalanced by the identification with the leader and his general approach of universalizing problems, which helps unite the members so that they identify with one another.

To further strengthen the group therapeutically, the therapist promotes the building of the "therapeutic group envelope" (5). The energy for building this setting arises in each patient—from his or her need to be close, from the realistic need to be independent and to find self-expression, as well as from the unconscious need to transfer old relationships from the past onto people in the group. (It is this process that gives rise to the apparent dichotomy in views between the here-and-now and the there-and-then.)

At first, the nature of the cohesiveness fragments easily; soon, it turns into an infantile rigid form and only gradually becomes flexible in an adult fashion. The therapist helps the patients move gradually from esteeming the consciously-apprehended ties holding them together to appreciating the personal, unconscious sources for their needs in the group. This leads to a strengthening of the therapeutic group envelope, paradoxically by increasing the flexibility of the ties which hold the group together, and to a strengthening of the individual egos. By the use of his own unconscious and conscious visions of intimacy, the leader helps the patients mobilize their visions in order to work together. He similarly is seen as responsible for the meaning of the environment and milieu in producing the particular character of the group envelope.

This process leads to an alliance on the group level, as well as to the beginnings of strong transference manifestations in each of the members. It takes about 40 meetings for these two phenomena—the group envelope and strong transferences—to develop. At the rate of meetings held twice a week, this should be present in 20 weeks or five months. Nevertheless, the envelope is not as total as this description sounds nor as one might wish it to be. It changes all the time, depending upon the frequency of meetings and the particular emotional makeup of the individuals involved in a given grouping. In practice, members get attached to other members to varying degrees and probably each member is attached to only a certain subset of the group membership. Each member develops a certain number of relationships within the group which are important to him; he may remain relatively indifferent to most of the other members.

In a group membership of eight or nine, people usually have four or five significant relationships. More isolated people, such as schizoid personalities or psychotics, may have only one or two. In such cases, the leader may have to lend himself more actively to support them, particularly when the member on whom the psychotic has been leaning leaves the group; otherwise, that schizoid member will also leave. (In one group, a recompensated schizophrenic woman attached herself to a paranoid woman and clung to her and to the group for a year and a half. When the paranoid woman moved to another part of the country, the recompensated schizophrenic left the group—untouched by it therapeutically.) In this way then, the envelope is composed of a series of networks of relationships, which are different for each of the members. What unites the group members is their continuing conscious and unconscious relationship to the leader. Further, the nature of the envelope changes, as old members leave and new ones come in, so that, in an open-ended group, the nature of the group and of the envelope changes for a given member over time.

My approach to the group is psychoanalytic in the sense that I assume and rely on:

1) the existence of an unconscious in myself and in all the mem-

bers of the group, as well as the importance of dependency yearnings and libidinal ties among us in holding the group together;

2) the significance of narcissism within the economy of each individual, which he can invest in other members, but which also leads to the necessity of dealing with the clashing narcissisms of all the group members, so that each member can live peaceably enough with the others to work out issues with them in the group;

3) the importance of aggression in competition, leading first to group disruption and then to cooperation and cooperative competition as a modus operandi for the group.

All of these factors must be kept in mind about each individual and oneself in relation to each individual in order to understand the problems of the individual and to help the members do the work of the group. This consists of their interacting freely, expressing feelings, comparing notes about any issue, discussing problems, reacting to psychological and interpersonal situations, making judgments, analyzing the meaning of events, relating material to childhood events in the others and in oneself, imitating others in trying out new approaches to problems and solidifying new ways of dealing with life.

After 11 years of doing and teaching group therapy, I devoted myself for nine years primarily to doing individual psychoanalysis, while still continuing to teach group therapy. Then, over 12 years ago, I resumed seeing therapy groups, meeting each group once a week for an hour and 15 minutes per session. I soon had to increase the frequency of meetings to twice a week when I found that people were hungry for more contact with me and with one another and were in need of more support from the group and from myself. They demonstrated this increased need by asking questions at the end of the meeting, writing me letters, and calling me on the phone with crises and with threats to leave the group. At the same time, it was seen that many of these requests for more contact appeared as individual transferences grew stronger and they simply did not have enough time to satisfy their yearnings for more understanding for themselves or one another. Generally, sessions twice a week have been useful for the membership, except in select cases where, for other reasons, such as excruciating marital crises, sudden deep depressions and other intrapsychic catastrophes, I have had to supplement group therapy with individual therapy supplied by another therapist.

When I began doing group therapy, I aimed to have four men and four women in every group. After a few years, more women approached me for group therapy than men, so that, at times, I have had groups with two men and six women—or even just one man who was very lonesome in a group of seven women. More recently, the trend seems to have shifted in the other direction; there are fewer women coming to group therapy with a male therapist. Consequently, I have more and more men in the group.

At first, when there is just one man or just one woman in a group, this is a hardship for the single member of a given sex, whether male or female, surrounded by many members of the opposite sex. The longer this situation continues, the more all the members adjust to it. Nevertheless, members avoid discussing certain personal sexual issues or fantasies as long as they feel isolated within a sea of members of the opposite sex. When the membership changes and there is more of a balance between men and women, the member who used to be the solo male or solo female will confess that he or she feels a loss of the former privileged position, but also comfort in having more members of the same sex in the group.

This group psychotherapy approach relies on the dynamics set in motion by eight members and the leader, using the psychoanalytic philosophy of encouraging individual responsibility for one's conscious and unconscious feelings, thoughts, fantasies and acts. I set this in motion two ways: 1) At the initial evaluation interview I tell the new members to be spontaneous and appropriate. This sets in motion whatever conflicts they have between libidinal and aggressive impulses (spontaneous), on the one hand, and their superego values (appropriate), on the other. 2) I tell the members that the more they "love" the other members, i.e., understand them emotionally and care about them feelingfully, the more they will strengthen themselves. This gives them a very selfish reason for involving themselves empathically with the other members. It also leads me to be reserved in my interactions in order to extend to the members every opportunity possible to work out issues. I step in only when the group misses something important with which they need my help. While this may lead some members to accuse me of being "sphinx-like, old-fashioned, analytic" or the like, it gives me enormous leverage so that each of my open interactions is valued and seen as being weighty. In the long run this makes my work more useful to the members. Sometimes I have to additionally encourage their spontaneous interaction by asking them, "What did you think of what so-and-so said?" or "Has this ever occurred to anyone else?" Sometimes, when the issue is particularly painful, such as when the group may be afraid that someone has committed suicide or that someone has become psychotic or some other catastrophe has happened, I have to poll the membership by going around the whole group. They then begin to see that they all have related feelings about the issue and this frees them up.

The members relate to one another individually and in combinations of several members. They relate to the leader individually or as a group. From the first meeting, members are preoccupied with dealing with the wish to expose themselves to the group and their defenses against these wishes, the wish to look at the other members and the defenses against this wish. Ultimately, there is the expectation of seeing only oneself—one's own outlook on life and values reflected in others—so that one will not be offended by something different or troubling.

Frustration with the leader's psychoanalytic approach of encouraging members to interact and to bear as much anxiety and depression as they can (6, 7) leads to an identification with the leader, who is at first seen as an aggressor. Because they are frustrated by his analytic philosophy and approach, they see his attitude as an aggressive one. They identify with that attitude and at first may aggressively analyze the others, themselves and the leader. They may also identify with the leader as a person who encourages and tolerates feelings and encourages understanding and interaction. This often occurs in connection with an individual's emotional suffering and often gets bound up with the request for medication. I explicitly tell the patient and the group that it is of value that he bear his sadness and anxiety rather than mask them with pills. We have to find out when these feelings crop up and what they mean, so that he will be able to tolerate more of them and strengthen himself that way.

COMBINED THERAPY

These observations apply not only to people who are in group psychotherapy twice a week, but also to those members who have individual therapy outside the group. There are two ways in which this comes about: 1) Sometimes individual psychotherapy appears insufficient to help a patient work out his or her problems. In such an instance, the patient may be referred to group therapy. 2) The patient is in group therapy already and then develops particular pressing problems of an interpersonal or intrapsychic nature which require more attention than the group can provide. This may be a sudden increase in phobias, a deep psychotic depression, a series of suicidal efforts, a psychotic reaction, a deepening rift and conflict with a mate at home and the like. At such a point, group therapy alone would be insufficient. When there is a marital problem, one can refer the patient along with the mate for couple or family therapy, along with the group therapy. For the other problems mentioned, hospitalization may be necessary; under any of these circumstances, individual therapy may have to be provided for more intensive individual work than the group can ever provide.

Depending upon the character structure and aim in life of the patient, such a referral in either direction has particular consequences. Patients with a more primitive character structure and more primitive aims in life (borderlines and psychotics) may continue in both therapy situations for an indefinite period of time. There are two sets of reasons for this—the patient's and the therapist's. The patient may have so little trust in any one therapist that he simply must provide himself with two situations, so that he does not feel he has to rely totally on one therapist; he must be given enough time to feel out the situation emotionally and see which therapist he will really rely on. The therapist's reason is related to the same issue. He may seek more help in providing the patient with yet another psychotherapeutic figure to meet systematically with the patient and help him pull himself together.

The consequences of combined therapy are different for neurotics and character neurotics. Such patients are usually attracted to whichever therapist they feel recognizes and respects their transference needs more forthrightly, consistently and strongly. It may end up being either the individual or the group therapist. If an individual therapist has been treating a patient for some time and a muted, erotic transference develops which he does not attend to or a healthy negative transference develops which the therapist cannot bear, his referring this patient to group therapy where the group therapist welcomes either transference will lead the patient to gravitate towards the group situation. Simply paying attention to the patient's intense yearnings of a positive or negative nature, which the other therapist has been ignoring, will attract that patient to the present therapist. At times, although highly aware of the intense nature of the patient's transference feelings, the group therapist may simply not be able to provide enough time and attention to the transference feelings and therefore permit the patient to gravitate towards the individual therapy situation.

Occasionally, neurotic patients in my therapy group may require individual psychotherapy to finish working out erotic issues in the privacy of individual therapy. Although the arena for action for erotic issues seems to be interpersonal, most of these issues are ultimately lived out intrapsychically. The group setting is essentially an interactive situation so that less intrapsychic material can come out. One is often amazed at how much sexual and erotic material does emerge in the group situation, but it is a small portion of what actually exists in the individual. There is simply not enough time in the group situation for the myriad forms of an individual's erotic fantasies to be examined, much less understood. Erotic material is usually offered by psychotic, borderline and more disturbed character neuroses—rarely by genuine neurotics. Such patients usually are too shy about exposing such fantasies in public. On the other hand, patients who talk freely about sexual fantasies are often really concerned about other issues, such as tenderness, that they find harder to deal with.

I no longer try to serve both functions—that of a group therapist and individual therapist for the same patient. In several such experiments, where I served both functions for the same patients, the rivalry in the group for getting individual therapy from me as well grew so intense as to paralyze the group. At the same time, those members who were already in individual therapy with me simply directed all their work to the individual situation and were content to sit back, while paying money, in the group therapy situation and expose very little of their efforts there. When I stopped this kind of work, one of the sequelae was that the members whom I had not seen in individual therapy felt so unwanted and felt so rivalrous that these feelings sapped the constructive efforts of the group for two more years.

EVALUATION FOR PSYCHOANALYTIC GROUP PSYCHOTHERAPY

Evaluation of the patient is the crucial part of group psychotherapy, as it is for any therapy. It is essential to know why the patient comes for help and how he sees this help. Just as important is the need to determine the reasons for the decompensation; it may take four to six months at times to figure out why someone really came for help at a certain time. One patient presented himself with obvious signs of a paranoid decompensation; he felt that his boss had homosexual designs on him. It took about a year to discover that what had led to the paranoid decompensation at this time was his breaking off his relationship with a woman whom he had loved and who cared for him. There was no inkling of this during the evaluation itself nor for some months to come. In the evaluation, it had been clear only that he was desolate about a very unsatisfying relationship with a mean, abusive father who now was declining from a stroke in a nursing home. These two aspects of his life had to be tied together subsequently in therapy to make sense out of what he complained about, the help he wanted and what seemed to be the underlying reason for the decompensation. It is also important to evaluate the interpersonal and intrapsychic problems which led to the decompensation, including underlying childhood developmental problems. Only then can we decide the most appropriate treatment plan for this patient and whether group therapy can be of use to him.

Some patients referred to me for group psychotherapy do not end up in my therapy group. Often they are sent back to the individual therapist to continue work on an unattended erotic transference or a powerful negative transference. When the transference has not been recognized by the therapist, a hint usually helps him proceed with the work. Some therapists feel, for ideological reasons, that they should not refer to the transference in once-a-week psychotherapy, despite the contrary findings of such workers as Malan (8) and general clinical experience. Usually, good will and clarification by the consultant and, occasionally, a reference to authority encourage the therapist to continue. For such patients, coming to group psychotherapy really serves more as a consultation than as a change of therapy. Once the individual therapist accepts the hint and addresses himself freely to the transference, the patient continues in individual therapy and works matters out.

Some therapists are reluctant to face a particular transference for personal reasons which one can only guess at. A patient with such a therapist may be referred to group psychotherapy and work out his/her fate there. Even more tricky is an unrecognized transference from a former individual therapy some years back. It is often a source of powerful feelings that have been pushing the patient around in life for many years until it is finally recognized and worked out in the group. It may take a considerable amount of time (up to a year and a half or two) before such a dormant transference becomes apparent and workable in the group. At any rate, in the case of patients who have had prior meaningful therapeutic contact, these various possibilities must be considered.

In the case of psychotic patients and borderlines who are likely to have a psychotic decompensation, I ask that they have some reliable relative available who will bring them to the group from the hospital if it seems that they might very well have to be hospitalized for decompensation during the process of group psychotherapy. At such a juncture, there may be a need for medication as well. In such cases, too, the additional support of individual psychotherapy for the patient may have to be considered. This is similar to the therapist's providing several helpful, sane objects for the patient to interact with on the ward, while he himself carries the main burden of the therapy (9).

> In one case, a woman who had been dependent on her mother
> until her mid-thirties had worked for several years trying to undo
> her yearnings to be cared for reasonably by that mother. Against
> the advice of the male group therapist, she began to see a female
> therapist who had a positive dislike for the male group therapist.
> In a sense, this was a reenactment in transference of the childhood
> dilemma of the patient, whose parents had split apart before she
> was born. She had constantly yearned to glue together the two
> parents, who would have nothing to do with each other. She re-
> peated this with the two therapists. The male therapist found what-
> ever of value he could in the reports that the patient brought back
> from her female therapist. He accepted all undermining efforts by
> that female therapist without comment. In the end, the patient
> grew from the efforts of both situations but this might have ended
> up as a very confusing multi-therapy situation.

In the evaluation interview, I also explore the expectations that the
patient has of group psychotherapy, as well as his resistances towards
it and reservations about it. I remind him of the problems of joining an
ongoing group, with the hazing of the newcomer and the difficulties of
trying to break into a well-entrenched clique. Alerting patients to the
fact that such hazing may go on for two months (16 meetings), during
which they may be blamed for the sins of recently-departed members,
is enough to help most patients fit into the group. An occasional patient
may leave at this juncture, very early in this process.

Sometimes, certain leading conflicts or problems presented during the
evaluation interview may be evident in the very first therapy session.

> When his father had yet another stroke, a paranoid man developed
> fears that his boss had homosexual designs on him. He had had
> three other such episodes in recent years. He had endured a very
> lonely childhood in which his father frequently abused and as-
> saulted his mother, himself and his siblings. He was attached to
> his father and visited him frequently in the nursing home where
> he now resided. This material came out clearly in the evaluation
> interview.
>
> In the first group psychotherapy session that he attended, the
> three women had stayed away, fearing the newcomer. The three
> men who came listened to the newcomer as if hypnotized by him.
> He entranced them, talking to them at great length about himself,
> his childhood and his pain regarding his father. He was able to get

these three older "fathers" to listen to him as he had never been able to get his father to do.

The knowledge of his relationship with his father and his wanting to be able to make a point with the parents clarified the emerging transference in this session. I interpreted this to him and to the group, saying, "You now have gotten three older men to listen to your pain with your father of recent years and from your childhood, as you've never succeeded with your father and always wanted to; the three oldtimers in the group, on the other hand, are so nervous about the newcomer that they sit here listening patiently rather than getting acquainted."

It became clear to them all that he was exposing himself while they were avoiding exposing themselves and, in the meantime, no one was getting acquainted. This, then, freed the four of them for the freer interaction more characteristic of an initial meeting. Nevertheless, this interaction indicates how powerful a transference can be from the evaluation session or first therapy session on.

Obviously, the evaluation for psychoanalytic group psychotherapy is extremely important, since the future course of therapy, as well as later psychotherapeutic interpretations, may very well be outlined then.

The reasons for coming for psychoanalytic group psychotherapy are, in the main, no different from those for coming for individual therapy. We see the whole gamut of the patient population—neurotic, character neurosis, borderline state and psychotic—come for basically the same three kinds of reasons—a loss, including a relative loss; a chronic slide into frustration and defeat; and, occasionally, life-cycle stress.

> 1) *Loss or relative loss*. This may be an absolute loss of an individual who was a gratifying object in the case of neurotics, a supporting object in the case of the borderline states, or a sustaining object in the case of the psychotic. Relative loss refers to the loss of a particular function of the love object as is true for a man when his wife goes out to work or has another baby.
> 2) The *chronic slide into frustration and defeat* is usually a series of repeated losses over many years.
> 3) *Life-cycle stresses* include puberty, the end of adolescence with its need for one's own identity and one's own direction in life, engagement, marriage, childbirth, the birth of a particular child and the order of births, promotion, the menopause, mid-life, self-reevaluations and so on.

Some virgins to therapy who are merely neurotic ask for group therapy for ideological or doctrinal reasons, although ideally one might think about psychoanalysis for them. They, however, "believe" in group therapy and insist on it.

WHO SHOULD NOT COME TO GROUP PSYCHOTHERAPY

In general, patients who do not want to be in a psychotherapy group, whose needs are too great for a particular group to deal with, or who have a particular symptom which they treasure or feel too ashamed to disclose cannot be helped in group psychotherapy.

Analytic group therapy takes place within the context of the "group envelope" (5)—that psychological setting in which the mutual identifications of the members with the therapeutic aims of the group leader hold everyone together, so that mild or even moderate infractions of the rules of the "group envelope" can be safely analyzed within that setting. Ideally, this leads to growth of the various individuals in the group. Where the pressures within given members are so great or where the group therapy milieu is so weak or unsupportive of the needs of a given patient that the particular member cannot be contained within that setting, such a member is automatically ruled out of that particular group therapy setting.

Certain patients are suitable for group therapy only under special circumstances. It is possible to treat manic patients in a group therapy setting within a hospital, but not in an outpatient setting or in a private office. The therapeutic container is simply too fragile to contain them and help them settle down to do the group work. In the holding environment of group therapy in a hospital setting, manic patients may be "sedated" by only a few sessions (10). This environment generally accepts them while disapproving of their loss of control. Similarly, the acting-out sociopath may be safely contained in a therapy group in a prison situation, or in an outpatient situation where the probation officer acts to contain the patient within the therapy situation by ordering him to attend. Such patients might not last more than one meeting in an ordinary outpatient situation without these containing supports.

Similarly, patients whose needs are extremely great because of a sudden acute loss of a supportive figure or because of a panic may also not be safely contained in an outpatient situation. For instance, a phobic individual who, in the midst of therapy, loses a person who has given him vital support, may not be able to even get to the group session for help. Just as often, potentially violent psychotic or sociopathic patients, self-mutilating psychotics, patients with extreme tics, and patients with other bizarre and unusual symptoms may simply not be accepted by a group of mixed patients.

There are others who should not be in group therapy. People who insist for whatever reason that they cannot be in the therapy group should not be encouraged to come there against their will. Every beginner, especially when he is hungry for more patients, may try to seduce such patients to come to the group. It does not work out well for the therapist, the patient or the rest of the group. The patient will not work on his problems, the other members will feel defeated and the leader will feel therapeutically impotent and blame himself for it. Similarly, although patients with perversions can be helped in groups consisting of individuals with related perversions, in a group of patients with other diagnoses such patients may sometimes fritter away a year or two in a group without ever revealing their symptoms or getting to work on their problems. Such patients have to be faced with this contingency before they come to the group; if they feel they cannot be frank about their particular perversion in the group, they should not be in that therapy situation.

THERAPIST'S EXPECTATIONS OF THE GROUP

The therapist must be clear in his own mind as to what kind of group he wants to have. It may take experience with several groups over some years to begin to clarify for himself what he would like to see in his group. Once he knows this he behaves in every way possible, whether actively or passively, to bring about that kind of group. Ultimately, he wishes to help each member of the group become totally responsible for all his or her feelings, wishes, needs, fears and acts. In this way each person will become most useful as a group member and most integrated as a human being.

Most of the transactions in the group move the members and the whole group in that direction. The leader conducts himself in such a way as to encourage the members to assume as much responsibility as possible for their interaction, for understanding one another, for creating breaches in the group envelope, for healing these breaches, for looking at the past, and for understanding every aspect of everything that goes on. The leader encourages the group to understand every issue as it occurs.

Even when a question or a problem is addressed directly to the leader, he treats it as simply another association, turns to the group and asks: "What do you think about it? How do you feel about it?" Usually, this is sufficient to keep the group going. Occasionally, when a thorny subject is brought up, such as the communal hatred of a psychotic by the other neurotic members, or the aversion with which people react to a particularly obnoxious attitude in one member, the leader must "take the bull by the horns," verbalize the issue to the members and even poll them one by one to make sure all members bring their feelings out into the open.

> In one group, the neurotic members were afraid of a paranoid member. When this paranoid member lost a girlfriend during one summer vacation, he felt especially hurt that his poetry was not valued and he took a knife and stabbed himself in the belly four times while living at a halfway house. The group was disgusted and overwhelmed by the feelings of pain, terror, hurt and rage aroused by his behavior. In his absence, they were helped to verbalize these feelings. At first they were reluctant. They had to be polled person by person before they began to express their feelings out loud; with such "practice" they were able to tell him these feelings on his return to the group. This was useful for them in that they realized that they could trace even such painful feelings and useful for him in that he heard a frank discussion of the feelings he had aroused in them. With such experiences, members begin to realize that such frank facing of feelings is helpful to every individual involved.

The leader's intuitive and empathic understanding of the individual members and of the group is of ultimate importance in the working of the group. Intuition and empathy are innate qualities which can be sharpened by personal psychotherapy or analysis and are still further increased by treating many groups and teaching and supervising group therapy. It is important that the leader expose himself to many different kinds of people so that he can sharpen his intuitive understanding in many directions.

Both qualities, intuition and empathy, shade over into the area of countertransference (11), when specific feelings raised by the patient pose a problem for the therapist for defensive reasons and because of his own past, so that he does not feel free to deal empathically with that member in the group. As he realizes this, he may sit back and listen carefully to the members of the group. They may be allowed to take over the burden of the psychoanalytic work until he can work his problem out for himself, on the spot, with consultation or with further psychotherapy (12). Ultimately, he must work with and analyze these countertransference feelings in himself and use them to help the patient.

A therapist with an unrequited wish to be a novelist permitted a would-be writer to pay a smaller fee than the other members of the group. That member came late. Repeated attempts to analyze his tardiness had no impact on his behavior. The therapist realized that he was treating the member in a privileged manner, counter to his own interests and those of the group, to satisfy his old yearning to be a novelist. As he grew aware of his resentment and his impotence in helping this member work with the group, he became aware of his own wishes that he was satisfying through the patient. He then re-set the fee for this patient so that it was the same as everyone else's. That member came regularly thereafter. The therapist was able to work out his own feelings without help from others in the group or anyone else and to use them to help the member as well as the group. He came to terms with his own feelings, began to treat the patient like any other member and the countertransference impasse was resolved.

GOALS OF GROUP THERAPY

There are nine general areas of work, of increasing levels of complexity, that can be accomplished in group therapy. These include: 1) compensation of the ego of the patient, 2) resuming one's daily life, 3) changes in interpersonal relationships, 4) working out losses and grief, 5) analysis of ego mechanisms, 6) analysis of the transference, 7) analysis of the transference neurosis, 8) working out libidinal problems and 9) the work of termination.

1) Compensation of the Ego of the Patient

Compensation refers to the process of returning to the level of functioning that existed before the breakdown period. This is a goal for neurotics, borderlines and psychotics, particularly in reaction to a loss. The change in functioning and behavior is more prominent in the individual who shows much anxiety (unrecognized by the psychotic), depression and regressive infantile ways of responding to people in the environment. A therapy group can be very useful for a decompensated individual (13, 14) at such a point in his life since he feels accepted by the other members who have suffered similarly. They all recognize common factors in themselves and this creates bonds among them. The very presence of these feelings in the other members encourages him to try

and do what he used to do in his daily life by way of work and interactions with people who are important to him. The discharge of feelings
of distrust of others, of the fear of not being accepted, of the panic of
the decompensated state and of related anger leads to relief. This lightens
the burden for the decompensated patient. Identification with the other
members strengthens him so that he can begin to function more effectively, as he did before. This is particularly true of neurotics; their former
state may return in a few weeks. Compensation may take six to eight
months with acutely decompensated borderlines and psychotics.

2) Resuming One's Daily Life

A related process of longer duration occurs in the case of patients
(particularly borderlines and psychotics, but also neurotics), who have
slid slowly into a nonfunctioning state over a period of many years.
There is really no prepsychotic or preneurotic state of effectiveness to
return to. Therapy is a matter of slowly helping the patient mobilize
himself so that he can take stock of whatever assets and talents he
possesses and begin to put them to work, often for the first time. It may
take several years in the group before the patient will again try to carry
out new activities in his life in order to get some personal satisfaction.
Similar factors are at work in this process as in the case of recompen-
sation. The process of universalization of problems and the facing of
distrust, fear and rage in the group are the techniques for the patient
until acceptance by the other members encourages him to take some
steps in doing something for himself. Gradually, as such a member is
accepted, he may begin to look at the disastrous state of his life and try
other approaches from the lives of other people or from members in the
group to see what he can do for himself.

> A schizophrenic member had given up college and work and
> had hidden out at home to play the piano, attack various forces
> in society, dream about sex and fight with the family, especially
> blaming all of his troubles on his father. It took more than two
> years in a therapy group of individuals with mixed diagnoses for
> him to air his distrust of people, to speak of his various theories
> about young women flagrantly showing off their charms and keep-
> ing themselves unavailable to him, of his ugliness in being bald at
> so young an age, of his distrust of his father who was mean and
> niggling and unsupportive. He then began again to try and make
> some money mowing lawns and to think of just taking a few
> courses to finish off his degree. By the time two more years had

passed, he had given up the high-flown ambitions of being a Professor of Physics without ever having taken a course in physics to completion. The group listened to him; they did not fight with him, they accepted him, and this gave him the courage to try out some of these things. This pattern is followed by many kinds of patients who have been out of commission psychically for many years.

The neurotic who has been involved in a lifelong pattern of enmeshment with compliant objects may have a very difficult time finding some strength in order to manage in life. The borderline poses a similar kind of problem. He is often enmeshed with objects who offer him a particular kind of stability in what usually seems to the therapist to be an unstable way of life. In fact, it is extremely stable and rigid and is given up only with great effort and difficulty. Going on with one's life after the acute decompensation means going back to that kind of way of life—but that has to be analyzed carefully before the patient can begin to make progress. Sometimes the patient may have to decide to relinquish such objects and grieve for them and find others that are healthier so that he can free himself from this rigid, unstable way of life. For this reason, resuming one's way of life may take many years for such patients.

3) Changes in Interpersonal Relationships

Since group therapy is essentially an interactional type of therapy, it is particularly useful for the study of interpersonal relations *in statu nascendi*. Many group therapists stress that group therapy may be superior to individual therapy since one can see the individual interacting simultaneously in many different directions. One can study many different aspects of his behavior as it goes on. This is certainly true. It does not, however, necessarily facilitate changes in interpersonal relationships. It is merely that the behavior is more obvious.

The group situation lends itself nicely to an intense study of the problems of aggression, as well as to application of techniques for dealing with aggression. It is also an excellent setting for studying self-assertiveness, competition and cooperation in interpersonal matters. Very quickly, the particular patterns used by each member become apparent. This leads to a further study of genetic roots as each member is able to offer such data from his past. In this way, group therapy becomes a mixture of current interaction and introspection for the past sources of such behavior. The mutual identifications of the members give them courage to look into their own individual pasts. This revives old conflicts which are partly remembered and partly acted out in relation to the other members and the leader. Then, the members are in a better position to try out different techniques, often borrowed from one another in the group or from the therapist, first in the group and then outside.

4) Working Out Losses and Grief

Group therapy is very useful in helping people deal with problems of grief for recent or old losses. The group members listen supportively and help the member by bringing examples of their own grief and loss. This can be just as useful for the listeners as it is for the member whose loss is being reviewed. The group is also quite supportive in helping the individual bear the rage connected with his loss; tears, however, are sometimes harder for some people to face in a group situation. Sometimes they resort to weeping in private.

It may be difficult in group therapy to deal with the childhood determinants of the disaster which lays the groundwork for later grief and gives form to the illness of the particular individual. The deficits in the earliest relationship with the mother leading to the current depression often cannot be dealt with sufficiently in the group situation. Sometimes, too, group therapy alone cannot deal with some of the identifications with the lost individual as openly as one might like. Nevertheless, the social supportive side of helping an individual grieve make up for many of these deficits.

5) Analysis of Ego Mechanisms

To varying degrees, analysis of the ego may take place in the group situation, with particular attention to those aspects of the ego that are prominent in interpersonal relations and interactions. Members begin to be aware of parts of themselves or to see aspects in others that they have not been aware of before. They start wondering why they cannot understand or control this particular aspect of themselves. Sometimes they first recognize it in relation to someone they are interacting with outside the group and sometimes in relation to another member in the group. This leads to a careful survey of the particular techniques used by this patient and a search into their historic origins and the conflicts with significant figures that gave rise to this particular pattern. Certain problems, however, such as interlaced defensive layers seen in certain character neurotics, are analyzed only with difficulty in the group situation. Such people may need additional individual therapy.

6) Analysis of the Transference

Transference—the displacement of a series of attitudes, emotions and conflicts from a significant figure in the past to an individual in the present environment—is at work in every member in a psychotherapy group from the first contact. The use of transference is one of the major tools of group therapy. The study of transference is important for the group therapist in helping him and his patients understand the various kinds of unreal reactions that they have in their outside world and in the group.

Beyond the problem of the beginning therapist developing experience and recognizing transference, there are probably three levels of recognition that pose problems:

> 1) Easiest is the member who shows a very bizarre and stridently inappropriate attitude to the leader or another member. It is clear from the beginning that this is a transference attitude, although it may not yet be clear whom it is being transferred from.
> 2) Sometimes a patient recounts some personal data in the evaluation session and begins to act out these data in the transference in the first session. The paranoid man described earlier, whose father had suffered a stroke, illustrates this. In the first group session, when the women stayed away, the three men serving as "listening" fathers brought to a head the emerging transference and allowed for a most useful interpretation.
> 3) Most difficult to deal with is the member who shows an attitude to the leader or some other member which may pass as being reasonable. Only after much experience with this member and only after much historical data are presented does it become apparent that, in fact, this apparently reasonable attitude is the beginning of a silent transference relationship. With certain kinds of borderlines and even psychotics, one often sees what looks like a working alliance with the therapist; in fact, it is often the beginning of an idealized relationship with the therapist, which never existed in fact in the past, but is meant to make up for all the old unsatisfied yearnings (15).

In general, transference manifestations are very gross and obvious in the case of psychotics and borderlines, although their meaning may be vague. In the case of neurotics and character neuroses, they may be more heavily disguised but are, nonetheless, present from the beginning.

Transference may seem perplexing to the patient in individual therapy when all the attention is focused on him. In the group situation, other members can see the therapist's analysis of the unreal part of the patient's relationship to the therapist and support this view. However, in a psychotherapy group, the transference may appear even more fragmented to the patient and, therefore, more mysterious to him. For this reason the therapist must keep an eye on each of the transferences and make them clear to the member and to the group as they become evident. The therapist may have to connect many apparently unrelated interactions over a period of months and even years in the light of his knowledge of the transference of the patient in order to make it clear and convincing to the patient himself. As the group members begin to understand this, they help one another keep track of their own transferences and are very constructive in helping one another see and analyze these unreal feelings.

7) Analysis of the Transference Neurosis

Those periods of intensified transference neurosis in individual psychoanalysis, when the patient seems to be sane and unneurotic in his everyday activities outside the analysis but suffers his symptoms most acutely in the analytic situation, seem maddening to the beginning psychoanalyst and confusing to the patient, who is always a beginner to the situation. Ultimately and paradoxically, this experience is the most convincing part of the therapeutic experience to the patient, demonstrating the importance and impact on his daily life of his childhood neurosis. Living through the transference neurosis safely and settling it by seeing it in the perspective of childhood help the patient give up his neurosis. The energies then released attach themselves to individuals and activities in his present-day life. The patient can then invest himself emotionally in areas of legitimate interest as well as some areas previously not even seen as being important to him.

The group therapy situation seems to be better set up to deal with problems of interaction, aggression, sadness, loneliness and emptiness, but not with erotic problems. In a group psychotherapy situation, there is simply less of an opportunity, in terms of time, attention and energy, to develop a transference neurosis surrounding the leader and to resolve it. The group will not tolerate this expenditure of time and energy for any one individual, despite the remarkable tolerance the group shows in letting people develop shorter episodes of this nature. This is determined by the nature of the material involved and by the character structure of the individuals involved.

To the extent that the patient is a high-functioning neurotic, the nub of his neurosis concerns erotic material which he will not bring into the group. At the same time, borderlines and psychotics will freely bring in such erotic material, often as a defense against more serious material having to do with aggression, sadness, loneliness and emptiness. Consequently, episodes of transference neurosis are more likely to be worked out for borderline and psychotic patients in a therapy group than for neurotics.

8) Working out Libidinal Problems

It is still an open question for me how much libidinal material can be dealt with in an analytic psychotherapy group by neurotics. My experience has been mixed so far.

Since the details of sexual life and fantasy life are harder to face and verbalize in the group situation, there may be certain limitations as to how much of sexual problems in neurotics can be worked out in a group. Certainly, whatever can be shifted by the patient into the interpersonal arena will be worked out in a more or less satisfactory manner by that member. What cannot be shifted to that arena may require individual therapy or analysis. Hysterical women, in particular, tend to leave the group to go into individual therapy to work out the rest of their inner libidinal concerns, since these are essentially intrapsychic and do not get presented to, reviewed in or analyzed by the group.

9) The Work of Termination

Some of the best work in group psychotherapy, as in individual psychotherapy or psychoanalysis, is done during the process of termination. In a sense, much of the previous work has merely been a matter of laying the groundwork so as finally to work things out and make them stick during the termination process.

The first signs of the coming termination for a patient may occur in the therapist's feeling of sadness as he recognizes that he will not be enjoying a given patient much longer. This may be true even before the patient has said anything overtly. It comes up from the patient's side when he shows his independence as private interests open up more for him, often in conflict with the aims of the group.

A member who had previously come steadfastly and religiously to group therapy decided to skip a night and go out bowling with her husband, whom she had been ready to divorce three years earlier, when she had first come to the group. She was even willing to pay for the missed meeting. The group members simply could not understand such "perfidy." Every group resents and resists a member's getting better and leaving, because the separation is so painful for all the members. The therapist had to recognize this as an important signal for the coming termination of this member.

In helping a member terminate, one should set aside a large portion of time (three to six months or 25 to 50 meetings) to review systematically the work required for termination and to build solidly on the work that has been done until then. One asks the patient to review why he came for therapy in the first place, which of these problems have been taken care of, which new problems have been uncovered, which problems have *not* been taken care of. Above all, in which ways has the group or the therapist been a disappointment to him? This will usually help the member to review what has realistically taken place, as well as to begin to face the disappointment and resentment of the unrealistic or realistic matters that have not been helped.

The other members of the group are encouraged to review these data with the member who is contemplating leaving. They are usually very frank in pointing out his assets as well as his deficits. The members of the group may want him to leave quickly so as to get the pain over with; he may want this himself. He should be encouraged to stay on for the agreed upon period of time so that he may study the process in a leisurely and detailed fashion. This will help him to know his own patterns of taking leave for the future.

The patient may seem to get sicker in the psychotherapy group as he approaches the point of termination, so that the therapist begins to doubt whether he has done anything worthwhile with him. The returning anxiety comes in the form of the anxiety that brought the patient to the group in the first place, but is an expression of the ultimate anxiety of saying goodbye. The therapist must have the experience of a number of safe and reasonable terminations to begin to see how much of such anxiety has to do with the normal, reasonable termination and how much has to do with work not done.

SUMMARY

I have tried to indicate the common elements shared by psychoanalysis and psychoanalytic group therapy in theory, technique and practice.

Nevertheless, certain differences emerge in the kinds of patients that can be treated, the kind of treatment that can be offered and how much can be done and cannot be done because of the nature of the setting. All in all, psychoanalytic group psychotherapy can deal effectively with present-day issues and with issues such as grief, loss, depression, aggression, loneliness and the ego techniques involved in dealing with such matters. It is not as well set up to deal with the erotic part of the neurotic individual's intrapsychic life. Concurrently, it is a difficult situation in which to explore all the genetic aspects of the problems that individual psychotherapy can deal with successfully or the niceties of analyzing and changing ego structure, especially intricately interwoven ego structure. Nevertheless, it is useful for a wide spectrum of patients from psychotic through borderline, narcissistic character neurosis to neurotic, who can learn from it and who can teach the therapist a great deal about life, people and himself.

REFERENCES

1. Bion, W. R.: *Experiences in Groups*. New York: Basic Books, 1959.
2. Wolf, A. and Schwartz, E. K.: *Psycho-analysis in groups*. In *Comprehensive Group Psychotherapy*, H. Kaplan and B. Sadock (Eds.), Baltimore: Williams & Wilkins, 1971, pp. 241-291.
3. Durkin, Helen E. and Glatzer, H. T.: Transference neurosis in group psychotherapy: The concept and the reality. In *Group Therapy 1973: An Overview*, L. R. Wolberg and E. K. Schwartz (Eds.), New York: Inter-Continental Medical Book Corporation, 1973, pp. 127-144.
4. Foulkes, S. H., and Anthony, E. J.: *Group Psychotherapy: The Psycho-Analytic Approach*. Baltimore: Penguin Books, 1965.
5. Day, M.: Therapeutic group envelope. *Psychiatric Spectator*, 1964, p. 5.
6. Zetzel, E.: Anxiety and the capacity to bear it. *Int. J. Psychoanalysis*, 30:1-12, 1949.
7. Zetzel, E.: Depression and the incapacity to bear it. In *Drives, Affects and Behavior*, Vol. II, M. Schur (Ed.), New York: International Universities Press, 1965.
8. Malan, D. H.: *A Study of Brief Psychotherapy*. New York: Plenum, 1975.
9. Day, M., and Semrad, E. V.: Schizophrenia. In *The Harvard Guide to Modern Psychiatry*, A. Nicholi (Ed.), Cambridge, MA.: The Belknap Press of Harvard University Press, 1978.
10. Winnicott, D. W.: Transitional objects and transitional phenomena. *Int. J. Psychoanalysis*, 34:89-97, 1953.
11. Day, M.: Countertransference in everyday practice. In *Issues in Psychotherapy*, Vol. I. Schippers, L. (Ed.), Boston: Boston Institute for Psychotherapies, 1977.
12. Glatzer, H. T.: The working alliance in psychoanalytic group psychotherapy. *Int. J. Group Psychother.*, 28:147-161, 1978.
13. Standish, C., and Semrad, E. V.: Group psychotherapy with psychotics. *J. of Psychiatric Social Work*, 20:143-150, 1951.
14. Day, M., and Semrad, E. V.: Group therapy with neurotics and psychotics. In *Theories and Techniques in Group Therapy, Vol. VI, Group Treatment of Mental Illness*, H. I. Kaplan and B. J. Sadock (Eds.), New York: Jason Aronson, 1973.
15. Kohut, H.: *The Restoration of the Self*. New York: International Universities Press, 1977.

Chapter 7

Psychotherapy Within Social Systems

Lee Birk, M.D.

Approximately 15 years ago I became convinced of the advantages of combining some aspects of psychoanalysis and some aspects of behavior therapy in my own clinical practice. In this paper I shall describe briefly the evolution of this notion from its beginnings as an essentially untested set of ideas and intuitions to its current state as a hybrid clinical methodology of broad general applicability and demonstrated unusual effectiveness in a number of special settings. This hybrid clinical approach has by no means been codified into a rigid "system of psychotherapy"; rather, it is clearly still evolving in major ways. In fact, I hope it will continue to be guided empirically by what "works best"—if so, of course, it should continue to evolve indefinitely, instead of becoming rigidly crystalized (ossified) into yet another discernable "school" of psychiatry.

From the outset, it was clear that all the therapeutic advantages of such a combination flowed from and were the result of a basic factor having to do with a central epistemological point, i.e., establishing access to the broadest base of information about each patient which would prove both usable and reliable. It has been my opinion, in a nutshell, that psychoanalytically-oriented therapists, albeit generally very conscientious about collecting and organizing patients' self-report data, have nonetheless deliberately limited the scope and, therefore, the reliability of their data by excluding from their professional purview other sources of information about the patient that are actually independent of the patient's own account. Behavior therapists, on the other hand, because of their conceptual reliance on direct observation and quantification, have tended to disregard one whole class of crucial data, i.e., thoughts, feelings and mental events in general.

Since my early professional education was a dual one, touching on both psychoanalytic therapy and behavioral research and therapy, it was natural for me to wonder why one therapist could not call upon both disciplines in his clinical practice—dealing with significant thoughts and feelings and also emphasizing direct observation and management of relevant behavior. Even *a priori*, there is an obvious epistemological advantage in such a combination in that it offers the therapist access to a broader range of clinical phenomena than either professional discipline alone can provide and an opportunity for independent verification of therapeutically significant material.

In my first attempt at a representative terminology for this combined clinical approach, I used a simple conjunction of the two terms: "psychoanalysis and behavior therapy" (1-6). Subsequently, it became evident that the process of "doing both" was far more complicated, and also much more specifically useful, than such a simple conjunction implies. I then began to use the terms "behavioral psychotherapy" (7) and also "the learning therapies" (8) in order to emphasize the hybrid nature, interdependence, cross-fertilization and synergism of the combination or process of "doing both." But those names also have fallen short of the mark in that they fail to convey the central feature of the combination as it evolves clinically—*and that is its necessary reliance on a systems approach to psychotherapy*. In essence, the therapist who seeks to know more about the people he treats, and seeks to know more with greater accuracy and reliability, and also seeks to treat those people effectively, finds himself gravitating toward the use of social networks within the therapeutic setting—hence the phrase and title of this chapter "Psychotherapy within Social Systems."

In the remainder of this paper, I would like to cover only very briefly some of the theoretical aspects of doing psychotherapy that borrows extensively from psychoanalytic and behavioral principles, because I have addressed this more fully elsewhere (1-8, 16), and to make the primary goal of this chapter a very practical review of some major lines of clinical work I have carried out while using both psychoanalytic and behavioral frameworks while working within differing kinds of social systems.

Although it has long been my contention that the conceptual and technical frameworks of psychoanalysis and behavior therapy are susceptible to combination, it is only fairly recently that I have realized the extent to which maximally effective psychotherapy demands such a combination. The practice of psychoanalysis, including what has come to be known as psychoanalytically-oriented psychotherapy, is based upon a well-defined body of assumptions held in common by most practitioners of psychoanalysis. These assumptions are about, for example, the nature of mind, the development of ideas about oneself and others, the major factors influencing personality, character and "neurotic symptoms." These and other compatible assumptions comprise the conceptual framework of psychoanalysis, which in turn serves as a generative base for the technical framework, the principles and techniques of psychoanalytic treatment. Behavior therapy also relies on a conceptual framework: a tradition of assumptions about the nature of brain-organism-environment adaptations, about the plasticity of personality and of all behavior, adaptive and maladaptive, and so on. The technical framework of behavior therapy is comprised of a set of principles and techniques for analyzing and modifying particular behaviors in actual clinical cases.* Although these conceptual and technical frameworks are associated with different traditions, one more clinical and one more experimental, there is no reason inherent in the principles and treatment techniques themselves that would militate against integration and combination.

When I began my clinical practice, the great majority of my cases followed the traditional course—individual psychotherapy. In this setting, what one might call pressing epistemological questions presented themselves to me, at first sporadically and then more frequently and urgently: Is what the patient is saying and feeling really "true," in any broader sense than as a purely subjective report? Is any of a particular account susceptible to verification or corroboration by independent sources? What is the actual evidence for a patient's feeling or belief?

Often such questions were prompted by a patient's emphatic and steadfast presentation to me of a strong, clear, rather exclusively negative view of his mother, or his father, or of both parents, or of his whole

---

*For those readers who are not familiar with behavior therapy, may I suggest a brief primer: the American Psychiatric Association Task Force Report, *Behavior Therapy in Psychiatry* (14).

family. The nagging questions which recurred was: Was it really so? Or, to put it more accurately: Was it so, but only when viewed only through the eyes of the patient? And further: What independent evidence was there for the patient's view of things?

Corollary questions existed and of course multiplied when I began to gather social systems data: data drawn from the direct behavioral observation of the patient interacting with those people in his family about whom he had earlier provided self-report data. Some of the corollary questions were: What role did the patient himself or herself play in provoking negative parental behaviors? What function in the family as a whole system was served by the patient's behaviors and by the behaviors of the patient's family members? What positive interactions and feelings might there be which, no matter how long or deeply I probed, were *not* presented to me?

Thus, in evaluating the kinds of human problems that people bring to psychiatrists, I became more and more struck by how easily I and other "well-trained" therapists could be seriously misled by falling into accepting, more than we realized we had, the black-and-white thinking of our patients, especially after seeing them for prolonged therapy. Such "absolutes" occur, of course, but ordinarily only through the eyes of certain beholders: patients in individual psychoanalytic psychotherapy who have (or feel they have) the unqualified support of an understanding psychotherapist.*

Einstein, in his briefest description of his own Relativity Theory, said simply that it was that, "There are no hitching posts in the universe, so far as we know." By this he apparently meant that in the universe there are no points which can be assumed to be fixed and stationary, and that all motion must be defined relatively between particular specified points; even the points themselves have meaning only in relation to other points. In a parallel way, in human relationships the equivalent of motion is "who does what to whom, and for what reason," and this, of course, as with motion in the universe, is intrinsically relativistic, in that the "doing" person has one set of internal cognitions and feelings about what he is doing, and yet, even for the very same event, the person being "done to" has an entirely separate and ordinarily very different set of internal cognitions and feelings. Very frequently, almost typically,

---

*Something similar occurs of course with certain husbands, wives, and special friends who feel they are being loyal, helpful and somehow therapeutic by providing absolutely unqualified support and unlimited endorsement for painting others black—most commonly parents, grown-up children and ex-spouses—in the interest of appearing white oneself.

the two persons even have clashing views about who is doing and who is being done to!

Since there obviously are no "hitching posts" in human relationships, why, I began to ask, should we foster the illusion of them in psychotherapy? As my relativistic view of psychiatry deepened and I experienced how catalytic for a person's therapy it could be to have even a few "leveling" family consultations, it became my practice to do every reasonable thing within my power to help my patients grow beyond a destructive, mistaken, fixed-egocentric-"hitching-post" view of their relationship with their parents, with other family members, and with other people generally. Of all the interventions which might achieve this result, I believe none is so powerful as the use of direct observation and reality-oriented feedback within therapeutic social systems—couple, group and family. It is hard to overstate the power of seeing patients actually interact with family members who have shaped their lives and attitudes and whom they have previously spent hours describing and analyzing in individual and/or group therapy. The sophisticated psychotherapist who never meets with family members is, of course, not automatically taken in by patients' absolute thinking. However, even if the therapist escapes the error of partially "buying into" some of his or her patient's distortions, without actually meeting with the patient's family he can have no directly observed evidence for his view. He is left with very little therapeutic leverage to get patients to work through their distortions.

Family therapists and couple therapists have known this for decades. No couple therapist then or now would elect to treat an unhappy couple by doing therapy with the wife exclusively or the husband exclusively. And for many years, family therapists have been clamoring for the attention of psychotherapists, with gradually improving results, to get us to see the realism, the wisdom, and the strategic importance of seeing whole families, at least diagnostically, and of refusing to accept as simple truth the fiction of "the identified patient."

My own private practice, however, when I began it in 1965, was not composed of couples or families or "identified patients." On the contrary, as already mentioned, most of my professional effort then went into seeing people for "individual psychoanalytic psychotherapy." At that time, generally I did not take the initiative to create the opportunity to observe directly and *in vivo* the people I was working with individually while they were functioning within a social group.

Most of my first private patients had been referred by colleagues at the Harvard University Health Services, where I was then a Fellow;

accordingly, my early private patients for the most part were young adults, people who lived hundreds or thousands of miles away from their families. And, not only were they not coming to me as decompensated "identified patients," but they were functioning well enough to have been admitted to Harvard and to remain there. It therefore required strong conviction on my part to insist on having at least two or three or four opportunities to see some of these early patients together with their parents, because this necessarily involved believing and getting them to believe that it was "really worth it" to get family members to make a special trip of hundreds or thousands of miles for family consultations.

In the early years, I was able to justify this wish to have some data derived from the direct observation of the patient together with his or her family only in cases where there existed some compelling extenuating circumstance, such as a dangerous acute crisis. Later, after accumulating some experience in family consultations, I became emboldened by what I came to feel was their great value. In this way I gradually began to weave family consultations into my general therapeutic strategy and method; this meant, of course, that I had to work through the inevitable reluctance and resistance in order to have the benefit of directly observed data drawn from the social system which had generated both the patient's problem and the patient himself. Now it is not unusual for me to work actively to create an opportunity to do this with older patients (people in their thirties, forties or even fifties) and also with people who are functioning at a very high level in terms of their working life (scientists, physicians, professors, attorneys, executives, etc.).

HISTORICAL CONTEXT

Psychoanalysis was developed, refined, and expanded through intensive work with individuals; it deliberately avoided direct observational data about the social matrix within which individuals must live and function. It is, of course, true that in analysis and in individual psychoanalytic psychotherapy both an individual's current social matrix and the social matrix of his or her personal-historical development are scrutinized in great detail, with appropriate emphasis on tendencies to replicate painful aspects of the primary developmental matrix in the present. Always, however, this is retrospective—even for events in the very near past—and accomplished exclusively from the vantage point of, and even through the eyes of, the analysand. Data derived from directly observing the social matrix and/or from conjoint interviews with the patient together with those individuals who in aggregate comprise the matrix are not obtained.

Within individual psychotherapy or psychoanalysis the view of the therapist or analyst of course plays a role, but a limited one, in that he or she is permitted direct access only to data which have been filtered through the percepts and world-view of the patient. Further, since it is true that situationally everything—or everything except the transference—is retrospective, the therapist must content himself or herself with after-the-fact comments, clarifications and interpretations. With the sole difficult exception of observing the patient's social behavior in his or her interactions with the therapist, *the pure individual therapist has and can have no opportunity to observe and influence ongoing social behavior directly*.

Live data, drawn from live observation of the live interacting couple, the live interacting family, and/or an "artificial" but live interacting social group (as in group therapy), not only were not a part of the method of psychoanalysis, but until very recently in many quarters were rigidly proscribed, at least during the period of the analysis. The early behavior therapists based their techniques on "learning theory"; in general, both they and the founders of "learning theory" worked with individual organisms, not with mated pairs, families, or social groups. Thus both the early pioneers of psychoanalysis and those of learning theory and behavior therapy were steeped in work with individuals and were not accustomed to working with or thinking about social systems.

THE DELIBERATE CREATION OF A SOCIAL SYSTEM: GROUP THERAPY

When a biologist wants to know about the physiology of an organism, he engages in detailed observations of individuals, and then systematically alters variables in order to discover how the animal functions and maintains homeostatic balance. On the other hand, if he wants to know about the *behavior* of social animals, as for example wolves (9, 10), lions (11), or gorillas (12), he is obliged to seek out an opportunity to study social groups—extended families really—and the behavior of individuals within those groups; as with people, the natural adaptation of these animals occurs within a social group. Thus the biological scientist interested in behavior and/or in the "personality" of individual animals cannot simply study individuals; rather, he must find a family—a pack, a pride, or a band—and study how it functions, how individuals function within it and how they behave toward other family members, as well as toward members of alien families in the area.

If champanzees had been studied only individually, we would never

have learned much about grooming and mating, about nurturant, play-
ful, aggressive or communicative behaviors, about emotionally expressive behaviors or dominance/submission patterns, or, most relevant for
psychotherapists, about individual personalities. A biologist observing
only individual chimpanzees one by one as they interacted with him or
her, rather than directly observing individuals functioning naturally
within a social system (13), would obtain only a fraction of the information about the widely differing personalities of the individuals studied.

Observing one individual closely, including his interaction with the
observer, is the method of classical psychoanalysts and of individual
psychoanalytic psychotherapists. Directly observing individuals functioning within a larger and more nearly natural social system is the
method of group, couple and family therapists.

EPISTEMOLOGICAL ADVANTAGE

There is a large epistemological advantage accruing to the psychotherapist who creates the opportunity to observe his or her patient functioning within a social system. A therapy group is such a system.

The advantage referred to is no mere theoretical nicety; more often
it is of crucial importance in how the therapy situation unfolds, in that
it can enable a therapist to transcend blanket empathy, support and
endorsement for the socially dysfunctional patient, and to make accurate
behavioral "diagnoses" as to precisely what the unhappy person actually
does which "turns off" other people.

> Quite recently, a man in his mid-forties entered weekly individ-
> ual therapy with a colleague because he was in a chronically un-
> happy marriage and was getting divorced, but most of all because
> he felt that people didn't like him.
> On talking with him individually, one received the impression
> that he was both exceptionally bright and quite likeable. He had
> been an honors student throughout high school and college and
> held a doctoral degree in a scientific field. He had become a tenured
> professor in that field, then changed fields entirely, to an artistic
> field in which he also soon became eminently successful. Both the
> referring therapist and I liked this man very much from the time
> of the very first contact—and still like him. The patient's individual
> therapist, however, wisely referred the patient for concomitant
> group therapy.

During this man's first group meetings, both the referring therapist and I were surprised to have it as certain observed knowledge
that this bright, accomplished, versatile, polite, modest and un-
assuming man found a number of different ways to precipitate
controversy and anger toward himself and to become (initially at
least) the object of considerable dislike from several highly differing
people within his therapy group.

THERAPEUTIC ADVANTAGE

Between 1971 and 1973 I was extremely fortunate in having the opportunity to serve as the Chairman of an American Psychiatric Association Task Force on Behavior Therapy. The people who comprised the
Task Force were both M.D.s and Ph.D.s, and ranged from traditionally
trained clinicians to experienced behavior therapists and laboratory investigators of animal learning. Somewhat surprisingly, the Task Force
eventually achieved a true consensus (14). One of our most important
conclusions was this:

Group Therapy and Family Therapy: In Vivo Behavioral Shaping

Group therapy, with its *in vivo* display of habitual maladaptive
social behaviors, is an ideal medium in which to use therapist-
mediated social reinforcement as an agent for behavioral
change. . . . In group therapy and family therapy. . . , the therapist has the enormous practical advantage of seeing maladaptive
behavioral patterns unfold and develop *in vivo*. As a result, he can
shift his strategy from relatively weak techniques of attitude change
through verbal conditioning, and of "corrective" extinction of
emotional experiences, to a much more rapid and powerful
method, and one which is especially appropriate for patients whose
primary problems center around their relationships with others.
*Many patients have problems that involve habitual, subtle, maladaptive
interpersonal behaviors. Bringing them into a group or family setting
where they actually experience problems with other people can be extraor-
dinarily important and catalytic both diagnostically in terms of what the
patients' actual maladaptive behaviors are and therapeutically, because
these settings allow for the direct behavioral shaping of alternative modes
of behavior* (p. 39).

These ideas were not new to me, in that my first organized thoughts
along such lines were published in 1967 (2) and in 1971 (15); the Task
Force members, however, were an extremely stimulating group, and the
experience of working with them helped give me the courage to imple-

ment an idea that I had been incubating for about 10 years, since late 1961.

The idea I had had was to put some of these notions to a difficult clinical test by means of an intensive five-day-per-week therapy group to be composed of people who had had very extensive prior therapy in traditional psychoanalytic psychotherapy and/or psychoanalysis. Late in 1971 I finally began this group, with eight charter members. Between them the charter group members had had seven hospitalizations, four analyses lasting a total of 16 years, and a mean of 9.3 years (1038 hours) of prior therapy per person. One had been addicted to heroin and still sporadically used heroin, and three were seriously preoccupied with suicide when they began therapy. All eight considered their previous traditional psychoanalytic therapy to have been unsuccessful and were skeptical about what they might gain from still further therapy. Six of the eight were particularly skeptical about treatment in a group.

After the first 18 months I published a paper (16) describing the intensive group therapy treatment format and reporting that seven of the eight people treated had achieved moderate to marked success in treatment, as gauged by ratings which they made on themselves, as well as by group-peer ratings and therapist ratings. After the paper was written, one patient became worse and left the group prematurely against advice. On the other hand, another patient, who at the time the paper was written had to be considered a treatment failure, subsequently made some very dramatic gains and these have been maintained post-termination over a four-year period of follow-up. When this man entered the group, at age 40, after 2100 hours of treatment, he was meek, extremely lacking in confidence, and upset that he was "still a virgin." Also, he was markedly passive-aggressive, habitually late for work, and in danger of being fired. During his work in the group he dated and had sexual experiences with several women and had intercourse for the first time. Simultaneously, he made an important invention out of which he was able to create a desirable new job for himself within which he could refine his invention. After leaving treatment, he married and has remained married to a woman he respects and likes. He has also prospered in his career—he has been granted about six patents and recently has had still another major professional promotion.

What was the source of all this therapeutic leverage? In my opinion, the major source was the use of the group setting as an "artificial" but therapeutically powerful social system within which a therapist who was sophisticated both psychodynamically and behaviorally could function, *as a part of the social system,* first to achieve a relatively precise understanding of what the relevant maladaptive behaviors were, and second, once he understood them, to change them, directly, by behavioral shaping, *while the behaviors were actually going on*:

> As is well-known by behavior therapists, the most effective and efficient method for eliminating maladaptive behavior is to isolate it *in vivo*: to point out, label it, and punish it while at the same time systematically reinforcing alternative, increasingly adaptive modes of behavior. Within a group setting maladaptive social behaviors easily become conspicuous target symptoms. As the other group members begin to understand and imitate the therapist's actions, these target behaviors become especially responsive to group interactional pressures. (Previously these target behaviors served exclusively as defenses, maintained by negative reinforcement—that is, by the contingent avoidance or reduction of painful feelings.)
>
> Interrupting these behavioral patterns by punishment (mere exposure or negative comment) and focusing on them elicits a feeling linked to the behavior and leads to group examination of the analytic origins of the particular feeling-behavior liaison—an insight in the psychoanalytic sense that serves to potentiate behavioral change . . .
>
> One of the key elements in (this) approach to intensive group therapy is individualized behavioral diagnosis. For each patient in the group the therapist arrives at a precise, fine-grained description of one or two pivotal maladaptive behaviors actually operative and observable within the group. When these target behaviors are interrupted and thus exposed, the associative group process works to uncover the meaning underlying them—that is, the basic, faulty world-view/feeling-disorder in the context of which the behaviors appear to make sense. If the choice of key target maladaptive behaviors is a correct one (correct behavioral diagnosis), if the punishment is sufficient to interrupt and suppress the habitual maladaptive pattern, and if the chosen alternative reinforced behavior is truly more adaptive in the real world outside the group, the new behavior will permanently replace the old. In behavioral terms, this happens because the new behavior successfully competes with the old behavior inasmuch as it "works better" and brings more reinforcement (16, pp. 11-12).

FURTHER WORK WITH "INTENSIVE" GROUPS

At the time I presented the results of the first 18 months of experience with this group, a number of the therapists listening speculated that part of its unusual success might have had to do with insights, analytic sophistication, and self-understanding gained in their prior therapy but not "worked through" successfully. I'm convinced now by my subsequent experience that they were right. Altogether, with new patients coming in as others terminated, several dozen people have now been treated in this same group, and those who have had prior psychoanalysis or extensive psychotherapy have tended to do somewhat better than those who have not. In particular, they have tended to be more tenacious about persevering in treatment until they were ready to terminate. A significant number of people without extensive prior therapy have terminated prematurely, usually within the first six months. The "loss rate" for such people has been about 30 percent vs. 0 percent for the charter members, and near 0 percent for subsequent members with a great deal of prior therapy. On the whole, however, clinical results with this treatment method have continued to be good to very good. Furthermore, as the reader might have suspected, "intensive" has proved a relative term, in group therapy as in classical psychoanalysis. I have experimented with essentially similar groups that meet four, three, and two times weekly. Twice weekly seems to be much more powerful and "intensive" than once weekly. And, whereas two, three or four times weekly sessions seem to be very similar, moving from four to five times weekly also seems to add significantly to "intensiveness" and therapeutic power. I also continue to see many patients in groups that meet once weekly but which utilize the same concepts and methodology.

Whether the groups meet five times weekly or once weekly, what sets them apart from traditional psychoanalytic therapy groups is that there is a primary reliance on the group as a social system within which maladaptive behaviors can be directly observed, precisely specified, and directly changed, by direct operant conditioning and behavioral shaping.

In these groups the therapist consciously and systematically employs operant conditioning and behavioral shaping in order to modify *directly* those interpersonal, communicative, and emotional patterns which the therapist, the patient and the group can agree are "maladaptive." (Within the group, consensus about which behaviors need modification, and in what direction, usually develops within weeks or, at most, months.) Thus, operant conditioning is treated as an absolutely primary therapeutic mechanism. When a therapist functions in this way, he is clearly doing something very different from what the leader of a traditional psychoanalytic psychotherapy group does. Although the differences are much less stark, he is also doing something different, at least in explicit emphasis, from what more broadly-based eclectic group therapists tend to do intuitively. Yalom, whose approach to group therapy is much broader than a purely psychoanalytic one, in his excellent and deservedly influential book *The Theory and Practice of Group Psychotherapy* (17), makes the following point:

Considerable evolution in psychoanalytic technique has occurred over the last half century, but until recently certain basic principles regarding the role of transference in psychoanalytic therapy have endured with relatively little change:

1. Analysis of transference is the major therapeutic task of the therapist;
2. Since the development (and, then, the resolution) of transference is crucial, it is important that the therapist facilitate its development by concealing his real self so that the patient can encloak him in transference much as he might dress a clothing store mannequin (this is, of course, the rationale behind the traditional "blank screen" role of the analyst).
3. The most important type of interpretation the therapist can make is one which clarifies some aspect of transference (Strachey's "mutative interpretation").

Within the past few years, however, many analysts have perceptibly shifted their position as they have recognized the importance of other factors in the therapeutic process. For example, a lead article in the *International Journal of Group Psychotherapy** by a prominent analyst stated: "Psychoanalysts have begun, in general, to feel more free to enter into active communicative exchanges with patients instead of remaining bound to the incognito 'neutral mirror' model of relative silence and impassivity." He continues by pointing out that therapy is a learning process wherein patients acquire new models of thinking, feeling, and behavior:

Moreover, these new models are not always achieved cognitively and consciously; as often as not they are acquired subtly, as a result of overt or covert suggestion, unconscious identification with the therapist, corrective emotional experiences in the interaction with him, and a kind of operant conditioning via implicit or explicit expressions of his approval or disapproval. In this process, the nature and quality of the patient-therapist interaction, the real personalities of both patient and doctor, and the degree of faith, hope, trust, and motivation that the patient brings to the therapeutic situation are of paramount importance in enabling the new learning to take place successfully.

Few would quarrel with the importance of the development, appreciation, and resolution of transference in individual dynamically oriented therapy. What is at issue, however, is the priority of the transference work relative to other curative factors in the

---

*I. W. Graham: Observations on Analytic Group Therapy. International Journal of Group Psychotherapy. Vol. 9, 150-157, 1959.

therapeutic process. *The problem is a substantial one since the tasks are not complementary but, to an extent, mutually exclusive—the therapist cannot focus his attention solely upon transference and at the same time hope to utilize the large number of other potential curative factors* (pp. 192-93, italic added).

On this latter point especially, I agree completely with Yalom.

Like Yalom, I also believe that there are quite a number of other "curative factors" in group therapy, in addition to operant conditioning *and* the analysis of transference feelings. In many clinical situations these other factors may be *at least* as important as analyzing the transference. These other factors include cognitive recognition of self-defeating patterns; "insights" in general; grieving, when this is needed; the slow progressive extinction of learned fears of people, or women, or men, or of façade-free communication; "corrective emotional experiences" involving people in the group, including but by no means limited to experiences with the therapist; and, finally, identifications with the therapist and with other group members in various ways. In addition, like Yalom (and obviously like psychoanalytic group leaders), I know full well how important it can be for some patients to work through transference feelings excited by the therapist or by other group members. In fact, almost every group therapist would probably agree that the elicitation of multiple transferences provided by the group setting constitutes a very major advantage of group over individual psychotherapy.

However, a therapist who is not only broad-based in his view of "the curative factors of group therapy" but who is also behaviorally oriented will consider it his first and foremost responsibility *in every group meeting* to pay attention to what behaviors each member is emitting and which of these are maladaptive. Using all the experience and learned art at his disposal,* he will then give first priority to maximizing the chances that within the group non-neurotic adaptive behaviors are reinforced while

---

*The therapist also tries to promote adaptive behavioral sequences over maladaptive ones by the systematic conscious use of "discriminative stimuli." These are used to enhance the probability of a favorable response which then can be reinforced once a discriminative stimulus has successfully "set the stage" for the response to occur. Although at first the therapist will be very liberal in his use of discriminative stimuli to influence behavior which can then be reinforced, he will use "stimulus fading" to reduce progressively reliance on the use of discriminative stimuli. In this way adaptive behaviors occur gradually with less and less prompting, and finally occur completely "autonomously," which is to say supported only by the natural consequences of the behaviors themselves. (For those readers who need to be reminded about what exactly constitutes a discriminative stimulus, I suggest review of the last chapter of the primer on behavior therapy recommended earlier (14).)

maladaptive behaviors not only go unreinforced, but are instead followed by punishment, and at least on occasion actually interrupted by punishment. (Optimally, the punishment comes primarily from other group members but may come from the therapist to the extent this proves necessary.) Needless to say, all these tasks needed to implement a behavioral treatment strategy require a good deal of moment-to-moment monitoring and attention. In the group work itself, it is the therapist's commitment to attempt to do this, not to the exclusion of, but, in terms of priorities, *before all other matters*, which is what distinguishes this approach from the related therapeutic stance advocated by Yalom in which "interpersonal learning" and even "a kind of operant conditioning" are acknowledged to be of some importance, but are not accorded such explicit and systematic emphasis.

Another matter of very great importance which distinguishes the approach being advocated in this chapter from what most experienced eclectic group psychotherapists do is the emphasis on the flexible use of a relevant variety of social systems in working with troubled people. In other words, a troubled person is seen not just in one social system—like a therapy group, which is a collection of unrelated peers—but also in the other social systems, or combinations of systems, which are relevant to him or her. That is, a person may be seen regularly in group therapy, while also being seen periodically or regularly in dyadic couples work with his spouse, and while also being seen for family consultations over the course of therapy for relevant work with his parents, and/or with his children, and/or his children plus their spouses, and/or his in-laws, and so on. *The point is that the therapist follows the clinical data wherever they may lead him in terms of relevant social systems.*

THE CREATION OF A SPECIALLY DESIGNED SOCIAL SYSTEM FOR
HOMOSEXUAL MEN: GROUP PSYCHOTHERAPY WITH
MALE/FEMALE CO-THERAPISTS

People who are homosexual comprise a group as diverse as people who are heterosexual. Of those who come to psychotherapists for treatment, many come for problems unrelated to their sexual preference. For them, my approach to treatment is no different from what it would be for a heterosexual person with a comparable life problem.

Some others come because of sexual or other dyadic problems occurring in the context of a relatively stable and satisfying same-sexed couple relationship. For them, of course, sex therapy and/or couple therapy is what is needed.

Some other homosexual people, however, come because of a genuine wish to broaden their lives to include the pleasures of sexual intimacy with the opposite sex and/or because they wish to open up the possibility for themselves of marriage, children, and family life. My own experience in working as a therapist with homosexual people who are in this latter category has been very predominantly weighted toward work with men rather than women. For this reason, I will focus here on my experience of working with homosexual men who came to me interested in "heterosexual shift," by which I mean not a total metamorphosis, but a definitively effective broadening of a person's ability to enjoy sex and intimacy with persons of the opposite sex.

Most homosexual men who come with treatment goals of this kind have experienced particular distortions in their own primary developmental social systems, their own families. Usually they have been chronically exposed to a situation in which emotional closeness to the man (their fathers) was virtually always at the expense of continued closeness with the woman (their mothers). As Bieber (18) has documented, the mothers tend to be "close-binding-intimate" persons, with very strained relationships with their husbands and with unmet needs of their own which they tend to try to fill by means of an unusual and exclusive allegiance with their sons. The exclusiveness of the "close-binding-intimate" allegiance which such mothers need and seek apparently prompts them to undermine the father in the eyes of the son and to punish in the son—sometimes subtly, sometimes quite baldly—any nascent tendency to identify with his father or to become closer to the father emotionally.

In 1966, I began working with homosexual men having an interest in heterosexual shift within a social system which was intentionally structured to replicate triangular aspects of the social matrix in which the patient grew up. It was my belief at the time that it would be very useful to do the therapy within a social system of this kind. I felt it might afford the patient a sort of "corrective emotional experience"—that is, an *in vivo* desensitization—in the area of his being able to have a close triangular relationship with a man (the male therapist) and a woman (the female therapist) at the same time. In the therapeutic situation, usually quite unlike the situation in the patient's family of origin, the patient is afforded a new experience in which he can be emotionally close to the man (the male therapist) without experiencing threats, punishment, scorn, or withdrawal from the woman (the female therapist), who, also usually quite unlike the patient's own mother, works cooperatively and respectfully with the man rather than undermining the man and the patient's nascent identifications with and attempts to become closer to the man. During therapy within this purposely structured social system, the patient can learn to discriminate between this new woman and his own original female object, his mother. In addition, the patient can eventually learn to discriminate between this new man/woman team and his own father and mother. It is this discriminative learning that, in fact, really constitutes the specific "corrective emotional experience" which is afforded by doing the therapy within such a social system (19).

Within this special social system, what behaviors do the therapists choose to enhance by social reinforcement,* and to promote through modeling and through the progressive process of *in vivo* operant shaping?

First, like nearly all other experienced therapists of all theoretical persuasions they model and selectively reinforce certain modes of behavior which have widely generalized if not universal adaptive value: honest recognition and conscious acceptance of feelings (vs. unconscious "acting out" of feelings), genuine façade-free communication with other people, appropriate assertiveness, coming to be able to see (or remember) one's own family of origin in historical perspective, yet without having to blur any of the deep and frequently conflicted feelings toward family members, coming to be able to deal with other people in the here-and-now with empathy, honesty, and when possible, generosity, and finally, becoming able to face constructively the finiteness of life and the inevitability of one's own death. Beyond this, in these particular groups they also reinforce other particular behaviors which in the author's opinion frequently have special or unusual adaptive value for this particular group of human beings. This is not an exhaustive list, but among these particular behaviors felt to be of special adaptive value, and therefore singled out for selective reinforcement, the following would have to be included:

1) Both therapists reinforce attention to the personal side of sexual relationships, male or female. For example, if there is someone with whom the patient is living and/or experiencing sex, or to whom he is attracted, both therapists are immediately and continuingly interested in the personal side of this: What

---

*By social reinforcement, I mean any active participation on the part of the therapist which serves to encourage or deepen a line of thought or a direction of feeling. Operationally, social reinforcement gestures can be as "simple" as interested looks or nods, or as complicated as evocative interpretations or clarifications.

is his/her name? What is he/she like? Is he/she caring and thoughtful, or impersonal and uninvolved? Or is he/she actually destructive and exploitative?

2) Both therapists attempt to model a free, open and nonjudgmental attitude toward sex, whether between people of the same sex or of the opposite sex, and to model and reinforce the attitude that sexual pleasure is in itself good. As a corollary of this, relevant details of sexual interactions, homosexual, heterosexual, or masturbatory, are openly discussed. Nearly all group members are initially at least a little inhibited about some of the details—as have been all the therapists initially—but with many repetitions, the fears and inhibitions undergo extinction, and gradually both therapists and patients become freer. Many times the therapists elect to reinforce discussion of constructive wholesome homosexual experiences because they represent a shift away from guilt and/or isolation toward pleasure and a real person.

3) Both therapists try to model and reinforce viewing men and women as people first, with good and bad qualities, and as sexual partners second.

4) Both therapists try to help group members to discriminate between exploitative and nonexploitative people and relationships. Obviously, as in psychotherapy with heterosexual people, often this necessarily involves analyzing and working through underlying masochistic wishes.

5) Both therapists try to break down the often-false, self-protective black-and-white dichotomizing of self and others into "gay" or "straight." In other words, group members are reinforced for acknowledging fully *all* their conscious sexual feelings and fantasies: more often than not, though not certainly in every case, most group members, even those who are Kinsey 6 behaviorally, have at least some heterosexual feelings concealed within their operating concepts of themselves as purely and simply "gay."

6) Both therapists reinforce patients for trying to analyze what neurotic elements there may be in their homosexual urges, and also in their heterosexual behaviors. Some patients learn that they seek an anonymous homosexual outlet when very angry, or when afraid of some recent success. Several pedophiles have learned that the powerful urge for sex with a young boy for them has to do with a wholesome though misdirected wish to escape from the stodgy thoroughly unplayful conservatism of their parent(s) generalized onto all adults. Not a few group members who begin zealous "to go straight" or "become nor-

mal" need to be prodded into and then reinforced for an examination of the neurotic elements that drive them toward
compulsive pseudoheterosexual behaviors.
7) For those group members who do have or discover some
genuine elements of conscious heterosexual interest, both therapists reinforce experimentation in relationships with men *and*
women.
8) Both therapists try to reinforce movement toward healthier
relationships with less exploitative human beings, whether
those human beings happen to be men or women (19).

Turning to the results of doing therapy within such a specially designed social system, the following can be said: Over the past 13 years,
about 100 men have been treated in this way. Approximately 50 percent
of them valued the therapeutic experience enough to remain involved
in treatment within this specially designed social system for two and a
half years or more. Almost all of them considered their therapy to have
been very valuable in one way or another or else they would not have
continued in it.

Of the group who did persevere in this treatment, 29 were exclusively
homosexual at the time they began therapy and had never once experienced heterosexual intercourse prior to therapy. Of these 29, 15 were
only mildly or ambivalently interested in heterosexual shift as a goal,
and 14 were very strongly interested in achieving a heterosexual shift.
In terms of the new emergence of heterosexual behavior, 18 of 26 (69
percent) of these men achieved a heterosexual shift; for 11 men, the
heterosexual shift was "solid" enough that they married and remained
married. Almost all of these 11 men have one or more children.

Parenthetically, and not really surprisingly, there was a very large
difference between the group who began treatment with only an ambivalent or mild interest in a heterosexual shift vs. the group who began
with a stronger interest in heterosexual shift. Of the group strongly
interested in heterosexual shift, purely in terms of the new emergence
of heterosexual behaviors 14 of 14 achieved a heterosexual shift! Ten of
these 14 (71 percent) achieved a "solid" heterosexual shift which has
already led to a lasting marriage. On the other hand, for those patients
who were more ambivalent about interest in heterosexual shift as a goal,
only four of 15 achieved a shift, and only one of 15 (7 percent) achieved
a "solid" and lasting shift.

WORKING WITHIN NATURAL SOCIAL SYSTEMS: FAMILY THERAPY,
COUPLE AND SEX THERAPY

Family Therapy

The family is a truly natural social system. A family includes potentially all the significant persons who make up, or have made up in the past, the evaluative and distributive system of reward and punishment which served in some cases to generate, in other cases to shape or maintain, most of the behavioral patterns—adaptive and maladaptive—which comprise the total behavioral repertoire or manifest personality of each member of the immediate family.

There are two important strategic maneuvers which the family therapist can make in order to facilitate the development of truth-seeking, cooperative behaviors and the replacement of old, dependent, stifling, distancing or scapegoating patterns. Diagnosis and treatment begin almost simultaneously, for the family therapist can use the data collected during the initial, history-taking interview both to promote insight in the form of a generally consistent retrospective account which reflects the perspectives of all family members, and to point out, interrupt and shape the immediate interactional patterns elicited by the interviewer. In other words, the family therapist is operating with directly observable data of two kinds: 1) reflecting the attitudinal or interpretational style of each family member, and 2) evincing typical intrafamilial behavioral patterns.

The family history which is gradually developed by all the family members serves to expose the differences in perspective and interpretation which each individual brings to the account of a shared reality. An early goal, both diagnostically and therapeutically, is corroboration by all family members of a retrospective reconstruction of their common history; anything short of such a corroborated account creates a mounting pressure on all involved, the reduction of which, when skillfully handled by the therapist, serves as a negative reinforcement for cooperative, truth-seeking behaviors.

(It may be wise here to remind the reader that, despite wide misuse of the term, negative reinforcement is not synonymous with punishment. Rather, it is an ongoing stimulus situation which —because it is "negative"—when ended serves to reinforce the immediately preceding responses. Thus negative reinforcement increases the frequency of responses while punishment decreases their frequency.)

A later goal of family therapy is the exposure and elimination of troublesome interactional patterns: father-son, mother-father, parents-children, sibling-sibling, and so on. In order to expose to view the focal problem area, the therapist should arrange to interview the family in various combinations. For example, he will see the parents alone, the children alone, the mother and the children, and the father and the children, as well as seeing the whole family all together. In some cases, he will elect to meet with the youngest children only, and to exclude deliberately, although temporarily, the oldest one or two siblings. This is often necessary because it is not rare for the oldest siblings to function as silence-enforcers or agents provocateurs for the younger siblings. Direct behavioral shaping strategies, employed by the therapist and gradually learned by family members, when applied to the problem interactional patterns that emerge *in vivo*, move the family as a unit toward the replacement of painful, perpetually angry, evasive or self-isolating behavioral ruts with warm, frank, autonomy-seeking-and-granting interactional patterns (8, pp. 57-9).

Couple and Sex Therapy

Married couples or unmarried but mated couples comprise a natural dyadic social system. In all cases, however, each member of the couple brings to the relationship "baggage" derived from the social system of his or her own developmental matrix, the family of origin. In addition, even though a couple may seek therapy primarily because of difficulties between them, if they have natural or adopted children, the situation intrinsically is still more complicated. Thus it very often may make sense in the treatment of individual couples to supplement the primary therapeutic work with the dyadic social system, the couple, with family consultations involving families of origin, or the children, or both. This seems to make sense when there are specific problems which the couple has which affect the children directly or which can be seen to be derived in part from difficulties that one spouse has with his or her own parents or in-laws.

If either member of the couple presents with a frank sexual dysfunction, such as a partial or absolute inhibition of sexual arousal or of orgasm, or with either of the hyperexcitatory dysfunctions, premature ejaculation or vaginismus, whatever couple therapy may also be needed, it is essential also to work with the couple in sex therapy. Not to do so, given the brevity and success rate of modern sex therapy techniques

(20-22), constitutes, in my opinion at least, inexcusably bad clinical management.

At the core of sex therapy is, of course, the basic behavioral strategem of using a competitive response, sensual and sexual pleasure, to displace and supplant maladaptive responses such as anxiety, shame, guilt, embarrassment, fear, "spectatoring" or "monitoring." As in many other behavioral treatment paradigms, desensitization is accomplished very gradually by means of a series of experiential "tasks" which need to be fun, not work. These are prescribed or assigned by the therapist to the couple at a controlled pace which allows assimilation, desensitization, and genuine pleasure. In the case of premature ejaculation, the principal therapeutic mechanism is one of training or retraining the man to focus on his own erotic sensations, rather than falling into the pattern of consciously or unconsciously denying them. In this way, a man can learn to pace the amount of incoming sensory stimulation occurring during intercourse so that he can learn to have reliably the capacity to remain at a level of arousal below the level of reflex ejaculatory inevitability. Initially, mild punishment may be needed to forestall ejaculation and permit the new learning of a capacity for paced stimulation. Most often the punishment is in the form of temporarily stopping pleasurable stimulation. In more demanding and intransigent clinical situations, punishment may be used in the form of the "squeeze technique."

Sex therapists do not actually observe directly the sexual interactions of couples they treat. In this way they are at a disadvantage behaviorally in comparison to group, family and couple therapists, who *can* directly observe the problematic responses they need to help patients to modify. Thus, sex therapists must cope with this disadvantage in much the same manner that traditional individual psychotherapists must do all their work—they must meticulously inquire about and painstakingly reconstruct the details of relevant interactions. Unlike individual therapists, however, and advantageously for them, sex therapists do this for an explicit practical purpose—so that they can assign appropriate experiential tasks for the week to come.

In couple therapy not involving sexual dysfunction, the therapist can have the enormous advantage which individual therapists do not have and which group and family therapists do have: *the advantage of working directly within the problematic social system.* In this way, the therapist can directly observe adaptive and maladaptive interactions. In addition to using cognitively mediated interpretations, the therapist can employ the much more powerful strategy of direct behavioral shaping to modify problematic responses.

In cases where couple therapy is indicated, it has been my experience that I can learn much more about the individuals who comprise a couple, and about the dyadic functioning of the couple, if I am able to afford myself the opportunity to observe directly each member of the couple participating in a same-sexed therapy group and also am able to observe the couple interacting with other couples in a group of husband-wife pairs. Good couple therapy depends on knowing each individual in the couple as well as possible. Just as it would be impossible for a biologist to know as much about individual chimpanzees by studying only one chimpanzee at a time, it is impossible for the couple therapist to know the individuals who comprise one-half of a couple he or she is working with as well as the person could be known if there were an opportunity to observe the same individual relating to a group of peers. In a parallel way, I find I can get to know a couple as a dyadic system much better by seeing how they behave with other couples than I can by meeting with them alone. Almost universally, in working with couples in a couples group, the comparison and contrast phenomena in various attitudes and behaviors are enormously helpful to the therapist and to the couples themselves. All of these thoughts have led me to invent a treatment method for couple therapy which over the past eight years has become my strongly preferred mode in tackling difficult problems with couples.

As the reader might have surmised from the foregoing, the method involves getting together about five or six couples for a period of about two and a half hours. For roughly the first 45 minutes I meet with the men as a therapy group while the women meet in an adjacent room in a leaderless group. (One week I meet first with the men and the next week first with the women.) During approximately the next 60 minutes, I meet together with all the men and all the women for a therapy group composed of all five or six of the couples. This particular combination of meetings, which, for want of a more elegant name, I refer to as "group-group-group," not only allows the therapist to work with an individual couple as a dyadic social system, but also allows each person and each couple to be observed and worked with from within two social systems, one of same-sexed-peers, and one of couple-peers.

In addition to this, the "group-group-group" has some other important advantages:

> 1) the facilitation of more genuine same-sexed friendships, which in turn seems to promote progress in the couple work;

2) the powerful effects of peer interpretation (particularly same-sexed peer interpretation);

3) the handling of "secrets"* within a couple; and

4) the creation of a therapeutic pressure toward the forging of a consistent account of the couple's history and current function: who has done what to whom, and who still does what to whom, and why and how.

Over the past nine years five of us** have led a total of seven such groups. In aggregate, we have treated well over 50 couples (100 individuals). When we are able to work through the often strong resistances to such a "public" form of therapy, we have been quite impressed with the efficacy of the group-group-group as compared to dyadic couple therapy.

WORKING WITH MEMBERS OF THE DEVELOPMENTAL SOCIAL SYSTEM TO CATALYZE WORK WITH INDIVIDUALS

Individuals, in my opinion at least, are *usually* more treatable if the therapist can work with them within a social system such as a therapy group. In specific cases, however, I do elect to do the primary work with some individuals in one-to-one therapy. In either case, whether I see an individual in group therapy or in individual therapy, as the process unfolds, if it goes well, the patient talks a lot and with great feeling about his mother, his father, his siblings, and often other important figures in his development. Very often the important people live in scattered places and at great distances. As mentioned at the outset, however, I have found it useful in many cases to arrange to meet with the patient together with other important members of his or her family.

I usually do not present this idea until the patient is well launched into an affective description of family members. At such a point I will often say something like, "Well, why don't you get your father to come in—then we can talk to him directly about all of this . . ." The therapist's

*For example, when one partner has had an affair, it may or may not be important and productive to discuss this at a particular time in the couple work. On the other hand, if one partner is actively pursuing a still covert affair, this creates a situation which usually seems to call for disclosure, even though this may be very painful unless full and prompt resolution can somehow occur. The same-sexed therapy groups in practice have proved to be very wise in their judgment about such "secrets" so that when a person's same-sexed group as a whole decides that he or she really needs to talk about a matter of this kind, they typically exert a very strong and usually effective pressure to that effect.

**Rosalind Barnett, Ph.D., Ann Birk, Ph.D., William Huddleston, Psy.D. candidate, and Stephen Schoonover, M.D.

making such a suggestion, provided it is done in a timely and judicious way, in my experience usually leads to an immediate sense of both exhilaration and disbelief. Patients typically respond with excitement at the suggestion, but simultaneously with a denial, for example: "That would be really something . . . *that* would really be the day! . . . Of course, he/she would *never* come. . . ."

If, after making the suggestion, the therapist follows it up assiduously and continues to inquire about it often, week after week, the general effect seems to be to deepen the patient's sense of the immediacy, relevance and power of the therapeutic process. Even in those cases where the parent or sibling or child indeed *does* adamantly refuse to come, which is rare, the therapeutic process seems to have been facilitated and rendered much more vivid and meaningful at the therapist's serious suggestion that this should be done despite obstacles of geography, resistance and inherent difficulty in the subject matter.*

It is not rare for it to be useful to see more than one family member together with a primary patient:

> A brilliant, but chronically unhappy and work-inhibited scientist in his forties entered intensive group therapy. During his early work in the group, he was able to disengage successfully from a rather long relationship with a woman whose attentions he had found gratifying but stifling. Despite his great versatility and brilliance, some months before he began therapy he had quit his job with a feeling of righteous protest, ostensibly because of his anti-war feelings. He did this, however, with anger of such intensity that it was clear that not all his feelings had to do with his philosophical pacifism.
>
> After this patient had succeeded in extricating himself from the problematic relationship with the woman he had been living with, he floundered for many months, using up his savings and getting himself in a worse and worse position professionally, all while ostensibly attempting to find himself a new job. Throughout a period of many months he was consciously attempting to get himself a job. During this period he appeared to be thoroughly "stuck"; he was spending enormous energy in perfectionistically drafting and sending out hundreds of resumes, all of which came to naught, while the content of his therapy vacillated between superficiality

---

*In a very recent case for example I had the opportunity to meet with the wife and one of the sister-in-laws of my primary patient, a current patient in the "intensive" group, in order to open up for the first time between these two sisters the subject of their father's incestuous behavior toward each of them during their adolescent years.

(many details of his frustrations in looking for another professional position), and unmanageable depth (his very great anger at his father, whom he described in terms which were almost totally negative). He felt that his father was "totally self-absorbed. . . ; he just doesn't give a damn about anyone, including me, my mother and my brother . . . and never has. . . ." Among other sins, he held his father responsible for a suicidal attempt his mother had made many years before, following the parents' separation and divorce some years after he had left home.

Despite the fact that his father lived in Detroit, his brother in California, and his mother in Louisiana, and despite the fact that his parents had been divorced for more than 10 years, I felt that it might be crucially important to meet with the other family members. The patient's reaction when I first proposed this was the standard one which I have described, but he was one of the most certain people that I have ever seen that his father would *never* come for such a consultation. After a good many weeks of working this matter through, the patient finally decided to accept my suggestion that he write to his father, to invite him to come to Boston for a consultation—several meetings together with the patient and me. After some delay, the father, also a scientist, responded with a two-page single-spaced letter which was explicitly intended as a summary of everything that was important about his son that any doctor might ever want to know about him, in lieu of the requested family consultation! This, of course, fueled the fires of the patient's anger at his father still further.

I reassured the patient that in almost every case parents will come eventually if they are asked and continue to be asked in a serious way. Eventually and without great difficulty, I did also have the opportunity to meet separately with the patient and his brother, as well as with the patient and his mother. As hoped, both these consultations were helpful.

The crucial intervention, however, as predicted, proved to be actually meeting together with him and his father. When his father finally did come, I was able to facilitate in our first meeting the patient's candidly expressing his anger directly to the father about the same things he had discussed in the group. By the middle of the second hour with the father, the patient began to be able to listen to how the situation, especially with his mother and the marriage, had looked to his father. Most important of all, the patient was deeply and directly touched by his father's obvious concern for him and his willingness to travel in his seventies to meet with him and me and to talk about these old and unpleasant matters. *The patient himself could directly see his father's caring and concern for him*. This I believe was the crucial element in the whole series of consultations with the brother, the mother and the father.

This seemed to free the patient from his angry, perfectionistic and competitive impasse—remember, his father was in the same line of work—in his efforts to get himself another job. As a result, soon thereafter he began working again. Beyond this both he and his father were extremely moved at the opportunity to be closer to each other than they had ever been before. Although some other aspects of this patient's treatment were not entirely resolved, this positive gain proved durable.

* * *

Psychotherapy is or should be an art based on science. As every committed therapist knows, it can also at times be both a profoundly human and creative process. Psychotherapy which goes beyond retrospective narration, and which emphasizes direct here-and-now behavioral observation and intervention—that is, psychotherapy within social systems—can be an even more powerful and thrilling experience for the therapist, and for the patient can lead to a much clearer perception of the relativity which is an intrinsic characteristic of interpersonal reality, as well as to demonstrably better treatment outcomes.

REFERENCES

1. Birk, L.: Social reinforcement in psychotherapy. *Conditional Reflex, A Pavlovian Journal of Research and Therapy*, 3:2, 116-123, 1968.
2. Shapiro, D. and Birk, C. L.: Group therapy in experimental perspective. *Int. J. Group Psychother.* 17:2, 211-224, 1967.
3. Birk, L.: Behavior therapy—Integration with dynamic psychiatry. *Behavior Therapy*, 1:4, 522-526, 1970.
4. Birk, L.: Psychoanalytic omniscience and behavioral omnipotence: Current trends in psychotherapy. *Seminars in Psychiatry*, IV:2, 113-120, 1972.
5. Birk, L.: Psychoanalysis and behavioral analysis: Natural resonance and complementarity. *Int. J. Psychiatry*, 11:2, 160-166, 1973.
6. Birk, L., and Brinkley-Birk, A.: Psychoanalysis and behavior therapy. *Amer. J. Psychiatry*, 131:5, 499-510, 1974.
7. Birk, L.: Behavior therapy and behavioral psychotherapy. In *The Harvard Guide to Modern Psychiatry*, A. M. Nicholi, Jr. (Ed.), Cambridge, MA.: The Belknap Press of Harvard University Press, 1978.
8. Birk, L., and Brinkley-Birk, A.: The learning therapies. In *Overview of the Psychotherapies*. G. Usdin (Ed.), New York: Brunner/Mazel, 1975, pp. 51-67.
9. Mech, L. D.: *The Wolf: The Ecology and Behavior of an Endangered Species*. New York: Natural History Press, 1970.
10. Allen, D. L.: *Wolves of Minong: Their Vital Role in a Wild Community*. Boston: Houghton Mifflin, 1979.
11. Bertram, B.: *Pride of Lions*. New York: Charles Scribner's Sons, 1978.

12. Schaller, G.: *The Year of the Gorilla*. Chicago: University of Chicago Press, 1964.
13. van Lawick-Goodall, J.: *In the Shadow of Man*. Boston: Houghton Mifflin, 1971.
14. Birk, L., Stolz, S., Brady, J. P., Brady, J. V., Lazarus, A., Lynch, J., Rosenthal, A., Skelton, W. D., Stevens, J., and Thomas, E.: *Behavior Therapy in Psychiatry*, American Psychiatric Association Task Force Report. pp. 1-75, July, 1973.
15. Guttmacher, J. and Birk, L.: Group therapy: What specific therapeutic advantages? *Comprehensive Psychiatry*, 12:6, 1971.
16. Birk, L.: Intensive group therapy: An effective behavioral-psychoanalytic method. *Amer. J. Psychiatry*, 131:1, 11-16, 1974.
17. Yalom, I. D.: *The Theory and Practice of Group Psychotherapy*. (Second Edition). New York: Basic Books.
18. Bieber, I., Dain, H. J., Dince, P. R., Drellich, M. G., Grand, H. G., Gundlach, R. H., Kremer, M. W., Rifkin, A. H., Wilbur, C. B., and Bieber, T. B.: *Homosexuality*. New York: Basic Books, 1962.
19. Birk, L.: The myth of classic homosexuality: The view of a behavioral psychotherapist. In: *Sexual Inversion*, (Second Edition). Boston: Little, Brown, 1979.
20. Kaplan, H. S.: *The New Sex Therapy: Active Treatment of Sexual Dysfunctions*. New York: Brunner/Mazel, 1974.
21. Birk, A.: Sex therapy: A behavioral approach. In: *The Harvard Guide to Modern Psychiatry*. A. Nicholi, Jr. (Ed.). Cambridge, MA.: The Belknap Press of Harvard University Press, pp. 459-470, 1979.
22. Birk, L.: Shifting gears in treating psychogenic sexual dysfunction: Medical assessment, sex therapy, psychotherapy and couple therapy. In: *"Sexuality Issue" Psychiatric Clinics of North America*, J. K. Meyer (Ed.), 1980.

Chapter 8

Contract and Alliance in the Supervision of Psychotherapy

Christopher Gordon, M.D., and Edward Messner, M.D.

For both supervisor and student, supervision of psychotherapy can be gratifying or grueling, a satisfying experience of growth or a frustrating struggle. For the teacher, supervision may be a time of sharing didactic and clinical knowledge, of fostering the development of a colleague, and of growing self-esteem; or supervision may be as exasperating as trying to teach someone to repair a machine one has never seen, over the telephone with a bad connection! And for the student, the experience may be a time of growing understanding, or acquiring new skills, and of sharing with a teacher a curiosity about the richness of the human experience; or supervision may be a ghastly exercise in pretense: pretending to know more and to feel less than is really the case, disguising doubt and error and uncertainty.

At the time we began this paper, one of us (E.M.) was a senior supervisor and psychoanalyst and the other of us (C.G.) was a junior resident in psychiatry. We had experienced the vicissitudes of this remarkable dyad from both sides. We wondered what factors contributed to making supervision a rewarding or unfulfilling experience. In extensive discussions with our colleagues, as well as in scrutinizing our own work, we tried to identify those areas of conflict which are most likely to disrupt the supervisory relationship, and to describe procedures for minimizing the impact of these conflicts.

Differences in supervision may arise from rational disagreements about the nature of the work, or from affective aspects of the relationship and of the experiences of doing therapy. Disagreements regarding the nature of psychiatric intervention are especially apt to arise because of the relatively recent explosion of information in psychiatry, neurobiology, chemotherapy, family and behavior therapies, and the profusion of analytic and innovative psychotherapies. With all of this information available, practitioners must choose among a host of models of mental illness and as many types of treatment. The potential for disagreement in supervision, therefore, is great. The supervisor and supervisee may harbor vastly different ideas of what the patient experiences, why he experiences it, and what should be done to help him.

Affectively derived differences can be even more troublesome and may underlie discussions which focus on differential diagnosis and decisions regarding medications. For the supervisee, experiencing and discussing the patient's material inevitably bring up personal areas of conflict, and may mobilize anxiety which is combated by heightened use of defenses. This response to the patient can be of great use in both therapy and supervision, if the response and the source of conflict within the therapist are regarded as useful for understanding the patient. Unexplained, unprepared and overly broad exploration of such experiences can lead the supervision into psychotherapy without explicit ground rules or an alliance. The therapist may then feel threatened, invaded, or "sick," and unsuited to do the work of psychotherapy. While supervisors may feel the pull into a role more therapeutic than pedagogic, the inexperienced supervisor, particularly, may find the role familiar and appealing, and may actively pursue it.

Since acknowledgment and use of these inner reactions to the patient and the supervision form a major base for learning to use one's self as a therapeutic instrument, the student-supervisor dyad needs to find a way to incorporate these issues in the learning process. Special attention to development of an alliance can strengthen the dyad's ability to accomplish this and mitigate sources of interpersonal differences from affective experience and models of psychiatric intervention. This alliance, like that between a therapist and patient, in Greenson's (1) phrase, embodies the "non-neurotic, rational relationship that allows the [supervisor and supervisee] to work purposefully." An alliance, in this sense, presupposes an explicit understanding of the goals of the work and the means used to achieve them. It provides a sense of personal safety and comfort, based on having acknowledged ground rules for the work, e.g., what can be talked about. The alliance can be a fortuitous occurrence, a "good fit" between people, but most often it must be fostered by specific procedures.

One crucial factor in developing an alliance in supervision is the early, explicit negotiation of a contract, which details the goals of supervision, the means, ground rules, and other details of the relationship. While such a contract is not in itself sufficient to develop an alliance (which is a more personal, comprehensive and less legalistic sense of mutuality), it may be an important precursor to an alliance. Certainly we have found that contracts maximize the chance that an alliance will develop.

This chapter, then, will discuss in some detail the use of a supervisory contract and the development of a supervisory alliance.

LITERATURE REVIEW

The most exhaustive and most eloquent work on the alliance in psychotherapy has been done by Greenson (1), as noted earlier. Greenson elaborates the alliance as the *sine qua non* of psychoanalytic psychotherapy. He provides telling examples of the interminable, fruitless, and sometimes harmful work that can occur when this non-neurotic, non-transferential sense of mutuality is absent. In some cases the development of the alliance in itself is the substance of treatment, as in the case of borderline patients.

The concept of alliance has been broadened and applied to the supervision of psychotherapy. Fleming and Benedek (2) discussed the "learning alliance" as an important component of psychoanalytic supervision. They emphasized the need to develop a keen awareness of the inner experience of the analyst. They underscored the difficult role of the supervisor in attending to both the patient's difficulties and the emotional troubles of the student analyst. They outlined problems of the learning alliance contributed by both the student and supervisor, with emphasis on the unconscious and preconscious transference and countertransference aspects of each.

Lazerson (3) examined the learning alliance in detail and applied the concept of alliance to all teaching situations. He paid particular attention to teachers' resistances within the learning alliance, based on understanding their needs and defenses.

Chessick's (4) excellent 1971 paper examined "how the resident and supervisor disappoint each other." He carefully outlined the needs, goals, and conflicts of both the supervisor and the resident and asserted that the development of a "supervisory alliance" is the "primary task" of supervision. He then described maneuvers for working in supervision once this alliance is established, to meet the needs of both supervisor and resident.

Greben, Markson and Sadavoy (5) wrote informally but clearly about their experiences as supervisors and supervisees. They discussed the utility of a supervisory alliance and remarked on the need to begin with a supervisory contract as a basis for their work.

Lower (6) discussed the usefulness of an alliance in supervision to deal with countertransference issues in the relationship.

Others have written on the concept of contract and alliance in supervision (e.g., Ornstein (7)). Some authors, however, have taken the alliance for granted (e.g., Berger and Freebury (8)); overlooked the alliance entirely (e.g., Gaoni and Neumann (9)); or disputed its primary importance (Gale (10); Goin and Kline (11)). Aside from a brief mention by Greben, Markson and Sadavoy, the importance of the supervisory contract has been unexplored.

CONTRACT AND ALLIANCE IN PSYCHOTHERAPY

The therapeutic alliance is the foundation of the psychotherapeutic process. Mutuality, rapport and basic friendliness between the therapist and patient help the patient to bear painful affects, to entertain new ideas about himself, and to engage actively in the work. The alliance enables the patient to see the therapist's maneuvers as directed at helping him. It permits the patient to feel safe enough to examine transference reactions to the therapist. In fact, it is the alliance that permits the patient to appreciate transference reactions and resistances for what they are, as they contrast with the basic sense of mutuality and cooperation. Without an alliance, transference reactions and resistances seem to the patient to be merely justifiable reactions to the therapist. These experiences are then uninterpretable until the alliance is developed or restored.

In sum, then, the alliance enables the patient to feel safe enough to look beyond the neurotic solution that brought him to therapy and to engage in meaningful cooperative effort with the therapist. The alliance provides an atmosphere in which transference can develop, and promotes insight and working-through as these reactions contrast with the mature, non-neurotic relationship in the alliance. The alliance enables the patient to bear the privations of silence and the discomfort of clarifications, confrontations and interpretations as part of the psychotherapeutic process.

Therapies with weak or absent alliances do not necessarily stop; they may just not go well. These stalled therapies may continue for years, the patient believing the therapist knows what he is doing, the therapist lulled by the continuing apparent compliance of the patient. On inspection, however, these therapies often seem to be on a sort of "automatic pilot," with little involvement by the participants. These therapies are characterized by pseudocompliance by patients who may produce abundant "material" without any change in their day-to-day lives, or by remarkable "insight" which remains intellectualized.

Langs (12) has detailed an added dimension of failures of therapeutic alliance, in describing various sorts of "misalliance" which can develop. These are not failures so much as distortions of alliance. The therapist and patient work mutually, but not toward the aims which the therapy originally was designed to attain. Rather, some neurotic bargain is struck between the therapist and patient which both then seem unwittingly to work to maintain. These alliances foster symptom relief in the patient and satisfaction in the therapist through pathologically shared defenses and inappropriate gratifications. These too may occur in therapies that appear to be progressing well.

Misalliances may lead to serious regression and acting-out. In fact, all therapies that are based on either a weak alliance or a misalliance are imbued with acting-in or acting-out, as the patient and therapist go through the motions of therapy. What is so dangerous about the situation is that this sort of acting-out is likely to be invisible to both parties and uninterpretable until a good alliance is restored.

We believe that an extremely important factor in alliance formation is the use of a therapeutic contract. A therapeutic contract fosters mutuality of purpose in the early stages of therapy. It details the reasons for therapy, the goals, the means, and a variety of administrative details such as fees, vacations and so on. Such a procedure is a valuable precursor to the sort of rapport which comprises an alliance. A contract minimizes the chances of misalliance developing, by keeping in focus the purpose and ground rules of the work.

The therapeutic contract helps the patient to feel understood at the outset. In elaborating his reasons for choosing treatment and outlining his goals, the patient is encouraged to feel that he is teaming with his therapist to alleviate suffering. In discussing questions about technique, the process of therapy is somewhat demystified, and the patient may feel more comfortable and engaged. This process of beginning therapy explicitly introduces the patient to the value of his inner experience, and may set the stage for increasing trust and openness. The contract is not in itself the alliance, but it may well be a necessary support for it.

CONTRACT AND ALLIANCE IN SUPERVISION

Having examined the importance of the contract and alliance in psychotherapy, we wish now to apply these concepts to the supervisory relationship. First we will discuss the use of the supervisory contract in mitigating conflict and setting the stage for alliance. Then we will elaborate the characteristics of the supervisory alliance itself.

In introducing this chapter we mentioned two distinct areas of conflict within supervision: content-based differences of opinion about the nature of mental illness and its treatment; and affective difficulties growing out of the treatment and supervisory processes themselves. Setting a supervisory contract effectively deals with the first, the theoretical sort of problem. The supervisory contract makes the goals of supervision explicit (e.g., to supervise a course of psychotherapy based on psychoanalytic principles, or to supervise the pharmacologic management of a chronically psychotic patient). The contract makes explicit, too, the means of such work, (e.g., listening together to tape recordings of therapy sessions, theoretical discussion, and speculation about transference and countertransference themes). In this way, ideological differences between the therapist and supervisor may become apparent. Each can make explicit what conceptual models of psychiatry (13) he prefers and/or is familiar with. Expectations and means of mutual evaluation can be clarified. The administrative details of location, fees, vacations, and so forth can be discussed. Confidentiality and opportunities for modification or renegotiation of the contract should be addressed. Potential difficulties and covert conflicts may be revealed, and technique can be developed to resolve them.

Setting a supervisory contract may make apparent other potential sources of conflict. The supervisor and supervisee can discuss the use of the therapist's inner reactions to the patient, and decide together how these will be brought into the supervision. In this way the value of the therapist's inner experience in understanding the patient can be made clear. Supervision at the same time can be differentiated from psychotherapy. Potential difficulties, such as the therapist's feeling exposed, can be anticipated. These subjective revelations by the therapist should be protected by explicit agreements about confidentiality.

By setting a contract in this way, the supervisor provides an excellent example for the therapist. This then becomes for the trainee his first experience in supervision by learning through identification. The supervisor's openness about his expertise and goals and his willingness to discuss the method to be used provide a role model for how a therapist might behave. In this way, the supervisor demonstrates the utility of an explicit contract. The supervisee can experience firsthand the comforting effect of the contract. It can enhance his appreciation of the reality-based aspects of his relationship with the patient.

In spite of the great utility of the supervisory contract, there seems to be reluctance by both supervisors and students to engage in the work of contract setting. For the student, it is difficult to reveal what may seem to be a sense of vast ignorance, especially at the outset. Without some formal reassurance, the student may feel frightened by his inner reactions to the patient and tacitly conceal them in supervision. He may feel he should know more about therapeutic technique than he does, and carry on with false bravado, or retreat into stony, safe, "analytic" silence. One way to handle such problems is to keep the goals and means of supervision fuzzy and inexplicit, "winging it" from hour to hour.

There are difficulties in contract setting from the supervisor's side too. As psychiatry has grown more complicated and the areas in which to be expert have multiplied, no single supervisor can be equally competent in all areas. In making the goals and means of supervision explicit, the supervisor may feel compelled to expose areas of less expertise. It may feel safer to both to keep the ground rules vague.

If this occurs, both therapist and supervisor may find themselves obscuring the nature of their work. Expectations may seem unclear, and the student may hesitate to voice feelings, doubts, experiences or ideas which he feels might conflict with these tacit, possibly erroneous expectations. Because he does not report these aspects of his therapy, the work may go poorly, or he may feel misunderstood without knowing why. Similarly, the supervisor may assume that the fundamental process of therapy, its goals, rationale, and technique are agreed upon when in fact they are not. The supervisor may feel frustrated that the therapist makes obvious errors, or is too obsequious, or too combative—all ostensibly issues in therapy—when the crucial issue may be the supervisory contract itself.

If these pitfalls are avoided, then the stage is set for an effective supervisory alliance. Like the alliance in psychotherapy, the supervisory alliance embodies trust, rapport, and mutuality between the participants and creates an atmosphere of safety in which doubt, ignorance, and creative speculation can be explored.

A flourishing supervisory relationship strengthens the therapist to bear the painful affects of his patients and to encourage their vocalization. The supervisor's help enables the therapist to be comfortable in discussing the patients' and his own dilemmas, in supervision, and to sit with the patients during therapy. Such a relationship can promote self-reflection in the therapist and supervisor and make more of each other's experience available for the work. As such, it provides an excellent model for the therapist-patient dyad.

The supervisory alliance enables the student to use the supervisor's pedagogic maneuvers, much as the therapeutic alliance helps the patient to use therapeutic maneuvers. The alliance makes visible transference and countertransference reactions within supervision. Based on a good contract, the alliance permits both parties to limit the inevitable regressions that occur in supervision, and to avoid other conflicts altogether.

All learning involves risk—the risk of exposing ignorance and trying new ideas. The alliance makes supervision a safe place to take chances and to develop to the utmost the potential for creative, honest, meaningful exploration.

LIMITATIONS OF THE CONCEPTS

As with other aspects of therapy, the alliance and contract are subject to failure, adverse effects, limitations, hazards, defects and abuse. We have suggested that a potentially serious cause of failure is inattention to the contract. Indeed, it seems that many contracts and alliances are concocted unintentionally. As a result, success in supervision may be serendipitous, or the relationship which develops is not as effective as it could be—from both sides. Other causes of failure include premature closure on the contract, which may preclude important exploration of needs or goals. Too rigid adherence to a contract may prevent an alliance from achieving flexibility and vitality, the suppleness needed to incorporate change. An ill-conceived contract can trap the participants and leave both feeling helpless to change it. If contracts include provisions for revision and negotiation of new issues, many of these hazards can be overcome.

Even the best conceived contract may have limitations. No agreement can cover the numerous circumstances of the therapeutic or supervisory relationship, and an attempt to make a contract so complete runs the risk of miring the participants down in rule setting, instead of getting to the business at hand. Similarly the contract may be open to abuse. Therapy or supervision can be precluded by setting an impossible contract, and infractions of the contract can be exploited as excuses for terminating a difficult relationship, therapeutic or supervisory.

SUMMARY

The establishment of a workable contract, as well as a working alliance, between supervisor and supervisee facilitates trust and mutuality. It makes explicit areas of potential conflict and establishes ground rules for dealing with them. It conveys to the therapist the importance of this procedure for the patient. It opens the way for both therapist and supervisor to appreciate their subjective experiences more fully. It strengthens both of them during times of difficulty. While they are imperfect tools not free of risk, forging a contract and developing an alliance are essential early steps toward mutually rewarding supervision.

REFERENCES

1. Greenson, R. R.: The working alliance and the transference neurosis. *Psychoanal. Q.*, 34:155-181, 1965.
2. Fleming, J., and Benedek, T.: Supervision, a method of teaching psychoanalysis. *Psychoanal. Q.*, 33:71-96, 1964.
3. Lazerson, A. M.: The learning alliance and its relation to psychiatric teaching. *Psychiatr. Med.*, 3:81-91, 1972.
4. Chessick, R. D.: How the resident and supervisor disappoint each other. *Am. J. Psychother.*, 25:272-283, 1971.
5. Greben, S. E., Markson, E. R., and Sadavoy, J.: Resident and supervisor: An examination of their relationship. *Can. Psychiatr. Assoc. J.*, 18:473-478, 1973.
6. Lower, K. B.: Countertransference resistances in the supervisory situation. *Am. J. Psychiatr.*, 129:70-74, 1972.
7. Ornstein, P. H.: Sorcerer's apprentice: The initial phase of training and education in psychiatry. *Compr. Psychiatr.*, 9:293-315, 1968.
8. Berger, D., and Freebury, D. R.: The acquisition of psychotherapy skills: A learning model and some guidelines for instructors. *Can. Psychiatr. Assoc. J.*, 18:467-471, 1974.
9. Gaoni, B., and Neumann, M.: Supervision from the point of view of the supervisee. *Am. J. Psychother.*, 28:108-114, 1974.
10. Gale, M. S.: Resident perception of psychotherapy supervision. *Compr. Psychiatr.*, 17:191-194, 1976.
11. Goin, M. K., and Kline, F. M.: Supervision observed. *J. Nerv. Ment. Dis.*, 158:208-213, 1974.
12. Langs, R. J.: Therapeutic misalliances. *Int. J. Psychoanal. Psychother.*, 4:77-105, 1975.
13. Lazare, A.: Hidden conceptual models in psychiatry. *N. Engl. J. Med.*, 288:345-351, 1973.

Chapter 9

Psychoanalysis:
A Future Prospectus

Alan M. Jacobson, M.D.,
and Dean X. Parmelee, M.D.

INTRODUCTION

The authors of the previous chapters in this book have discussed selected features of psychoanalytic theory and its use in clinical practice. They have examined changing patterns in the history of psychoanalytic theory, the testability of analytic hypotheses, and some current applications of the theory to practice in teaching. These contributions reflect the great degree of change undergone by psychoanalytic theory and practice in the past 85 years. For example, Meissner outlined the major changes in psychoanalytic ideas from Freud's first conceptions of drive theory for explaining hysteria to more recent developments in object relations theory for explaining the clinical problem of patients with borderline or severe character disorders. In addition, Notman and Bernstein explored specific features in the evolution of the psychoanalytic theory of female psychology and severe character disturbances, respectively.

Parallel with this evolution of psychoanalytic ideas has been a dramatic change in the larger field of psychiatry, with a proliferation of new models for understanding and treating patients. These changes have led to an essential change in the position of psychoanalysis in psychiatry. Because of this new diversity, psychoanalysis no longer provides the single unifying theme for understanding patients in clinical practice. Rather, it competes with several newer traditions, such as: biologic psychopharmacologic, social system family therapy, and operant behavioral therapy approaches. As with psychoanalysis, each of these models incorporates general theories of human behavior linked to clinical experience. On the other hand, their evolutions have also been supported by important developments in the basic social and biologic sciences, e.g., new methods and models in neurobiology, pharmacology, and social and behavioral psychology. Since the social and biologic sciences utilize rigorous techniques of research, these traditions often use methods of inquiry which differ strikingly from those of psychoanalysis. Consequently (and in contrast to psychoanalysis), they have influenced psychiatry to increasingly use empirical research methods for evaluating new models and treatment modalities.

Since these newer traditions provide alternative conceptualizations of and approaches to assessing psychological issues, they pose a series of challenges for psychoanalysis and its future role in psychiatry. In this chapter we will explore these challenges further by examining three related issues:

> 1) the compatibility of psychoanalysis and empirical research approaches;
> 2) potentially meaningful contributions from the social sciences to new directions in psychoanalysis; and
> 3) possible effects of an empirically grounded psychoanalytic psychology on the field of psychiatry.

PSYCHOANALYSIS AS SCIENCE

Given the changing nature of psychiatry and its increasing use of empirical methods, any consideration of the role of psychoanalysis in the future of psychiatry must begin with a consideration of the extent to which psychoanalytic concepts are verifiable and disconfirmable by rigorous scientific methods. Can concepts which are rooted in the experience of clinicians be examined, verified and modified using systematic research methods?

To date, the evolution of psychoanalytic ideas has largely remained at what Klerman termed in Chapter 3 "the hypothesis generating phase of research." New concepts have enriched or replaced prior ideas with little or no systematic assessment of their validity, either as applied to patients or as the basis for a general psychology of human behavior. The testing of these ideas has been the product of clinical practice. Thus, refinement has depended on repeated presentation of cases and case examples that identify or support particular approaches to understanding and treating patients; as noted by Edelson (1), these reports have been anecdotal rather than systematic case studies.

This work by psychoanalysts has led to a complex and rich body of concepts layered on one another by the experience of each succeeding generation of clinicians and theoreticians. Indeed, there has been a major controversy among psychoanalysts, philosophers, and scientists over the value and even the possibility of scientific assessment (1-7). For example, some have insisted that psychoanalytic ideas are inherently not postulates for scientific validation. Ricoeur (4) has insisted that psychoanalysis is not science but hermeneutics. That is, the psychoanalyst is interested not in observable facts but only in the subjective meaning these facts have assumed in a subject's personal history. According to this approach, psychoanalytic postulates are not verifiable using scientific methods. Others have proposed that if psychoanalytic postulates are testable, they are so only within the framework of the scientific method itself (7). Alternatively, it may be that psychoanalytic postulates, while testable, are to date too complex to be assessed by traditional research means, which refine hypotheses to forms that can be evaluated by empirical research paradigms. These paradigms may demand so much simplification that the original and richer meaning may be lost by the process of testing.

How can we understand the variety of perspectives on the nature of psychoanalytic propositions? Slater maintains that Freud's views of the nature of science and psychoanalysis suggest one source of this controversy. He believes Freud became enamoured with subjective experience as the subject matter of psychoanalysis such that behavior became "but a pale reflection of the more vivid subjective world" (5). Behavior was a mere translation from the unconscious.

Popper (6) suggests that Freud believed that the scientific method he employed could not yield error. Even the arguments of opponents, therefore, could be reinterpreted by examining the motives underlying these alternative explanations. The theory, according to Popper, "appeared to be able to explain everything that happened." Psychoanalytic study "had the effect of an intellectual conversion or revelation—of opening your eyes to the truth hidden from those not yet initiated. Once your eyes were thus open you saw confirming instances everywhere; the world was full of verifications of this theory. Whatever happens all was confirmed. Thus its truth appeared obvious and unbelievers were clearly people who did not want to see the truth—either because it was against their class interest, or because of their repressions which were still unanalyzed and crying aloud for treatment" (6).

As Slater (5) suggests, Freud, while believing psychoanalysis was a science, also insisted he alone was qualified to judge the truth of its assertions. While he changed the system over the years, only he had the authority to sanction those alterations. The picture painted by these critics is of a system that, while it may call its work science, depends primarily on belief, built up by highly personal experience, for verification.

Kohut's (7) examination of psychoanalytic method suggests that its very nature is an essential source of these different views of the scientific validity. He has suggested that analytic concepts can serve as valuable hypotheses for social science and biologic research, but that the psychoanalytic frame of reference differs from those of biology or the social psychologies. The psychoanalyst uses introspection and empathic understanding to make sense of his patients and does not use the methods of inquiry of other scientists.

Indeed, introspection and empathy are to the analyst the "essential constituents of observation." Even though they may be "linked and amalgamated with other methods of observation, the final and decisive observational act is introspective or empathic" (7). Thus, the proof of this actual existence of unconscious longings depends on "their introspective or empathic discovery" (7). Conversely, the biologists and social psychologists test theories based on external observation. According to Kohut, one must be careful not to mix and confuse theories derived from such different perspectives. Consequently, we can infer that conclusions from each field may stimulate assumptions and approaches to the other but these conclusions can only be validated within their own frames of reference using their own methods.

To the extent that this position is accepted, psychoanalytic observations are not confirmable or refutable by empirical methods. Insights may be examined by using empirical methods in other settings but the only tests of truth in the analytic setting are the introspective and empathic observations in the analyst and analysand. Ricoeur's (4) position becomes a logical outcome so that psychoanalysis deals only with subjective meanings, rather than with scientific propositions. On the other hand, there has been a consistent attempt by psychoanalytic theoreticians, investigators, and clinicians to consider analytic propositions as scientific claims, even if only testable within the analytic method as Kohut suggests.

This leaves psychoanalysis in a complex dilemma which is captured by Meissner in Chapter 1.

> . . . psychoanalysis is fundamentally and at root a clinical theory. When psychoanalysis withdraws from the hard-rock clinical data it deals with, it begins to become pale and wane. When it can put its taproot into that rich clinical material of the immediate interaction between analyst and patient, then it flourishes. As Goethe observed long ago, all theory is gray—reality is green. In psychoanalysis, as in all sciences, this is an anomaly. It is a constant problem in the methodology of psychoanalysis. It creates special difficulties in trying to assess what psychoanalysis is and what it does, because there is also a mandate that says I cannot simply test the hypotheses in one isolated context, particularly just the context from which those hypotheses are derived.
>
> Consequently, psychoanalytic theory has to become a general theory rather than a specific theory of how analysis works in the analytic situation. Further, it has to be tested and validated as a general theory. It is in that transition, in that interface between the concrete reality of clinical data and immediate clinical experience on one level, and the formulations of the general theory, on another level, that many of the problems in trying to understand and validate psychoanalysis arise. So if you think about analysis as authentically a clinical theory and think about the problems of methodology that are involved in translating it into other kinds of testing situations, other kinds of validating situations, experimental contexts where it becomes necessary to define, delineate, specify, and clarify variables and functional interrelationships, the enterprise becomes very difficult indeed (8).

This type of controversy is not unique to psychoanalysis; disagreement over methods of inquiry occur within all social sciences. For example, humanistic traditions in the social sciences have suggested that quantitative methods strip context and therefore meaning from research findings; consequently these approaches emphasize a more qualitative, holistic approach (9). As noted earlier, these social scientists frequently point out the complexity of social science propositions and the failure of empirical methods to capture this in simplifying research designs. Cooke and Campbell point out, however, that no matter the starting place, quantitative research designs and methods are needed to resolve differences between investigators. "If the starting point for investigating an issue was qualitative humanistic scholarship, the results of the scholarship would be criticized in terms of specific rival alternative interpretation. Answering these criticisms would lead to reinventing quantification, control groups, the arbitrary intrusions of experimental manipulation, and randomization, since recognizing threats to the validity of conclusions would lead to a need for mechanisms that rule out such threats" (10). This suggests that even within psychoanalysis, systematic assessment could help validate clinical assumptions.

Edelson (1) has suggested that the problem of psychoanalysis stems not so much from an inherent inability to test postulates but from the vagueness of the postulates themselves. He suggests that formalization of psychoanalytic ideas in clear, decisive terms is a necessary next step in the evolution of a field which abounds with flabbily constructed notions. Such an emphasis on systematic descriptive approaches would seem to be well-suited to psychoanalytic case descriptions, which would be extended from anecdotal reports to carefully constructed systematic case studies linked to clearly formulated psychoanalytic postulates.

It seems to us that for psychoanalysis to consider itself a member of the social sciences, it must at some level utilize the methods of social sciences, including to some extent those of empirical scientific methods. While such an approach poses clear problems for a field that has depended almost entirely on anecdotal case reports and the intuitions of observers, the melding of these two methods of inquiry also holds some promise for the field. Observations from new areas of science inevitably enrich older, more established fields; such has been the case with new concepts in neurobiology for the field of psychiatry and such could be the case for both methods and ideas derived from the social sciences for psychoanalysis. In addition, such an approach would ensure an important role for psychoanalysis in the lively debates ongoing in the field of psychiatry. Psychoanalysis so constituted would contribute more effectively to a psychiatry that now has firm bases in scientific methods.

SCIENTIFIC RESOURCES
FROM THE SOCIAL SCIENCES

Social and developmental psychology provide methods of research which could play a major role for the further evolution of psychoanalytic theory and treatment. Derived from social psychology, conversation analysis provides the psychoanalytic researcher with quantitative techniques for systematically understanding the nature of verbal interchange between therapist and patient. New approaches in developmental psychology suggest ways of depicting maturational processes, thus impacting on psychoanalytic concepts of human development. In this section we shall present an example of how conversational analysis can be applied to understanding psychoanalytic interaction. In particular, we shall look at an example of how such an approach can be used to quantitatively examine transference interpretation in the analytic situation. We will then examine two examples from developmental psychology—moral development as developed by Kohlberg and ego developmental constructs as developed by Loevinger—to explore their potential influence on psychoanalytic developmental theory.

Conversation Analysis

Luborsky and associates (11) provide us with an example of social psychological methods for analyzing conversation, applied to the psychoanalytic situation. They have turned their attention to a clinical, yet quantitative, examination of the central intervention in psychoanalysis: the transference interpretation. While clinicians have developed guidelines regarding the use of transference interpretation, only one study has previously systematically examined analytic interventions. Therefore, the authors decided to study the timing and impact of interpretation during psychoanalytic sessions.

By carefully examining detailed transcripts of analytic sessions, clinically-trained readers were able to identify transference interpretations. They then examined the immediate preconditions and postconditions of the interpretation within the process of each session. The authors' purpose was to systematically describe preconditions in the hour which led to interpretations, the effect of interpretations on the patient, and the relationship of these effects to later clinical outcome.

The context of the interpretations was rated according to nine features important to the analytic process: 1) resistance, 2) involvement with the analyst, 3) affect, 4) understanding/insight, 5) transference, 6) positive transference, 7) manifest positive transference, 8) negative transference, and 9) manifest negative transference. Each of these was carefully defined and operationalized into rating scales used by the experienced clinical judges:

> The situations were judged against the expectation that an appropriate time for a transference interpretation is when transference

has increased, is negative and begins to impede the progress of treatment, and when the patient has begun to get some understanding and insight into it. A successfully timed transference interpretation under these conditions should begin to effect a decrease in resistance and transference. Involvement with the analyst and affect were also included because they seem to be relatively concrete aspects of these changes which are crucial in making judgments about the amount of transference present (11).

Judges were able to achieve high degrees of interrater agreement regarding what constitutes the transference interpretation and the degree each of the aforementioned nine processes were present.

The researchers found that while the timing of interpretations was similar for each of the three patients studied, distinct patterns of response were noted to the transference interpretations in each case.

TABLE 1

Statistically Significant Responses to Transference Interpretations and Ratings of Clinical Outcomes

	Response	*Clinical Outcome*
Patient A	resistance**	poor
Patient B	involvement* transference*	good
Patient C	involvement*** understanding** affect* transference*** positive transference* manifest positive transference* negative transference* manifest negative transference*	excellent

*p < .05   **p < .01   ***p < .001
This table is derived from the results presented by Luborsky, et al. (11)

Table 1 summarizes the major responses of the three patients to the transference interpretation. As noted, though the preconditions for transference interpretations were similar, responses to the interventions varied from increased resistance alone in Patient A, to increased understanding and involvement in Patient B, and to transference, understanding, involvement and affect in Patient C. When increased resistance was the predominant effect of an interpretation, the outcome was rated as poor. On the other hand, involvement, understanding, and alteration in both the positive and negative transference correlated strongly with better clinical outcomes from the analysis.

Patient A was a 31-year-old, unmarried, professional woman who entered treatment because of dissatisfaction with her relationships with men—the men were all much younger and with each one she felt terribly treated and therefore broke off the relationship. "The treatment, which lasted for 468 sessions, ended with patient and analyst agreeing that she had remained relatively 'untouched' by it. The following example indicates her negative response to interpretation such that their only demonstrable impact was a significant increase in resistance. After discussion about fees in Session 174, the analyst suggested, 'There's some pleasure in this kind of tug-of-war, as though associations were being extracted from you' The patient replied, 'Well, I just don't think so' " (11).

On the other hand, Patient C was a professional woman "in her late twenties, diagnosed obsessive compulsive neurosis, who entered analysis because of feelings of self-dissatisfaction and joylessness. She was upset by any situation calling for closeness and one of sexual intercourse." The outcome was considered highly successful by patient and analyst. In Session 1,028, the patient was complaining that she could not respond naturally to gestures or declarations of affection made to her; the therapist stated,

> "You don't know what to say. And you say this at a time when again you tell me how you feel fat. And so the question now is, what are you holding out for? And I think it's what you've always held out for. You're saying you can't have any relationship unless you have your father, unless you can have a daddy. And here it's been unless you can have me."
>
> The patient replied, "Yeah, well, uhm, I immediately think of something that F said on Friday when I saw her. And it was really how, in a way, I got into saying any of the things I did that had to do with, you know, more directly with my problem than I had ever said to her before. Uhm, and I thought of it now when I was wondering how I feel when M says he loves me. And, you know, how I feel I cannot say 'I love you' to him despite all—many good feelings that I have towards him. And, uhm, you know, that one element that's missing that I imagine with my father and with you."

Luborsky et al.'s method thus provides an approach for precisely examining clinical material in psychoanalytically-oriented treatment, in this case, the transference interpretation. The research depends on the development of careful, well-described definitions of terms with sufficient in-depth examples for different raters to reliably evaluate data. Such an approach allows for a precise, systematic delineation of the context and changes brought about by this technique. We shall later come to the impact such an approach linked to psychoanalysis might have on furthering our understandings in clinical psychiatry.

Structural Developmental Theory

Concepts derived from developmental psychology might have important implications for further refining psychoanalytic notions about maturational processes. These developmental theories, intellectual heirs to Piaget's studies of children, provide an approach for understanding social, moral, and cognitive development. Considered under the rubric of the structural developmental approach, the hallmark of such models is an attempt to describe the invariant sequence of developmental stages (qualitatively distinct ways of organizing and understanding a certain domain of experience) through which all individuals develop. In contrast to other approaches, the focus is on the structure rather than on the content of thought, on universal patterns rather than on individual or situational differences, and on patterns of thinking rather than on emotions or behavior. Since structural developmentalists search for evolving patterns of thought which form coherent and temporally stable attitudes, these theories may be compatible with the psychoanalytic models, which also emphasize enduring attitudes conceived in terms of deep structures in the mind. Thus, both approaches differ from behavioral psychology with its emphasis on externally observable behaviors as the critical manner for study.

While compatible and potentially synergistic, the two models differ in at least five main respects which are important to note:

> 1) Structural developmental theories have emphasized careful description of development; they have not evolved causal explanations of change. Psychoanalysis, on the other hand, examines social, familial, and intrapsychic causes of development.
> 2) For the structural developmentalists maturation proceeds in one direction. Development can be arrested short of maximum but regression is not built into the model. For psychoanalysts regression is both a defensive and adaptive phenomenon and is a critical part of their view of development.
> 3) Structural developmental theories explore cognition, be it

from a moral, social or characterologic perspective. The emphasis has been on how the self perceives and thinks. While psychoanalysis has a strong interest in cognition, there is also an important emphasis on non-cognitive aspects of development—for example, affects and their vicissitudes.

4) Psychoanalysis has generated a complex body of hypotheses but rarely has sought to empirically test their validity, while structural developmental theorists have a strong research emphasis and consequently have produced specific measures to assess and utilize their theoretical constructs.

5) Psychoanalysis is based primarily on clinical observation, while structural developmentalists have focused primarily on normal development rather than deviations from the norm.

Notwithstanding these differences, psychoanalytic and structural developmental theories have similar focuses, which make for some potentially interesting connections between these approaches. Our intent in this section is consequently to present two examples of structural developmental theoretical approaches as a basis for looking at some of these connections.

Moral Development

With his studies of development and cognition in children, Piaget described the essential outlines of cognitive structural developmental theory. It was Piaget and later Kohlberg who applied this approach to understanding transformation for moral reasoning during childhood maturation. "Moral development in the work of Piaget and Kohlberg refers specifically to the expanding conception of the social world as it is reflected in the understanding and resolutions of the inevitable conflicts that arise in the relations between self and others. The moral judgment is a statement of priority, and an attempt at rational resolution in a situation where, from a different point of view, the choice itself seems to do violence to justice" (12). Thus, moral reasoning consists of the justifications made in order to resolve an inevitably conflictual situation presenting non-commensurate values. The following hypothetical situation is one example of a dilemma which poses the value of life versus property rights. Using this story as a basis, Kohlberg has evolved a series of probing questions to examine the responses and concerns regarding these issues.

In Europe a woman was near death from a special kind of cancer.

There was one drug that the doctors felt might save her. It was a form of radium that a druggist in the same town had recently discovered. The drug was expensive to make, but the druggist was charging ten times what the drug cost him to make. He paid $200 for the radium and charged $2000 for a small dose of the drug. The sick woman's husband, Heinz, went to everyone he knew to borrow the money, but he could only get together about $1000, which was half of what it cost. He told the druggist that his wife was dying, and asked him to sell it cheaper or let him pay later. But the druggist said, "No, I discovered the drug and I'm going to make money from it." So Heinz gets desperate and considers breaking into the man's store to steal the drug for his wife (13).

Questions which elicit reasoning about the moral issues posed by this dilemma are then used to focus the discussion and elicit the respondent's consideration about this set of conflicts. For example, should Heinz steal to save his wife's life? Why or why not? If Heinz were discovered and prosecuted, should the judge impose a penalty? Why or why not?

Using this semi-structured interview format and a companion coding manual, Kohlberg and his colleagues have evolved a procedure to rate moral development stages (14). He has identified six stages in which an individual can theoretically pass during childhood. From his perspective, the stages are invariant and each represents a more adequate way of resolving moral dilemmas. At each stage the individual has a qualitatively different construction of a moral problem, so that passage from stage to stage is regarded as a major discontinuous transformation of the individual's perspective. Built into this transformational view of development is the conception that each stage reflects an overarching sense of oneness of the person's way of thinking. The stage reflects, therefore, an internally consistent structure of the mind. Kohlberg maintains that to attain high levels of moral reasoning, one must have obtained high levels of formal cognitive development, for moral reasoning is really a special subset of cognition. As we see, the focus of this work, as in psychoanalysis, is on the thought processes and attitudes rather than specifically on behavior. Behavior is seen as a possible but not inevitable outcome of these thought processes, as conflict in the psychodynamic perspective leads in a general sense to alteration of behaviors.

Kohlberg's stages form typologies of individual differences in the moral realm. The six stages may be grouped into three levels. The levels broadly define the individual's relationship to society. The lowest level (pre-conventional) individual does not yet understand or uphold conventional or societal rules, while the conventional individual at the next level upholds society's expectations just because they are society's rules. The individual at the highest level (post-conventional) understands and generally accepts these rules, but acceptance is based on a formulation and recognition of moral principles which underlie the rules of society (14). The post-conventional individual judges by principles when these principles come into conflict with society's rules.

> One way of understanding the three levels is to think of them as three different types of relationships between the self and society's rules and expectations. From this point of view, Level One is a pre-conventional person, whose rules and social expectations are something external to the self; Level Two is a conventional person in whom the self is identified with or has internalized rules for expectations of others, especially those of authority; and Level Three is a post-conventional person, who has differentiated himself from the rules and expectations of others and defines his values in terms of self-chosen principles (14).

Ego Development

Loevinger's approach to ego development is based on a conception of ego which emphasizes the individual's integrative processes and overall frame of reference. In many respects it is similar to and parallel with Kohlberg's concepts of moral development, for it has as one foundation structural developmental theory. Using this conception, Jane Loevinger and her associates have recently elaborated both a model of ego development and a related and linked assessment technique (15-18). Loevinger conceives of ego development as one of four lines of human development. The others—physical, psychosexual, and intellectual—are distinct conceptually though empirically related. From Loevinger's perspective, ego development most clearly parallels a broad concept of personality or character. The construct of ego development itself is drawn from several theories which have dealt with cognitive, character, self, and interpersonal development. Like Kohlberg, she assumes that individuals evolve through a series of stages which form distinct frames of reference for viewing and making meaning in the world. Thus, "Ego development is marked by a more differentiated perception of one's self, of the social world, and of the relationship of one's feelings and thoughts to those of others" (19).

At the most general level, Loevinger's concept of ego development refers to a framework of meaning which the individual subjectively imposes on experience. Thus, Loevinger views the ego as being unitary, unlike psychoanalysis, which conceives of the ego as having many related functions and capacities.

Loevinger has described seven sequentially ordered stages of ego development; these can be operationally defined and measured using a specific sentence completion test (16, 17). Although they may be correlated with chronological age, the stages are defined independently. Each stage is more complex than the last and in theory none can be skipped in a course of development. However, different individuals may arrest at different stages. Among adults, therefore, there are representatives of each stage who can be characterized in terms of the features specific to the stage at which they have stopped.

Each of the stages differs from the others along dimensions of impulse control, conscious concerns, and interpersonal and cognitive styles. In brief, individuals at the earliest stages are impulsive and fearful; they have stereotyped cognitive styles and dependent or exploitive interpersonal styles. The three stages which share these more primitive characterics are referred to as pre-conformist. In contrast, individuals at the conformist or middle level stages control impulses with defined standards and rules, demonstrate a concern for others, and show at least superficial niceness in their interpersonal style. In addition, they are consciously preoccupied with their social acceptability in groups and show a broad awareness of individual differences. In contrast, individuals who have reached the highest or post-conformist stages of ego development cope with inner conflict with high degrees of self-awareness, show much cognitive complexity, and have an interpersonal style which emphasizes mutuality and respect for individual differences. Table 2 provides a summary of the stages of development and their characteristic patterns. It is possible and indeed probable that the sequence can be arrested at any point. The consequence of this interruption is a character style corresponding to the features of a particular stage at which progress had ceased.

IMPACT OF PSYCHOANALYSIS ON CLINICAL PSYCHIATRY

We have noted the difficulties in treating psychoanalytic propositions as empirically verifiable, but have suggested that to the extent they are, psychoanalysis is in a better position to participate fully in the energetic debates between competing models in psychiatry. If we treat these propositions as solely verifiable within the analytic frame of reference, psychoanalysis may retain for a time a central position in psychiatry, but one which may erode from the force of more robustly evaluated approaches. We have also briefly reviewed two important research traditions in social psychology in order to expose the reader to some fields which may contribute valuably to the further evolution of psychoanalysis if it becomes linked more closely to the scientific tradition. We now turn to some potential impacts on clinical psychiatry of a psychoanalysis which does utilize findings and methods from the social sciences and in particular from these two areas.

Sociopsychological techniques for assessing interpersonal interaction seem relevant to psychoanalytic theory and its applications. For example, they can provide an alternative to the usual methods of studying outcome in psychotherapy. Such outcomes (20) invariably have depended on aspects of change between start and end of treatment. Outcome has been measured by patient and therapist reports, follow-up assessment interviews, reports of important others, and paper-and-pencil tests of psychological status. Luborsky's examination of the transference interpretation (11) provides an example of an alternative approach for assessment. By using similar methods it is conceivable that researchers could identify important techniques which facilitate change. Such microscopic change may be the building blocks for grosser alterations in the structure of an individual or in his behavior, which are the subject matter for the usual methods of outcome assessment. Psychoanalytic therapy has its initial, more subtle impact on the feelings and attitudes of individuals as picked up from individual sessions. Behavioral changes theoretically result from shifts in ways of thinking. Consequently, measures of within-session changes in attitudes and feelings are directly related to analytic assumptions about the process of psychotherapy.

An analogy may serve to underline this important point. While antibiotic effectiveness for pneumonia may be assessed by indirect measures such as fever reduction, returning to work, and appetite, the specific physiologic response of the therapy is best measured by more direct evidence of the resolution of pneumonia by physical exam and chest X-ray. Measures which assess transactions in therapy rather than behavioral changes similarly come closer to assessing the building blocks of therapeutic change.

It is sometimes argued that change depends on nonspecific factors in the therapist/patient relationship rather than on a specific therapeutic technique (21). However, to date, few attempts have been made to systematically look at the process of therapy in order to understand the nature of interventions and their specific effects. We think that such an approach could yield further information about the success of various techniques. Even if therapy is largely dependent on engendering hope, as Frank surmised (21), or on maximizing placebo effects, it should still

TABLE 2

Stages of Ego Development*

Stage	Impulse control, "moral" style	Interpersonal style	Conscious preoccupations	Cognitive style
Presocial (I-1)		Autistic	Self vs. nonself	
Symbiotic (I-1)		Symbiotic	Self vs. nonself	
Impulsive (I-2)	Impulsive, fear	Receiving, dependent, exploitive	Bodily feelings, especially sexual and aggressive	Stereotypy, conceptual confusion
Self-protective (Delta)	Fear of being caught, externalizing blame, opportunistic	Wary, manipulative, exploitive	Self-protection, wishes, things, advantages, control	
Transition from self-protective to conformist (Delta/3)	Obedience and conformity to social norms are simple and absolute rules	Manipulative, obedient	Concrete aspects of traditional sex roles, physical causation as opposed to psychological causation	Conceptual simplicity, stereotypes
Conformist (I-3)	Conformity to external rules, shame, guilt for breaking rules	Belonging, helping, superficial niceness	Appearance, social acceptability, banal feelings, behavior	Conceptual simplicity, stereotypes, clichés
Transition from conformist to conscientious; self-consciousness (I-3/4)	Dawning realization of standards, contingencies, self-criticism	Being helpful, deepened interest in interpersonal relations	Consciousness of the self as separate from the group, recognition of psychological causation	Awareness of individual differences in attitudes, interests and abilities; mentioned in global and broad terms

TABLE 2 (continued)

Conscientious (I-4)	Self-evaluated standards, self-criticism	Intensive, responsible, mutual, concern for communication	Differentiated feelings, motives for behavior, self-respect, achievements, traits, expression	Conceptual complexity, idea of patterning
Transition from conscienticus to autonomous	Individuality, coping with inner conflict	Cherishing of interpersonal relations	Communicating, expressing ideas and feelings, process and change	Toleration for paradox and contradiction
Autonomous (I-5)	Add: Coping with conflicting inner needs	Add: Respect for autonomy	Vividly conveyed feelings, integration of physiological and psychological causation of behavior, development, role conception, self-fulfillment, self in social context	Increased conceptual complexity; complex patterns, toleration for ambiguity, broad scope, objectivity
Integrated (I-6)	Add: Reconciling inner conflicts, renunciation of unattainable	Add: Cherishing of individuality	Add: Identity	

*Adapted from Loevinger (15) and Hauser (18).

be of interest to identify the specific behaviors and methods common or similar in all talking therapies that maximize hope in positive outcomes. A clear understanding of these behaviors may form a basis for further evolution of these therapies.

In one study, Sloane and colleagues (20) compared behavior therapy to psychoanalytic therapy. As part of their study, they taped psychotherapy interviews to find out whether the provided treatment actually utilized techniques and methods conceived to be central to each. They concluded that indeed the two treatments reflected accepted approaches for either analytic therapy or behavioral therapy. They also found both treatments to be of equal benefit in their various outcome analyses. What they did not do was to examine in detail the therapist/patient interaction so as to identify what may have been important similarities of therapist techniques around such issues as building a therapeutic alliance, history taking, etc. Such microscopic assessment could delineate significant techniques common to both therapies, along with critical differences that might account for therapy outcome divergences. For example, Sloane concluded that behavior therapy tended to yield superior outcomes for patients identified as more seriously disturbed. Studies of within-session contexts of intervention and their immediate outcome might further elucidate valuable procedures that relate to these various outcomes. This kind of examination is akin to anatomic dissection which uses both gross and histological methods.

Since analytic therapy techniques focus on the process of interaction between patient and therapist, further classification of these transactions could lead to a more precisely understood and consequently more effectively taught psychotherapy. This would be a psychotherapy approach, we might add, which would have at its roots not only theoretical assumptions but also empirical validation. Such an approach could also allow for further evaluation of new refinements in the procedures, and thus may benefit psychiatry by delineating a set of procedures which are more clearly defined. The process of studying psychotherapy in this way may also enrich our understanding of the work we do, even if it falls short of clearly developing a set of empirically derived techniques. At the very least it will provide a further refinement in our ability to operationalize concepts which are often difficult to define.

Previous attempts to predict outcome in psychotherapy have generally yielded poor results (22). While many factors may account for this, it is possible that our current methods for assessment of patients are simply inaccurate, inconsistent, or not sufficiently detailed to pick up important variations affecting therapy. Recent work on the development of the

Diagnostic and Statistical Manual III (23) have improved one feature of our nosology. Yet we depend for our assessments on a wider array of historical information and patient/therapist interaction for formulating our patients' problems. For example, from a psychoanalytic perspective, we assess ego strengths, including predominant defenses and intrapsychic conflicts. In addition, we assess the responses of patients to our initial interventions as a basis for understanding how the patient will respond in further sessions to additional interventions.

Relatively little work has been done on systematizing these initial interventions. As noted earlier, the methods derived from conversational analysis begin to provide a more systematic basis for developing these. Recent work on ego defenses has begun to evolve a series of more operationally defined concepts of ego functions. This work by Haan (24), Valliant (25), Hauser (26) and others uses operationalized criteria for evaluation of clinical interviews. Both Haan and Valliant have found that these procedures can be used to reliably measure adaptive capacities. For example, one study using Valliant's criteria of ego defenses found that defense evaluations could be used to predict outcome in short-term treatment for obesity (27). Further development of these important psychoanalytic concepts may be of help in refining the mental health professional's ability to formulate patient problems by using standardized and reliable methods—but ones which are not limited to description of symptoms alone. Then, ego functions measurement could apply psychoanalytic theory to rigorous assessment of coping skills of patients.

Similarly, structural developmental theory might be usefully employed in furthering important concepts in both psychoanalysis and clinical psychiatry. In particular, these approaches may hasten our understanding of psychological maturation. For example, Kohlberg's approach (14) provides a method for systemically describing moral development. Several questions are raised. For instance, to what extent does analytic theory modify levels of moral reasoning? Do patients at different levels of moral reasoning present alternative histories of experience, psychodynamics, or character structures? To what extent do semi-structured interviews used to define stages of moral reasoning also provide a basis for systematically defining superego functioning? Do experiences of guilt vary consistently with levels of moral reasoning? Since the stages of both ego development and moral reasoning provide character typologies, a broader question might also be asked by using these methods. That is the question about development of individual characterologic differences. Psychoanalytic theories of severe character

pathology utilize a developmental perspective, descriptively and etiologically. Biologic theories derived from infant studies suggest, however,
that children may be born with innate tendencies or temperaments
which evolve into fuller character structures, dependent in part on environment. Since Kohlberg's moral interview and Loevinger's ego development test provide means for tracking character from a developmental
perspective, we may be able to study the relationship of developmental
arrests to character pathology.

CONCLUSIONS

The underlying principle of applying empirical approaches to psychoanalytic propositions may benefit both psychoanalysis and clinical
psychiatry. Psychiatry as a field has tended to fracture into groups which
follow theoretical biases: biological, Jungian, Freudian, Kohutian, etc.
To some extent this fragmentation reflects the nature of psychiatric hypothesis testing, which until recently depended largely on clinical experience. While refutation of principles can be a painful process, hewing
to a principle of empirical inquiry may lead to a more unified field in
which alternative theories of causation or treatment may ultimately be
selected not only on clinical grounds but also on agreed-upon scientific
bases. While such unification is clearly far in the future, a process of
bringing psychoanalytic principles under the same rules of testing would
be an important step in this process.

We have presented but a few of the valuable approaches in social
psychology that might be useful as part of this process and suggested
some ways they might enrich both psychoanalysis and clinical psychiatry. Returning to the suggestions of Meissner (8), it would seem that
the process of change will be difficult and daunting, but perhaps fruitful,
in the continuing evolution of psychoanalysis as an important set of
concepts and frameworks within clinical psychiatry.

REFERENCES

1. Edelson, M.: Psychoanalysis as science. *J. Nerv. Ment. Dis.*, 165:1-28, 1977.
2. Fine, R.: Toward an integration of psychoanalysis and the social services. *Psychological Reports*, 41:1259-1268, 1977.
3. Olinick, S.: On empathic perception and the problems of reporting psychoanalytic processes. *Int. J. Psychoanalysis*, 56:147-154, 1975.
4. Ricoeur, P.: *Freud and Philosophy*. New Haven: Yale University Press, 1970.
5. Slater, E.: The psychiatrist in search of science: III The depth psychologies. *Brit. J. Psychiatry*, 126:205-224, 1975.
6. Popper, K.: Philosophy of science: A personal report. In: *British Philosophy in the Mid-Century*. C. Mace and G. Allen (Eds.), London, 1957.

7. Kohut, H.: Introspection, empathy, and psychoanalysis. *J. Am. Psychoanalytic Assn.*, 7:459:483, 1959.
8. Meissner, W.: The history of psychoanalytic ideas. In: *Psychoanalysis: Critical Explorations in Contemporary Theory and Practice.* A. M. Jacobson and D. X. Parmelee (Eds.), New York: Brunner/Mazel, 1982.
9. Mischler, E.: Meaning in context: Is there any other kind? *Harvard Ed. Review*, 49:1-19, 1979.
10. Cooke, T., and Campbell, D.: *Quasi Experimentation: Design and Analysis Issues for Field Settings.* Chicago: Rand McNally, 1979, p. 94.
11. Luborsky, L., Bachrach, H., Graff, H., Pulver, S., and Christoph, P.: Preconditions and consequences of transference interpretations: a clinical quantitative study. *J. Nerv. Ment. Dis.*, 167:391-401, 1979.
12. Gilligan, C.: In a different voice: Women's conceptions of self and morality. *Harvard Ed. Review*, 47:481-517, 1977.
13. Colby, A., Gibbs, J., Kohlberg, L., Speicher-Dubin, B., Candee, D., and Powers, S.: *Assessing Moral Stages: A Manual.* Cambridge, MA.: Harvard University Center for Moral Education, 1979.
14. Kohlberg, L.: Moral stages and moralization: The cognitive-developmental approach. In *Moral Development and Behavior: Theory, Research and Social Issues.* T. Likone (Ed.), New York: Holt, Rinehart, and Winston, 1976.
15. Loevinger, J.: *Ego Development.* San Francisco: Jossey-Bass, 1976.
16. Loevinger, J., and Wessler, R.: *Measuring Ego Development.* Vol I and Vol II. San Francisco: Jossey-Bass, 1975.
17. Loevinger, J.: Construct validity of the sentence completion test of ego development. *Applied Psychol. Measurements*, 3:281-311, 1979.
18. Hauser, S. T.: Loevinger's model of ego development: A critical review. 83:928-955, 1976.
19. Candee, D.: Ego development aspects of new left ideology. *J. of Personality and Social Psychology*, 30:620-630, 1974.
20. Sloane, R., Staples, F., Cristol, A., Yorkston, N., and Whipple, K.: *Psychotherapy Versus Behavior Therapy.* Cambridge, MA.: Harvard University Press, 1975.
21. Frank, J.: *Persuasion and Healing.* Baltimore: Johns Hopkins University Press, 1973.
22. Luborsky, L., Mintz, J., Auerbach, A., Christoph, P., Bachrach, H. et al: Predicting the outcome of psychotherapy. *Arch. Gen. Psychiatry*, 37:471-481, 1980.
23. American Psychiatric Association. *Diagnostic and Statistical Manual (Third Edition).* Washington, D.C., 1980.
24. Haan, N.: *Coping and Defending.* New York: Academic Press, 1976.
25. Valliant, G.: Natural history of male psychological health. V: The relation of choice of ego mechanisms of defense to adult adjustment. *Arch. Gen. Psychiatry*, 33:535-545, 1976.
26. Hauser, S. T., Beardslee, W., Jacobson, A., Noam, G., and Powers, S.: Longitudinal studies of ego development and ego defenses in early adolescents. Presented at Winter Meetings of Amer. Psychoanalytic Assoc., 1969.
27. Ellsworth, G., Strain, G., Strain, J., Knittle, J., Valliant, G., et al: Defensive maturity and sustained weight loss. Presented at the Amer. Psychosomatic Society meetings, March, 1980.

Index

221